CONVENTION ON WETLANDS OF INTERNATIONAL IMPORTANCE
ESPECIALLY AS WATERFOWL HABITAT (Ramsar, 1971)

Towards the Wise Use of Wetlands

Report of the Ramsar Convention
Wise Use Project

Edited by T.J. Davis

Ramsar Convention Bureau
October 1993

Published by the Ramsar Convention Bureau, Gland, Switzerland.

Citation: Davis, T.J. (ed.) 1993. *Towards the Wise Use of Wetlands.* Wise Use Project, Ramsar Convention Bureau, Gland, Switzerland.

ISBN 2 940073 07 4

Desktop published by T.J. Davis using Quark XPress 3.11 on a Macintosh IIci.

Printed and bound by Orchard & Ind Ltd, Gloucester, UK.

Available from: Ramsar Convention Bureau
                   Rue Mauverney 28
                   CH-1196 Gland
                   Switzerland

Contents

Acknowledgements

This report on the Wise Use of Wetlands Project would not have been possible without the work and contributions of a large number of people from many parts of the world.

The Ramsar Bureau wishes to thank in particular the Contracting Parties which were members of the Wise Use Working Group: Mauritania (Africa), Islamic Republic of Iran (Asia), Poland (Eastern Europe), Chile (Neotropics), United States of America (North America), Australia (Oceania) and Norway (Western Europe). Special thanks are due to: Steinar Eldøy, who was elected Chairman of the Group, Tom Dahl, Zygmunt Krzeminski, Lawrence Mason, Tim Richmond, Roberto Schlatter and Ibrahima Thiaw.

Technical expertise for the Wise Use Working Group was provided by: Peter Burbridge, Patrick Dugan, Carel Drijver, Jens Enemark, Geoffrey Howard, Paul Gumonye-Mafabi, François Lorfeuvre, Edward Maltby, Laurent Mermet, Michael Moser, Thymio Papayannis, Tobias Salathé and Jeroen van Wetten.

Special thanks are due to the Development Assistance Agency of the Ministry of Foreign Affairs, Government of the Netherlands, which funded the project; to the University of Leiden, Netherlands, and the IUCN Wetlands Programme which were instrumental in proposing and developing some of the case studies; and to the authors of the case studies whose names appear in the present report.

The editor wishes to thank Hervé Lethier, Director of Conservation and Coordinator of the Wise Use Project for the Ramsar Convention Bureau, Mike Smart, Assistant Secretary General of the Ramsar Convention Bureau, Tim Jones, IWRB/Ramsar Liaison Officer, and Diana Fowler and Sue Coyne of The Wildfowl & Wetlands Trust for their assistance in the production of this report.

Foreword

The most significant aspect of modern efforts for environmental protection has been the realization that conservation and development must go hand in hand. This was the main theme of the 1980 World Conservation Strategy and of several other important initiatives including the publication of 'Our Common Future' in 1987 by the World Commission on Environment and Development. Indeed, the need for sustainable development based upon sound conservation principles was the central tenet of the 1992 United Nations Conference on Environment and Development.

It is therefore interesting to note that one of the earliest legal provisions calling for a linkage between environment and development can be found in the 1971 Ramsar Convention on Wetlands of International Importance especially as Waterfowl Habitat. Article 3.1 of this Convention calls upon the Contracting Parties to formulate and implement their planning to achieve the 'wise use' of wetlands in their territory. Over the years, the Contracting Parties to the Convention have made significant efforts to clarify this responsibility. Guidelines and additional guidance for implementing the wise use concept have been adopted and several of the member States have undertaken innovative approaches for the creation of national wetland policies, as well as site-specific and regional management plans, to ensure that the conservation of wetland areas is achieved within the context of local and regional development activities.

Of course, calls for the integration of environment and development are not enough in themselves. What is urgently required is on-the-ground application of the concept. Hence the value of this publication in demonstrating that the wise use of wetlands is possible, by providing a variety of examples in different social, economic and ecological settings.

However, it is not possible to give the complete and final answer on how to achieve wise use of wetlands. Wise use under one particular circumstance or in one particular wetland may not be wise use under other circumstances, and changes over time may change wise use to unwise use. Wise use is therefore as much a question of focusing on the way of thinking, planning, organizing, verifying and adjusting, as to focusing on actual use itself.

I do believe, however, that this volume, containing as it does the guidelines for, and guidance on, the implementation of the wise use of wetlands, and the wealth of lessons learned from work already undertaken, will provide an important basis for the future wise and sustainable use of wetlands globally. I congratulate the Contracting Parties to the Ramsar Convention for this initiative and most notably the Netherlands for its continued support for Ramsar's wise use work. Norway, one of the first member States to the Convention, has been pleased to play its part in chairing the Ramsar Wise Use Working Group which has overseen the production of this volume. It is encouraging to note that the Kushiro Conference decided that the work of the Wise Use Working Group should be continued by the Convention's newly established Scientific and Technical Review Panel.

Sustainable development has been placed high on the political agenda, both internationally and nationally. Giving continued high priority to implementation of the wise use concept should therefore be an important part of a strategy to strengthen and give more political weight both to the Ramsar Convention and to wetland conservation in general.

Steinar Eldøy
Chairman, Ramsar Convention Wise Use Working Group

Introduction

Although wetlands are seen still by many people as unproductive and unhealthy, there has been a growing realization of their value during the last twenty years. Governments and scientists have devoted enormous attention to wetlands, and have reached a better understanding not only of their biological importance, but also of their social, economic and cultural functions (de Groot 1992).

The role of wetlands in regulating climate and in reducing the greenhouse effect, through their capacity for retaining carbon, has been scientifically established, especially as regards peatlands which make up almost half the world's wetlands (Maltby *et al.* 1992). It is now widely accepted that wetlands play an essential part in reducing natural risks such as drought and floods. Thus, after years of drainage and reclamation work in the Lake Thompson watershed, in South Dakota, USA, the local authorities took the decision to restore meadows in the lake basin in order to limit the devastating effects of flooding, which had been exacerbated by the destruction of the wetlands (Dahl, this volume).

Wetlands obviously store water but they also improve water quality, as shown by management action in the Chowilla floodplain in Australia (Phillips, this volume), restoration of water meadows in the Hortobágy National Park, Hungary (Végh, this volume), and the use made of wetlands around Calcutta, India, to purify waste water from the city (Ghosh, this volume). They supply numerous natural resources used by local people (Dugan 1990): wood and its derivatives such as tannin in the Sierpe mangroves, Costa Rica (Lahmann, this volume); fish, shrimps and shellfish in the Indus Delta, Pakistan (Meynell & Qureshi, this volume); game in the El Jocotal lagoon, El Salvador (Benitez, this volume); honey and natural essences in the Mekong Delta, Vietnam (Le Dien Duc, this volume).

Both coastal and inland wetlands thus support a very large number of human activities which depend directly on the proper functioning of the wetland ecosystem: farming and grazing in the floodplain of the River Logone in Chad (Kodi Dadnadji & van Wetten, this volume); forestry, fisheries, fish farming and tourism in Guinea-Bissau (Campredon, this volume) and the Cotentin marshes, France (Lorfeuvre, this volume); cattle raising, fishing and hunting in the Kafue Flats, Zambia (Jeffery, this volume). Such activities, which contribute to the gross national product and to the welfare of local people, are totally dependent on the maintenance of the ecological character of the wetlands.

Countries as different and as far apart in so many ways as Canada and Uganda have recognized what is at stake and have adopted national wetland policies. However, in addition to the initial decision made at the highest political level, adopting a national wetland policy requires a legal and institutional framework, consultation and coordination machinery, and monitoring and management tools to put the orientations, guidelines and strategies into effect. The study presented by the Commission of the European Communities on a particular region, the Mediterranean, provides a very useful example of the all too familiar limitations of well-meaning statements. Conversely, the regional approach adopted by Denmark, Germany and the Netherlands for the management of the Wadden Sea is an excellent example of how to deal with a wetland subjected to numerous constraints, and in an international context which makes traditional problems even more complex.

The case studies presented in this report show how important wetlands are, particularly in developing countries whose future, and in some cases even survival, is heavily dependent on wise use of resources. They provide examples of experiments in the search for wise use of wetlands and their resources. Other measures which might have been cited include the work to ensure sustainable management of the Kushiro-Shitsugen in Japan (Koumaru 1993), and the long-term approach to conservation in the Kosi Bay Nature Reserve in South Africa (Kyle 1992), with centuries-old traditional forms of animal and plant resource exploitation.

Without anticipating the case studies which follow, there is a clear, recurrent message running through all of them: a lack of political will at the outset, lack of coordination, insufficient use of existing knowledge, fragmentary management, lack of training and absence of follow-up are the main reasons for the continuing degradation and disappearance of wetlands, to the detriment of future generations.

It was no accident that the participants in the International Conference on Water and the Environment, held in Dublin, Ireland, in January 1992 under the auspices of the United Nations, listed the protection of water resources, water quality and aquatic ecosystems among the great development challenges of the 21st century. Two chapters of Agenda 21 adopted at the 'Earth Summit' in Rio de Janeiro are also devoted to the subject (Robinson 1992). Much still remains to be done if these obvious facts are to be translated into everyday reality: the disappearance of wetlands is not just a bad memory, it is still all too real (Lean *et al.* 1991).

There must be no ambiguity about the purpose of the present report. The case studies (Chapter 2) are mostly still at the experimental stage and their final results will not be known for several years, even though it is not too early to draw preliminary conclusions from the experiences obtained (Chapter 3). It would be wrong to expect this work to produce a set of recipes to suit all situations; its aim is rather to help promote the wise use of wetlands by providing eyewitness accounts of important initiatives.

Daniel Navid
Secretary General
Ramsar Convention Bureau
Gland
Switzerland

Chapter 1
In pursuit of the wise use of wetlands

Pursuant to Article 3 of the Ramsar Convention, "the Contracting Parties formulate and implement their planning so as to promote the conservation of the wetlands included in the List, and as far as possible the wise use of wetlands in their territory".

The first meeting of the Conference of the Contracting Parties, organized in Cagliari, Italy, in November 1980, approved recommendation REC C.1.5 which emphasized that "wise use of wetlands involves maintenance of their ecological character, as a basis not only for nature conservation, but for sustainable development" and expressed the conviction that "the establishment of comprehensive national policies would benefit the wise use of wetlands". Three years later in Groningen, Netherlands, in May 1984, the parties adopted recommendation REC C.2.3 on 'Action points for priority attention' which in its Annex presents a 'Framework for implementing the Convention' including national measures designed to achieve the wise use of wetlands. At the third meeting of the conference in Regina, Canada, in June 1987, the parties adopted (in the Annex to the recommendations) a definition of wise use and a first set of guidelines on implementation; furthermore, in recommendation REC C.3.1 they established a Wise Use Working Group whose tasks were "to examine the ways in which the criteria and guidelines for identifying wetlands of international importance might be elaborated, and the wise use provisions of the Convention applied, in order to improve the worldwide application of the Convention".

This working group, comprising one member from each of the seven regions represented on the Ramsar Standing Committee together with a number of expert advisors, met under the chairmanship of Norway at the fourth meeting of the Standing Committee in January 1988. There, and in subsequent exchanges, they produced a report on criteria and proposed a more detailed draft of guidelines on wise use (Appendix 1, this report). The fourth meeting of the conference at Montreux, Switzerland, in July 1990, approved recommendation REC C.4.10, which calls on Contracting Parties to adopt and apply the 'Guidelines for implementation of the wise use concept of the Convention' contained in the working group's report. These wise use guidelines call for the establishment of national wetland policies covering all problems and activities related to wetlands, including institutional and organizational arrangements, legislative and government policies, increasing knowledge and awareness of wetlands and a review of wetland priorities in a national context. Recommendation REC C.4.10 also called for the Wise Use Working Group to be reconstituted to continue the wise use work of the Convention and report back to the next meeting of the conference.

Two workshops specifically on the subject of wise use took place at meetings of the Conference of the Contracting Parties, one in Regina and one in Montreux. Their reports and the papers presented are published in the proceedings of these meetings.

The fifth meeting of the conference, in Kushiro, Japan, in June 1993, approved resolution RES C.5.6, which calls on Contracting Parties to "implement in a more systematic and effective manner, and at international, national and local levels, the guidelines on wise use". A further wise use workshop held during the conference discussed additional guidance for the implementation of the wise use concept. Resolution RES C.5.6 notes the 'Additional Guidance for the implementation of the wise use concept', contained in Annex 1 to the resolution (Appendix 2, this report), urging Contracting Parties to implement its provisions.

A key objective of the wise use project has also been to publish an Action Plan which would identify priority wise use activities in a number of developing countries. The Ramsar Bureau, in cooperation with the authorities of the countries concerned, will be submitting this plan to the Government of the Netherlands and other interested governments and development assistance agencies.

Definitions

As defined in Regina in 1987, "the wise use of wetlands is their sustainable utilization for the benefit of mankind in a way compatible with the maintenance of the natural properties of the ecosystem".

"Sustainable utilization" of a wetland is defined as "human use of a wetland so that it may yield the greatest continuous benefit to present generations while maintaining its potential to meet the needs and aspirations of future generations".

"Natural properties of the ecosystem" are defined as "those physical, biological or chemical components, such as soil, water, plants, animals and nutrients, and the interactions between them".

In this context, the wise use concept will promote national wetland policies through a long-term process and through emergency actions at specific sites, whether or not they are on the List of Wetlands of International Importance.

Implementation of the wise use concept

The concept of the wise use of wetlands has been even more of a focal issue to the Ramsar Convention since the Wise Use Working Group began its work in 1988. Much work has subsequently been done throughout the world on the wise use of natural resources. The present publication reflects part of this work which, thanks to a number of international organizations such as IUCN - The World Conservation Union (and in particular the IUCN Wetlands Programme), has permitted a clearer understanding of the sense and strengths of the concept, which will prove helpful in conserving wetlands.

According to the guidelines adopted in Montreux and published as the Annex to recommendation REC C.4.10, wise use of wetlands involves the establishment of national wetland policies. Whether or not national wetland policies are being prepared, priority actions at national level and at particular wetland sites should be defined. The principal elements of national wetland policies may be grouped in the following sections:

- improvement of institutional arrangements so that wetland policies can be fully integrated into the planning process; and the establishment of mechanisms and procedures for incorporating this integrated, multi-disciplinary approach into planning and execution of projects concerning wetlands.

- review of existing legislation and government policies (including subsidies and incentives) including, where appropriate, application of existing legislation and policies, adoption of new ones, and use of development funds for wetlands.

- increasing knowledge and awareness of wetlands and their values, including exchange of information, propagation of their benefits and values (a statement of which is given), review of traditional techniques, and training of appropriate staff.

- review of the status of wetlands in the national context, including compilation of a national inventory, and definition of each wetland's particular values and conservation priorities.

- addressing of problems at particular wetland sites, by integrating environmental considerations into their management, regulated utilization, establishment of management plans, designation as appropriate for the Ramsar List, establishment of nature reserves and, if necessary, restoration.

Defining a national wetland policy is often a very long process, and governments may wish to promote priority aspects of the wise use of wetlands before the actual adoption of a comprehensive policy. In this context, they need to identify short-term priority actions to be taken at national level, as well as priority actions at specific sites.

The Wise Use Project

After the Montreux conference, the Government of the Netherlands commissioned the Ramsar Bureau to carry out a three-year project, designed to draw lessons from between six to eight current experiments in the wise use of wetlands from developing countries, selected in such a way as to ensure the widest possible geographical representation in different socio-economic contexts. With the advice of the Wise Use Working Group, the IUCN Wetlands Programme and the University of Leiden, Netherlands, no fewer than seventeen case studies were selected during a meeting of the Wise Use Working Group held in Perth, Australia, at the 18th session of the IUCN General Assembly in November 1990. Australia, Canada, Denmark, France, Germany, Hungary, Netherlands, USA and the Commission of the European Communities complemented the project with case studies drawn from their own experience. Most of the studies present ongoing activities in which international organizations such as the Asian Wetland Bureau (AWB), Wetlands for the Americas, the Commission of the European Communities, the Common Wadden Sea Secretariat, IUCN and WWF, as well as governments, are directly involved.

Ultimately, more than forty countries, some developed, others developing, were associated with the project and took part in the evaluation of the case studies which were reviewed and analysed by the Bureau and its advisors, and discussed at two meetings hosted by the Netherlands in The Hague in October 1991 and at Texel in September 1992; these countries also participated in the elaboration of the conclusions of the project, notably at a meeting hosted by the United States of America in February 1993.

The recent enhanced understanding of wise use is illustrated by the case studies which follow. The studies examine the problems encountered, the methods employed, the results obtained or anticipated, and the lessons learned. An examination will reveal examples of the multitude of approaches adopted, with the ideal of reaching sustainable utilization of wetland resources while at the same time respecting the natural functions of the ecosystems.

Hervé Lethier
Director of Conservation
Coordinator of the Wise Use Project
Ramsar Convention Bureau
Gland
Switzerland

Chapter 2
Case studies

This chapter examines the problems, approaches, achievements and the lessons learned from seventeen widely varying case studies from around the world.

International studies:
- Towards integrated management of coastal wetlands of Mediterranean type.
- Wise use of the Wadden Sea.

National studies:
- Canada: The Federal Policy on Wetland Conservation.
- Guinea-Bissau: Coastal wetland planning and management.
- Uganda: The National Wetlands Programme.

Local studies:
- Australia: The Chowilla Resource Management Plan.
- Chad: Traditional management systems and integration of small scale interventions in the Logone floodplains.
- Costa Rica: The mangrove forests of Sierpe.
- El Salvador: Wise use activity in Laguna El Jocotal.
- France: Developing a wise use strategy for the Cotentin and Bessin Marshes.
- Hungary: Wetland conservation in Hortobágy National Park.
- India: Towards sustainable development of the Calcutta Wetlands.
- Pakistan: Sustainable management of mangroves in the Indus Delta.
- The Philippines: Wise use and restoration of mangrove and marine resources in the Central Visayas Region.
- USA: Wetland drainage and restoration potential in the Lake Thompson watershed, South Dakota.
- Vietnam: Rehabilitation of the *Melaleuca* floodplain forests in the Mekong Delta.
- Zambia: Wise use of floodplain wetlands in the Kafuc Flats.

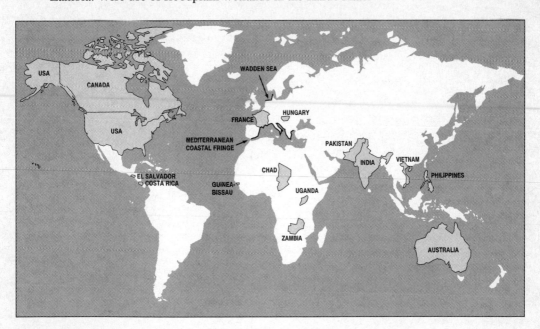

Towards integrated management of coastal wetlands of Mediterranean type

Tobias Salathé

Introduction

In 1987, the Commission of the European Communities, Directorate-General XI (Environment, Nuclear Safety and Civil Protection), Division for Nature Protection and Soil Conservation, instigated preparatory actions concerning the integrated management of coastal wetlands of Mediterranean type. A working group was set up in order to allow the necessary exchange of information amongst experts and to coordinate a number of studies which were financed by the EC.

The studies produced by the group cover many of the aspects proposed in the concept of wise use elaborated by the working group of the Ramsar Convention. They can make a significant contribution to a community-wide policy on wetlands, particularly where addressing the problems at specific wetland sites, identifying problems in a regional context, increasing knowledge and awareness of wetlands and their values, addressing legislation and government policies, and improving institutional arrangements (Ramsar Convention Bureau 1990) are concerned.

This paper summarizes and assesses the information gathered and the main ideas created through the work of the group. Some of the wetland areas analysed by the working group are already serving as models of the concepts elaborated by the experts. One such case, concerning the Odiel marshes in Spain, is discussed here. The paper closes with an overview of how the integrated approach to the multiple use of wetland functions and products could be applied at supranational level in order to give concrete procedures and actions to the term 'wise use'.

The problem

Wetlands are environmentally amongst the most sensitive areas in the European Community. Although they now probably cover less than one per cent of its territory, they are among the most productive and fragile ecosystems. Early Mediterranean civilizations were based around coastal wetlands and depended on them for food, water and building materials. In more recent times these same areas have often been regarded as wastelands. Consequently there has been a massive loss of wetlands, especially in the Mediterranean basin, although data to quantify this are scarce and difficult to obtain.

The rate of destruction of remaining wetlands has accelerated this century and has been rapid over the past 40 years. Wetlands are drained for intensive cultivation, to provide land for urbanization and tourist developments. They are reduced and degraded through infilling and inflow of polluted urban, agricultural and industrial waste waters. Over-fishing, over-hunting and excessive boat traffic deprives wetlands of many of their functions, such as wildlife habitat, food-chain support, and human recreation.

Wetland destruction and degradation often have adverse and unforeseen long-term costs, whilst organizations and individuals can make short-term profits from the conversion of wetlands. In the Mediterranean, drainage of excess run-off in winter can result in water shortages in summer and exacerbate drought situations. Irrigation to overcome water shortages for agriculture can be costly and is usually maintained by high levels of public subsidy. Soil and groundwater salinization, agro-chemical, industrial and urban pollution, and disruption of social patterns can result. Destruction of wetland habitat, by whatever means, reduces the abundance and diversity of wetland-dependent flora and fauna, including exploitable fish and shellfish stocks.

The vested interests which cause governments, administrations and individuals to use wetlands in a destructive way are powerful and well financed. Such destructive policies sometimes operate deliberately, for example through publicly declared policies to reclaim land for agriculture. More often, wetland destruction is wrought indirectly, unconsciously or inadvertently. There are strong political short-term disincentives to confront longer-term environmental problems. Financial constraints are of paramount importance. To improve upon insufficient management, unwise development, deterioration and pollution of wetlands and to conserve these sensitive areas more effectively, one has ultimately to confront indebtedness, inappropriate pricing and institutional arrangements that do not work. In order to tackle these problems, one needs good, large scale examples of case studies and guidelines for adequate management of wetlands.

The approach

The need for a programme on integrated management of coastal wetlands of Mediterranean type was realized following the Integrated Mediterranean Programmes (IMP) set up by the European Community in the mid 1980s to improve the socio-economic structures in Greece, southern France and parts of Italy. At that time, it was recognized that these regions suffer from structural weaknesses such as under-developed agriculture, difficult natural conditions, difficulties in marketing their products, the existence of extensive less-favoured areas with unemployment, a low technology level, industrial crises, and large tourist industries that create socio-economic imbalances and poorly organized administrations. IMPs are multi-annual, cover all sectors and must be consistent with other policies, including the Common Agricultural Policy (CAP) and the Community policies on nature conservation.

In this context, the service for nature conservation (DG XI, B-2) of the European Commission decided that it would be useful to elaborate a baseline concept of integrated management, taking into account the particular political requirements related to coastal wetlands of Mediterranean type. The intention was that this concept would serve as a guideline for actions to implement conservation objectives. The concept should enable conservationists to maintain and even to strengthen their position in the dialogue with politicians and commercial sectors. An important consideration was that it should help those in charge of the implementation of the Community environment policy at local level as an efficient administrative tool.

The work programme for the development of integrated management structures proposed by the Commission consisted of three types of preparatory actions:

1. The elaboration of a set of studies to analyse practical aspects of specific wetland sites and also the more generally important aspects, including a study on wetland sites of Mediterranean type outside the European Community.

2. The establishment of a technical working group for a period of about three years, consisting of the leaders for the commissioned studies, representatives of interested EC services and experts of national administrations, in order to allow the necessary exchange amongst experts and to coordinate the work of the commissioned studies; and, on the basis of the results of these studies:

3. The preparation of a generalized analysis and guidelines for policy implementation and practical work in the framework of the integrated management of coastal wetlands of Mediterranean type (Klein 1988).

A methodology for site-specific problem analysis was proposed which would consider the historical and current situation at a given site, with an analysis and assessment of existing problems. This would include an evaluation of the factors contributing to the current state, proposals for future actions, and an *a priori* assessment of the factors which may influence future developments of the area (Figure 1). Such analyses were undertaken for 31 coastal wetland sites in Mediterranean EC member states. Although the main focus was on EC wetlands, for comparative purposes an additional study dealt with five wetlands of a similar type in other parts of the Mediterranean. A number of studies on general management aspects also took place.

At the end of this first phase of the work programme, more than 60 experts gathered to exchange experiences and debate the concept of integrated management of coastal wetlands of Mediterranean type. General conclusions on progress with site-specific and problem-related analyses were drawn up and used by the EC Commission as a basis for further work during a second phase.

For this, two sub-groups were created to deal specifically with the Messolonghi Lagoons in Greece, and the Odiel marshes in Spain. Each group organized a field visit and workshop to discuss the management problems. A project-planning method, 'ZOPP' (German for 'objectives-oriented project planning'), was applied to both projects during the workshops. The method required a team approach to visualize the problems and their inter-relation. Team members representing different interests in the wetland identified their respective core problems, their causes and effects. This was built into specific multi-level branch models of causal links of the problems, and the activities needed to solve them for both Messolonghi and Odiel.

Figure 1. Methodology proposed by the EC for the studies on integrated management of coastal wetlands of Mediterranean type (cf. Klein 1988).

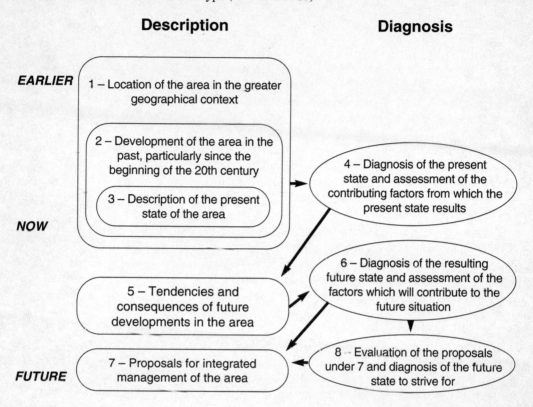

The first step of the ZOPP planning method, problem analysis, is concluded when the team is convinced that all the essential information has been used to build a causal network explaining the main cause and effect relationships characterizing the problem. The hierarchy of problems is transformed into a hierarchy of objectives which are then analysed. The next step is to identify potential alternative solutions and to develop a matrix of the actions required. At this stage it is important to identify whether assumptions were made which would influence the planned activities and adversely affect the desired end result. To ensure the success of the actions proposed, it is therefore important to re-examine how realistic the assumptions are which have been made during the planning process.

Additionally, the Wetland Ecosystems Research Group of the University of Exeter applied their Wetland Evaluation Technique to the Mediterranean sites analysed in detail in the earlier studies. Analysis of the questionnaires facilitated a basic understanding of the dynamics and functions of coastal wetlands of Mediterranean type (Maltby *et al.* 1988).

Achievements

Characteristics of Mediterranean wetlands

Coastal wetlands of Mediterranean type considered by the working group included river deltas and associated riverine habitats, estuaries, coastal lagoons, lakes and marshes, and endorheic lakes and marshes; most, but not all, are directly linked to the sea. Artificial wetlands, of which some are of ecological value (e.g. salt pans) whilst others provide valuable hydrological functions (e.g. reservoirs for irrigation or flood control), were also considered; so too were wetland sites on the Iberian Atlantic coast as they were considered to share the same features of the characteristic Mediterranean climate.

The contrast of cool wet winters and hot dry summers is reflected in a particular way in the hydrological regime, temperature, water chemistry and salinity of Mediterranean wetlands. Potential evapotranspiration exceeds rainfall for most of the year, during which run-off is infrequent and recharge of groundwater insignificant. Unless such wetlands are fed by external water supplies (either from higher rainfall regions or from the sea), the system is likely to be dry for at least part of the summer. Wetlands directly connected to the sea periodically become highly saline while those without such connections often dry out completely. Surface water run-off and groundwater discharge are essential in supplying coastal wetlands with freshwater, nutrients and other inputs which effectively link marine and coastal wetlands with a much wider hydrological catchment. Non-coastal wetlands situated further upstream and which are often influenced more by an orographically dominated climate and water regime (mountainous regions) were not considered.

Unlike many coastal areas, the Mediterranean has a very narrow tidal range. Water levels and wetland processes are therefore influenced more by storms and wind direction than by tidal cycles. Many of the coastal Mediterranean wetlands form a complex association with non-wetland habitats (dunes, open grassland, scrub, heath and matorral) which are intrinsically involved in the functional support of the wetlands themselves; e.g. dunes acting as aquifers, woodlands providing roosts for wetland birds. Most of the wetland functions are determined by the subtle interplay of freshwater and marine water.

The most prominent processes and functions of coastal wetlands of Mediterranean type can be summarized as groundwater recharge and discharge, flood storage and desynchronization of flood peaks, sediment trapping, shoreline anchoring, dissipation of erosive forces, maintenance of water quality, retaining and removing nutrients, food chain support, providing habitat for wildlife, fisheries support and different socio-economic values (recreational, economic, aesthetic and educational). Not all wetlands perform all functions and not all functions are performed to an equal extent (Maltby *et al.* 1988). Functions also interact (Figure 2).

The most important factors causing environmental problems in coastal Mediterranean wetlands are dam projects, water extraction, soil erosion, agricultural intensification with increasing use of fertilizers and pesticides, salinity control measures, pollution from sewage and industrial wastes, overfishing, hunting and tourist development. Resistance to conservation by local people, internal conflicts between management objectives, and the lack of adapted institutions, adequate finances, scientific resources, and skilled personnel further add to the management difficulties (Baldock *et al.* 1988).

Aquaculture

A specific study dealt with the problem of how best to integrate aquaculture activities into the management of coastal wetlands (Cataudella *et al.* 1988). Traditionally, Mediterranean lagoon fisheries have taken advantage of the fact that many marine fish species migrate regularly between the sea and shallow brackish lagoons which they use as spawning grounds. Thus, for centuries, fish traps were installed at strategic links between lagoons and the sea. Such installations are widely distributed along the Mediterranean coast and can be found in every country with coastal lagoons. The study summarized their function, ecology, and socio-economics, focusing mainly on the 'vallicoltura' in the lagoons of the northern Adriatic and

Figure 2. Matrix showing the interaction between different wetland functions (Maltby *et al.* 1988).

	Groundwater recharge	Groundwater discharge	Production/food chain support	Flood control	Sediment stabilization/erosion control	Water quality	Fisheries/aquaculture	Wildlife habitat	Recreation	Socio-economic
Groundwater recharge			●	✓		✓	●	●	●	
Groundwater discharge			✓		●	❀ ●	✓	✓	✓	✓
Production/food chain support						●	❀ ●	❀ ●	❀ ●	
Flood control	❀	❀	❀ ●		✓	✓	❀ ●	❀ ●	❀	✓
Sediment stabilization/erosion control	❀	❀	❀ ●	✓		✓	❀ ●	✓	✓	✓
Water quality			❀ ●	✓	✓				❀	✓
Fisheries/aquaculture			✓		●	●			✓	✓
Wildlife habitat			✓			❀ ●	❀ ●			
Recreation		❀	●	●	✗	✗	❀ ●	●		
Socio-economic		❀	●	●	✗	✗	❀ ●	●	❀ ●	

✓ Generally enhancing   ● Sometimes deleterious

❀ Sometimes enhancing   ✗ Generally deleterious

other sites on the Italian coast. In some lagoons, shellfish are also commercially exploited, either with ground-nets or by cultivating the desired species on artificial banks.

The danger of exploiting these resources above a sustainable level is real in several places. On the other hand, aquacultural installations often suffer from dystrophic crises during the hot summer months and from water pollution in the lagoons, which are still used in many places as collecting basins for only partially treated or untreated sewage. Additionally, piscivorous birds such as cormorants, herons, gulls and terns are seen by fishermen as competitors depleting a resource in which the fishermen have heavily invested. Several studies have investigated the extent of such damage and evaluated means of deterring the birds (with acoustic devices) or preventing access to the fish (with nets spanning smaller basins). The problems are, on balance, of lesser commercial importance than was initially believed and always restricted to specific localities and seasons.

In places where new aquaculture infrastructures are to be installed, environmental impact assessments (EIA) are needed to assess both the capacity of the hydrological regime and the long-term viability of the wetland to support the proposed installation. The sustainable exploitation of such renewable coastal lagoon resources by means of non- or semi-intensive aquaculture (based on traditional methods) is considered by the authors of the study to be compatible with the integrated management and conservation of coastal Mediterranean wetlands. However, this applies only where the coastal lagoons are clearly zoned in areas where aquaculture (and fisheries), tourism (boat traffic, surfing, swimming, etc) or conservation (wildlife refuges) are the dominant activities. Nevertheless, plans for regular restocking of the commercially exploited species (with fry from fish farms) need to be drawn up to ensure real sustainable exploitation. Further research into the ecology of the species exploited, and improved environmental training of personnel working in aquaculture are needed. Increased finances are likely to be required to compensate landowners, and to cover restoration costs and training programmes (Cataudella *et al.* 1988).

Integrated management

Sound integrated management of wetlands depends on a clear understanding of the physical, chemical and biological processes which control their functions. General recommendations concern: a) the importance of the catchment approach when examining processes and impacts, as well as appropriate management strategies; b) the need for active monitoring of the water table and hydrological budget of a wider range of wetlands than is currently the case, particularly in the light of increasing pressures on aquifers for alternative water use (e.g. irrigation, tourism); c) the assessment of sedimentation rates, inputs from soil erosion in the catchment, and erosion rates at the seaward edge of the wetland complex, together with analysis of the effects of water regulation structures and land use change on the stability and functions of the system; and d) the development of practical restoration or mitigation options (Maltby *et al.* 1988).

Integrated management can be divided into four main activities: shielding (against negative influences), control (of ecological and socio-economic influences), utilization (of natural resources), and design and structuring (i.e. planning for desired evolutions) (Szijj 1988). None of the studies came up with a concept of integrated management which would have been transferable from the region of its creation to another Mediterranean country, although some basic considerations were repeatedly mentioned. It was considered useful to direct a major effort to follow up the initial analyses in the site-specific studies, taking into account the special features of the different ecosystems, the apparent deficiencies of the direct application of existing methodologies, and the need for active collaboration with a variety of regional specialists (Maltby *et al.* 1988).

Above all, integration means the synchronization of opposing interests (in this case in a given wetland and its resources) towards a common goal of conservation and sustainable utilization. If this is done properly, i.e. when all interested parties participate in the process of finding a consensus or compromise, it is likely to be a difficult and time-consuming exercise. To achieve such integration, the roles of the various organizations – governmental, non-government, local, regional, national and supranational – need to be clarified.

To give adequate recognition to such an integrated planning procedure, and to demonstrate its importance to other administrations (ministries), it was proposed that an authority for integrated management be created at the appropriate administrative level, and that a manual on integrated management techniques and procedures be produced (Malakou *et al.* 1988; Pergantis 1988). Besides having to deal with the (supra)national policy for integrated management, such an authority would have to deal with the different wetlands on a case-by-case basis. It might be useful to regroup smaller wetlands into larger administrative units. Day-to-day management would need to be based on an integrated management plan, and the wetland area would need to be zoned. This zonation would have to include, at least for basic considerations, the whole hydrological catchment area.

An example — the Odiel marshes

The sub-group created to deal with the Marismas del Odiel, a coastal marsh at the mouth of the rivers Odiel and Tinto next to the industrial town of Huelva on Spain's southern Atlantic coast, met for the first time in October 1989. The ZOPP project planning method was applied to the

Local fishermen in the Messolonghi wetlands, Greece.
Photo: WWF/Vassiliki Psihogiou

Figure 3a. ZOPP analysis of management problems at the Odiel marshes.

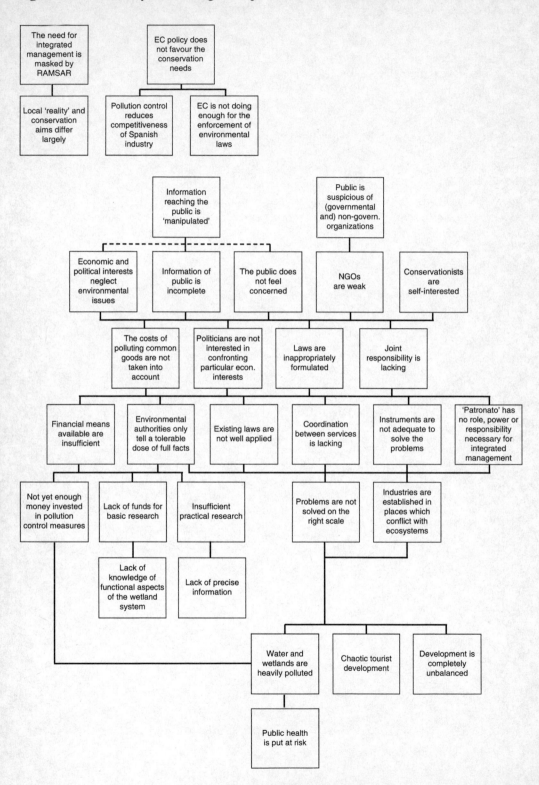

Figure 3b. ZOPP analysis of management objectives for the Odiel marshes.

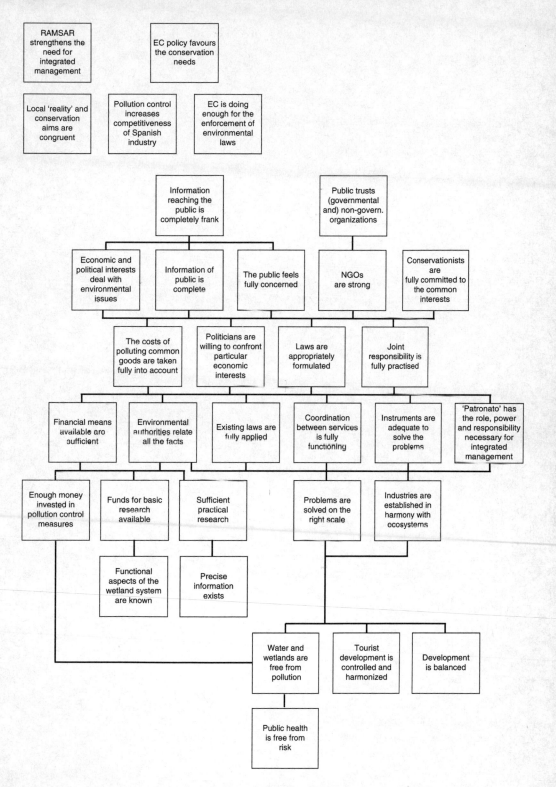

site (Figure 3) to clarify the issues at stake. This enabled the local office of the regional government environment agency, Agencia de Medio Ambiente (AMA), to coordinate a detailed study of the history, the environmental problems and pollution, and the development options for Odiel.

In November 1990, a group of Spanish and foreign experts gathered at the University of La Rábida to work specifically on functional aspects of and threats to the Odiel marshes, and on the administrative organization and the procedures for decision-making with regard to integrated management. Their conclusions were integrated in a detailed analysis of the history, environmental problems, and management constraints and proposals. Subsequently, AMA published this comprehensive document, including an exhaustive bibliography and specific action points for different organizations concerned with the integrated management of the Odiel marshes (Rubio & Martos 1991).

Lessons learned

Results of the EC programme

This 'Preparatory action concerning the integrated management of coastal wetlands of Mediterranean type' occupied a core group of about 30 experts for roughly three years of part-time work, spending an EC budget of nearly 300,000 ECUs on specific studies and meetings.

So far, other projects, co-financed by DG XI of the European Commission, have relied on the nature conservation sector of EEC regulation No. 2242/87 on Action by the Community for the Environment (ACE), which in turn was based on the Council Directive for the Conservation of Wild Birds (79/409/EEC). ACE projects were therefore selected for EC co-financing according to the benefits they proposed to contribute to the survival of threatened bird species (as listed in Annex I of the Directive) by conserving or restoring the particular habitat (in precisely delimited areas) upon which a number of these bird species depend. Article 4 of the Directive mentions specifically the conservation of wetlands, especially those of international importance as habitat for migrating waterbirds (i.e. sites listed or qualifying for listing under the Ramsar Convention). As a result, such ACE projects consisted mostly of land acquisition in order to protect and conserve particular natural habitats.

The programme of actions leading towards integrated management of coastal wetlands of Mediterranean type was therefore a conceptual novelty for DG XI since it addressed nature conservation issues of a more complicated nature. The partners involved needed to gain experience, and the efficiency of their work should be judged with this in mind. During the process, useful debate took place between the partners; important information on particular sites and the administrative and political structures was gathered, and, in some cases, was also presented to a wider audience. At seven sites, ACE projects for land purchase and habitat improvement were already running when the studies on their integrated management were commissioned; at two additional sites, ACE projects were soon to start. The elaboration of the studies on integrated management had a clear influence on many of the ACE projects in broadening their approach to include management aspects.

The mutual exchange of expertise, information and experience amongst the technical and regional experts of the integrated management working group proved to be highly valuable, both within the group and through outside contacts. The work of this group was essential in preparing the ground for the symposium on 'Managing Mediterranean wetlands and their birds for the year 2000 and beyond', held in February 1991 in the Adriatic town of Grado. During the symposium, participants developed 'A strategy to stop and reverse wetland loss and degradation in the Mediterranean basin' (Anon 1992). In September 1991, the first informal meeting of a 'Mediterranean Wetland Forum' drafted a three-year MedWet Action Plan to be implemented from 1992 to 1995 with co-financing (66%) to the tune of 4.4 million ECUs by the Commission of the European Communities (under the EEC regulation No. 3907/91 on Action by the Community relating to Nature Conservation; ACNAT), the remainder to be covered by southern EC member states and private organizations.

One may criticize the imbalance of the quantity of paper produced compared with the number of concrete actions following on the ground. Additionally, besides extremely important matters, much rather marginal information was also compiled and buried in a small number of internal draft reports. Some of these reports are unstructured, badly presented, unedited, and exist only in a small number of photocopies. They have most probably never been read by more than a few selected insiders. On the other hand, some authorities (e.g. the Junta de Andalucía) printed the reports of the different working groups and published them for wider circulation to concerned specialists, administrators and decision-makers (Martos *et al.* 1989; Rubio & Martos 1991). This is in line with the principle that the free flow of information is an essential prerequisite for achieving integrated management. The Camargue study even merited publication by a commercial publisher (Boulot 1991).

Although the Messolonghi Lagoons study did not produce an easily accessible written output, discussions between the study group members and local people were essential in furthering the understanding of the ecological and management problems of the area's wetlands. They also created awareness at the local and national level of the potential impacts of important developments in aquaculture and hydraulic works, particularly in the Acheloos river delta at the western end of the gulf.

According to the 'subsidiarity principle', the role of the EC is limited to initiating activities at Community level without interfering at the regional level. The preliminary actions towards integrated management of Mediterranean wetlands initiated by DG XI need therefore to be followed up by initiatives at the regional and local level. Where it has not already been done, the results of the valuable preliminary studies need to be edited, published and distributed widely amongst key people. Regions should be encouraged to follow examples set elsewhere. It should be seen as a way of instigating public debate on the issues raised, confronting the different interest groups, and commencing the integration of management proposals at a local and regional level. These follow-up activities, all part of good wetland conservation practice, should receive further EC support.

Ultimately, the implementation of integrated management of coastal wetlands of Mediterranean type should be refined in light of future experience. It can then be adapted and applied to all Community wetlands, including non-coastal wetlands and those of Atlantic type (e.g. peatbogs, tidal marshes). The present programme has laid solid groundwork to this end.

Integrated management and wise use

This paper addresses wetland conservation at the supranational level, i.e. not in the context of managing a particular wetland shared by different states, but trying to establish a policy for sound management covering different wetland sites in different countries. The EC is unique in its structure as a supranational entity with a central administration that was given the power to unify and streamline nature conservation policies, while, at the same time, the implementation of these directives has to be based on national laws and policies. This mix of administrative powers and the existence of powerful lobbies (e.g. agriculture, industry) at international and national level explains many of the difficulties and the slow progress experienced while working towards the wise use of wetlands and their resources within the EC.

Comparing the EC programme of integrated wetland management with the guidelines for wise use as prepared by the Ramsar Convention working group, it becomes clear that the EC programme has made a substantial contribution towards the implementation of the wise use concept, especially towards the establishment of a community-wide wetland policy, integrating the best parts of the different national wetland policies.

The work programme on integrated management has yet to contribute in any depth to the following fields of the concept of wise use:

1. The review of existing legislation and policies (including subsidies and incentives) which affect wetland conservation;

2. The application of existing legislation and the adoption of new legislation and policies;

3. The use of development funds for projects which permit conservation and sustainable utilization of wetland resources.

In addition, the training of appropriate staff in the disciplines which will assist in implementation of wetland conservation action and policies has barely been touched upon by the studies and the working group. These issues could form the basis for specific programmes in the near future. A study leading to the integration of different, recently-established national and regional wetland policies into a unified community-wide policy would be most beneficial. Above all, it would be preferable to seek to implement effectively, and without delay, the knowledge on integrated management already gained during the work summarized in this paper.

Tobias Salathé, EC Wetland Conservation Unit, Station biologique de la Tour du Valat, Le Sambuc, F-13200 Arles, France.

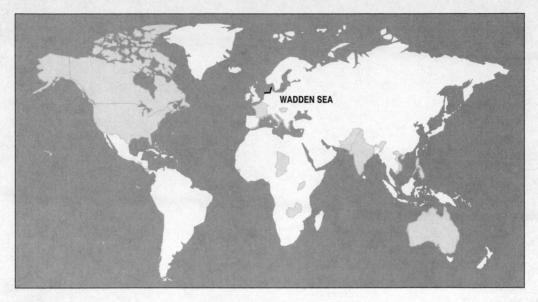

Wise use of the Wadden Sea

Jens A. Enemark

Introduction

The Wadden Sea is a marine wetland area shared by Denmark, Germany and the Netherlands. For more than a decade the three countries have cooperated to protect and conserve the Wadden Sea as an ecological entity and it is included in the List of Wetlands of International Importance under the Ramsar Convention. The Convention's concept of wise use has been of major importance in the framework of the trilateral Dutch-German-Danish cooperation as it constitutes a common organizing principle in terms of defining common principles and objectives for a wetland system shared by three countries.

The Wadden Sea is a shallow coastal area with extensive tidal flats, saltmarshes, sandbanks and islands, all subject to formation and erosion by wind and water. It has a coastline of about 500 km, from Den Helder in the Netherlands to the Skallingen peninsula in Denmark (Figure 1). Its width averages some 10 km, although in some areas it can reach a width of more than 30 km. Although it covers an area of almost 8,000 km^2, changes in tidal amplitude mean that the Wadden Sea lacks a clear borderline. Tidal amplitude, which changes with the phases of the moon and is affected by wind, is about 1.5 m at the northern and western edges of the region and about 3 to 4 m in the inner German Bight. Twenty-three islands with sand dunes and 14 sandbanks form a barrier to the North Sea.

For marine organisms, the Wadden Sea is a severe environment, yet it is characterized by high biomass production and an ecological importance extending far beyond its borders.

Saltmarsh, a transition zone between sea and land, is the habitat of a large number of plant species, most of which are salt-tolerant. Many invertebrates, especially insects and spiders, also depend on the Wadden Sea's saltmarshes, and there are more than 250 endemic species, sub-species and ecotypes.

Figure 1. The Wadden Sea region includes the entire coastal area from Den Helder in the Netherlands to the Skallingen peninsula in Denmark, a coastline of about 500 km.

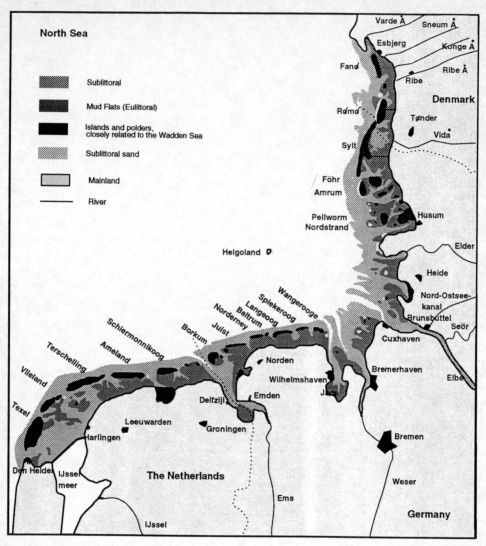

The Wadden Sea is important for breeding birds and for the numerous passage migrants which feed, moult and roost. Six to twelve million individuals of more than 50 species utilize the area throughout the year.

Of 102 species of fish recorded for the Wadden Sea, 22 species are common, 26 fairly common, 16 scarce, 12 rare and 22 extremely rare. Most are migratory and are therefore only present in certain periods of the year. A number of commercially important fish are dependent on the Wadden Sea, e.g. Plaice *Pleuronectes platessa* and Sole *Solea solea*, while in some years a large part of North Sea Herring *Clupea harengus* stocks are produced in the Wadden Sea.

Until 1974, the population size of the Common Seal *Phoca vitulina* decreased steadily, due mainly to hunting. The Dutch population only started to increase after 1980, pollution having depressed breeding success prior to this date. There were an estimated 10,000 seals in 1988, after which an epidemic reduced the population by 60%.

The problem

Traditionally, man has used the Wadden Sea for farming, fishing and hunting for many hundreds of years. The Wadden Sea borders on one of the most populated and industrialized areas of Europe where advances in technology allied to industrial development and an increase in recreational activities have had a substantial impact on the ecosystems of both the Wadden Sea and its adjacent areas.

The different forms of impact can be assigned to four categories:

1. Damage to or loss of biotopes as a result of new infrastructure, e.g. embankments and port facilities

The saltmarshes of the Wadden Sea are the largest of their type in Europe, but are a modest remainder of an extensive landscape of salt and brackish marshes, peatland and lakes which, up to some two thousand years ago, occurred in the border region between pleistocene and marine deposits. Embankment for human habitation and the subsidence of peat soil were quickly followed by storm surges which inundated the area. New saltmarshes formed through the sedimentation of sand and silt, often stimulated by human interference. One by one, the inundated areas were diked, yet only after 1600 was it possible to reclaim the land taken by the sea. The pace of land reclamation eventually outstripped saltmarsh formation and the area of saltmarsh gradually decreased. During the last fifty years, about 15,700 ha of saltmarsh have been embanked, an area equivalent to roughly half of the current saltmarsh (Common Wadden Sea Secretariat 1991).

2. Disruption of processes that maintain the productivity and health of the system through the input of nutrients and pollutants which reach the Wadden Sea via rivers, the North Sea and the atmosphere

Rivers are the major source of pollution in the Wadden Sea, the Elbe bringing by far the highest amounts of nutrients and contaminants. Dumping of dredged material, which includes roughly one third of all lead input, is another important source of heavy metals reaching the Wadden Sea. The atmosphere accounts for some 10% of total nitrogen inputs. Based on samples taken at one island in the German part of the Wadden Sea in the period 1988-1990, atmospheric inputs of cadmium are as high as 25% of the total cadmium inputs to the area.

No clear decreasing trend in nitrogen inputs can be found for the total Wadden Sea but phosphorus inputs seem to be decreasing slowly. There are strong indications that poly-chlorinated biphenols (PCBs) reduce the reproductivity of seals and that substances, or combinations thereof, attack the immune system of seals so that they become more susceptible to infection.

Possible sea-level rise as a result of the enhanced greenhouse effect may pose a substantial threat to the Wadden Sea ecosystem. It is estimated that an average 1-2 cm of sand and silt is deposited every year, against an expected sea-level rise of 0.5-1 cm/year in the coming decades. In addition to this, an increase in the height of the average tide and the subsidence of the sea bed should be added in those areas of the Wadden Sea where gas is extracted.

With the present rate of accretion, it can be expected that island saltmarshes will nearly all disappear, or will be diminished significantly, if future sea-level rise increases to 1 cm/year. Mainland saltmarshes may be able to withstand a 1-2 cm sea-level rise, whereas the tidal flats in the tidal basins with relatively small intertidal areas will tend to disappear even under the influence of a relatively small sea-level rise of 0.5 cm/year. Whether further sedimentation on flats in tidal basins with extended intertidal areas can keep pace with a 0.5-1 cm yearly sea-level rise is, as yet, uncertain.

3. Exploitation of renewable resources, e.g. blue mussels and cockles

Blue mussel fishing is a highly important economic activity in the Wadden Sea, total yields averaging about 100,000 tonnes. The mussel fishery is mainly carried out on culture beds, and currently about 10,800 ha of the Wadden Sea are designated as such.

Mussel and seed fishery have resulted in the complete loss of old (mature) mussel banks in the Dutch Wadden Sea and in a considerable reduction of their number and biomass in the German and Danish Wadden Sea. The impact of culture beds has local effects as well as wider ecosystem effects, such as changes in habitat and species composition, food competition with other organisms and a change in nutrient and primary-production balance in areas with culture beds.

There are further indications that culture beds cause food shortages for other filter feeders and result in lower levels of species abundance, including the number and distribution of birds, in adjacent areas.

4. Disturbance to wildlife as a result of recreation, hunting and military activities

The Wadden Sea region is an important area for tourism. Official figures put the number of tourists staying overnight at between 30-40 million annually, but the actual number is significantly higher; for some areas it may even be 100% higher. The tourist industry has developed into one of the most important activities in terms of income and employment. Most of the islands are fully dependent on income from tourism.

In addition to the loss of biotopes and changing structures within the ecosystem resulting from the construction of tourism infrastructure, e.g. hotels, and the over-exploitation of freshwater resources, tourism causes disturbance to wildlife. Disturbance during the critical May to September period, the peak time for tourism, can reduce the viability of animal populations by lowering reproductive success and by increasing mortality rates.

The approach

Protection

In order to protect the Wadden Sea as an area of international importance, a large part has been given protected area, nature reserve or national park status by the authorities responsible in the three countries. In addition, the Wadden Sea has been designated in the List of Wetlands of International Importance of the Ramsar Convention.

The three Wadden Sea countries cooperate to protect the Wadden Sea as an ecological entity. This trilateral cooperation is based on the Joint Declaration on the Protection of the Wadden Sea (1982), in which the governments undertake to consult each other in order to coordinate their activities to implement a number of international legal instruments in the field of nature protection, e.g. the Ramsar, Bonn and Bern Conventions. Within the framework of this trilateral cooperation, the parties established the Common Wadden Sea Secretariat in 1987.

The wise use concept

The assessment of the current state of the Wadden Sea leads to the conclusion that, although considerable progress in the field of nature and environmental protection has been made on a national, as well as an international, level, the quality of the ecosystem needs to be significantly improved in order to restore and maintain its natural potential, as required by the wise use concept of the Ramsar Convention.

To begin with, the protection measures of the national authorities must be enhanced in order to improve the quality of the ecosystem, and they must be harmonized between the three Wadden Sea countries to be effective. However, the legal and administrative systems of the three countries differ and, as a result, different solutions to basically similar problems impede their mutual effectiveness. It is here that the wise use concept of the Ramsar Convention comes into the picture.

Until now, the national and international Wadden Sea policies have primarily been concerned with the conservation of 'actual values' of parts of the ecosystem, e.g. protecting seals and birds. This, however, provides no guarantee for maintaining the values and potentials of the whole system. In fact there are, as stated above, many indications that the Wadden Sea ecosystem is still deteriorating. In conclusion, better guarantees for maintaining the natural properties of the Wadden Sea ecosystem can be provided by a policy based upon conservation *and* wise use.

It should be emphasized that the key concept is to increase natural values, which may mean a decrease in actual uses. The extent to which such a policy is implemented is determined by politicians.

The concept of wise use, as applied in the framework of the trilateral Wadden Sea policy, can be visualized by the flow diagram (Figure 2).

The *guiding principle* of the Wadden Sea policy is to determine the goal and the nature and direction of policy, based upon the wise use concept. The *actual situation* of the Wadden Sea can be described in terms of utilization, ecological values and threats, and is relatively well known, although differences exist as to the assessment of the situation.

The *reference situation* describes the potential natural values of the ecosystem. It is a hypothetical ecosystem composed of up-to-date scientific knowledge and serves as a calibration instrument. Ecological references are values assigned to parameters describing the reference situation. The ecosystem parameters must provide relevant information about an aspect of the ecosystem. Furthermore, the parameters should: a) be easy to measure and be based on sufficient scientific information; b) have political and social appeal; and c) be indicative of human influences on the ecosystem.

Together, the complete set of parameters must provide sufficient information about the quality of the ecosystem, while at the same time they must be limited in order to be applicable in practice. It should be emphasized, however, that there are many problems related to assigning concrete values to parameters describing the Wadden Sea. In evolutionary terms, the Wadden Sea is in its infancy, subject to very strong fluctuations which make it difficult to discern anthropogenic influences from 'background noise'. It is, furthermore, an open and heterogenous system.

Irrespective of the reference situation selected, a number of basic conditions apply with regard to (i) the chemical situation, (ii) the hydrodynamic/geomorphological situation, and (iii) the disturbance situation. Currently, the preliminary basic conditions necessary for achieving the reference situation are that:

- concentrations of chemical substances should be equal to or close to the natural background values;
- the present hydrodynamic/geomorphological situation should be maintained;
- the present level of disturbance should be reduced.

Figure 2. Flow diagram of the Wadden Sea wise use concept.

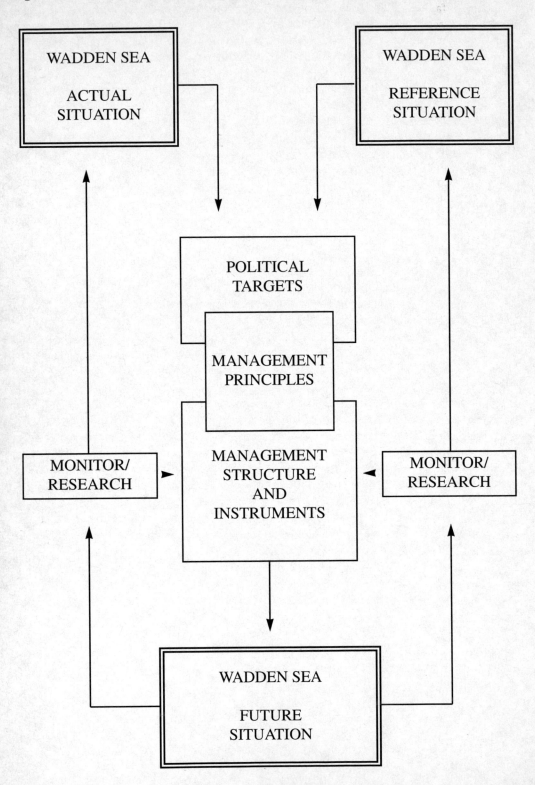

In conclusion, by comparing the actual situation with the reference situation, it can be assessed how far the actual situation is diverging from the reference. In consequence, political targets can be set in order to turn the actual situation in the direction of an ecosystem in which the quality is in accordance with the guiding principle.

Management principles are intermediate between overall policy and politics, linking the guiding principle with the actual situation in the area, where people live, work and pursue recreational activities. *Management structures* integrate the above elements and contain guidelines for the application of the elements in specific management plans. Feedback is achieved through *monitoring and research* in order to assess the effects of the measures taken. It can also influence the reference that is currently used in that it provides new insights and, possibly, results in the setting of new political targets.

At the Sixth Governmental Conference on the Protection of the Wadden Sea in November 1991, the above concept of wise use of the Wadden Sea was adopted, with the aim of maintaining the actual values and potentials of the ecosystem as a whole. The wise use concept is the cohesive element in the common, trilateral protection of the Wadden Sea.

Achievements

The guiding principle

The guiding principle of the trilateral Wadden Sea policy is "to achieve, as far as possible, a natural and sustainable ecosystem in which natural processes proceed in an undisturbed way". It aims to:

1. Maintain water flows and the attendant geomorphological and pedological processes;
2. Improve the quality of water, sediment and air to levels that are not harmful to the ecosystem;
3. Safeguard and optimize conditions for flora and fauna including:
   • preservation of the Wadden Sea as a nursery area for North Sea fish;
   • conservation of the feeding, breeding, moulting and roosting areas of birds, and the breeding and resting areas of seals, as well as the prevention of disturbance in these areas;
   • conservation of the saltmarshes and dunes;
4. Maintain the scenic qualities of the landscape, in particular the variety of landscape types and their specific features.

Management principles

The Wadden Sea is not an isolated nature area. It is used extensively by people, whose activities demand common management principles as a basis for the actual conservation and management of the area by the respective national authorities. These are:

1. The Principle of Careful Decision Making, i.e. to make decisions on the basis of the best available information;
2. The Principle of Avoidance, i.e. to avoid activities which are potentially damaging to the Wadden Sea;
3. The Precautionary Principle, i.e. to take action to avoid activities which are assumed to have a significant damaging impact on the environment, even where there is not sufficient scientific evidence to prove a causal link between activities and their impact;

4. The Principle of Translocation, i.e. to translocate activities which are harmful to the Wadden Sea environment to areas where they will cause less environmental impact;
5. The Principle of Compensation, i.e. that the harmful effect of activities which cannot be avoided are balanced by compensatory measures;
6. The Principle of Restoration, i.e. that, wherever possible, parts of the Wadden Sea should be restored if it can be demonstrated by reference studies that the actual restoration is not optimal, and that the original state is likely to be re-established;
7. The Principles of Best Available Technology and Best Environmental Practice, as defined by the Paris Commission.

Common objectives

For each of the common uses, impacts and human activities in the area, common objectives have been set, based upon the above-mentioned principles. Examples which demonstrate the implementation of the principles and the level of common regulations are:

Sea defence, saltmarsh management and dune protection

To harmonize the interests of nature protection and the essential safety of an area's inhabitants, there has been agreement on the prohibition of sea-walls and minimization of the unavoidable loss of biotopes through sea defence measures. Measures to protect saltmarshes and dunes have also been agreed in order to allow natural processes to take place, with special emphasis on flora and fauna; e.g. a ban on the application of fertilizers, pesticides and other toxic substances.

Fisheries

It has been agreed to close sizeable areas of the Wadden Sea to cockle and mussel fisheries, including intertidal and subtidal areas, in order to limit their negative ecological impact.

Tourism, shown here along the coastal strip at Büsum, Germany, must not constrain conservation and wise use. Photo: Jens Enemark

Recreation

To maintain the recreational values of the Wadden Sea, and to protect sensitive areas for birds and seals, it has been agreed to establish zones where recreational activities, including excursions by ship and recreational boating, is forbidden. In other areas, speed limits for boats are to be set and the use of jet-skis and similar motorized craft may only be carried out in small designated areas. The use of hovercrafts and jet-scooters will be prohibited altogether.

For civil air traffic, minimum altitudes of between 1,500 and 2,000 feet will be set. Lower altitudes of 700 to 1,000 feet will be allowed in designated flight corridors in less vulnerable areas.

Hunting

The hunting of migratory species in the Wadden Sea will be progressively phased out, and the hunting of non-migratory species will only be permitted if it can be clearly established that migratory species will not be harmed. The use of lead shot for shooting over the Wadden Sea is to be prohibited.

Pollution

Whilst the above activities are carried out mainly in the Wadden Sea and adjacent areas, the input of surplus nutrients and pollution, such as heavy metals and organic micropollutants, originates primarily from the catchment area of the North Sea, and also reach the Wadden Sea via atmospheric pollution. It is therefore necessary to take measures to reduce or, where necessary, eliminate such inputs. For a number of years, the countries adjacent to the North Sea have cooperated to combat pollution, and in this context it has been agreed to reduce by 50%, between 1985 and 1995, the input of nutrients in areas where they cause problems; and to reduce by at least 50% the input of a number of substances which are toxic, bioaccumulating and persistent (by at least 70% for dioxins, cadmium, mercury and lead).

In addition, the Wadden Sea countries have taken measures to reduce the direct input of pollutants into the Wadden Sea, prohibit discharges from off-shore installations, and reduce pesticide emissions.

Operational pollution and accidental discharges which originate from shipping will be eliminated or minimized by the establishment of a vessel-traffic-information system for ships carrying hazardous substances; compulsory pilotage for ships of a certain size; and making available adequate port-reception facilities for harmful ship wastes and garbage.

Birds

There is common agreement among the Wadden Sea countries with regard to the protection of migrating waterfowl along the East Atlantic Flyway, of which the Wadden Sea is a core area.

Implementation

The common wise use principles and objectives outlined above are currently being implemented in national instruments, measures and management.

The Wadden Sea countries have agreed the establishment of a special conservation area, for which a coordinated management plan will be prepared. The management plan will include a comprehensive set of measures aimed at achieving common ecological targets by the time of the next Governmental Conference in 1994.

The plan will also give consideration to whether zoning can be used to improve the protection of the Wadden Sea, in particular the designation of adjacent buffer zones in order to enable better regulation of activities outside the Wadden Sea but which impact on the Wadden Sea ecosystem; and to the need to harmonize zoning measures within the Wadden Sea, including the designation of special protection zones.

Lessons learned

The wise use concept plays a vital role in the trilateral cooperation on the protection of the Wadden Sea in that it is the common denominator linking together three countries, each with different legal and administrative structures. As such, it provides the basis for the maintenance of the natural values and resources of a shared wetland system. Such wetland systems often suffer from different measures being undertaken by the different countries involved, with the result that wise use is not achieved for the wetland system as a whole. The wise use principle may thus prove to be an outstanding tool for transboundary cooperation. Common principles of policy and management, and common goals, are therefore indispensable in attempting to manage shared wetland systems in a sustainable way.

Another very important aspect of the application of wise use in the Wadden Sea is the development of a conceptual framework and its implementation in terms of policy and management in the three countries. Two points are worthy of note here. Firstly, the wise use concept combines the conservation of the system's natural values and resources with its sustainable utilization. Secondly, the concept of wise use demonstrates the need to develop measures for assessing the state of the ecosystem, followed by the practical implementation of wise use principles. The development of the 'reference situation' may prove to be a powerful instrument for the setting of objectives, including the balance between conservation and sustainable utilization, as well as determining appropriate measures.

Constant monitoring of and research into the application of wise use practices are necessary to ensure that objectives are being met. Where new knowledge or insights are gained from such research, targets can be adjusted with the aim of improving still further the wise use activities being undertaken in the wetland ecosystem.

This Wadden Sea case study demonstrates the value of viewing wise use from an international perspective, and at different levels: on a global scale, wise use must address a reduction in the greenhouse effect; at the level of migratory flyways for waterfowl, it means adequate protection of habitats which are critical for their survival and life cycles; where it concerns the catchment area of the North Sea, it means a reduction in, and where necessary the elimination of, pollutants and surplus nutrients; at the level of the Wadden Sea as an entity, it means the conservation of the ecosystem and the regulation of human utilization; and at a local level, it might encompass the phasing out of certain activities, including the strict application of zoning.

The wise use concept is a dynamic approach to the problems that wetlands, national or shared, face and, as such, it is a powerful instrument for the conservation and sustainable utilization of wetlands. However, a profound challenge to the Wadden Sea, and the wise use activities being pursued, is sea-level rise as a result of the greenhouse effect. To lessen this effect, the sustainable development of the Wadden Sea requires the application of the wise use principle on a global scale.

Jens A. Enemark, Common Wadden Sea Secretariat, Virchowstrasse 1, D-26382 Wilhemshaven, Germany.

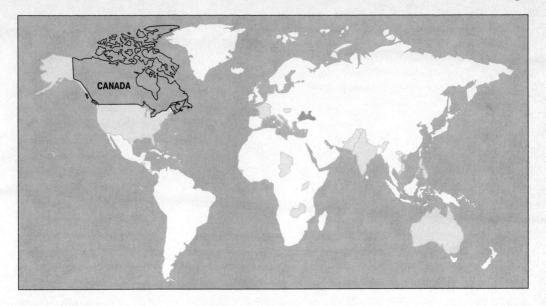

The Federal Policy on Wetland Conservation in Canada

Clayton D.A. Rubec

Introduction

Wetlands within Canada's borders cover over 127 million hectares (National Wetlands Working Group 1988) and comprise about 24% of the total global wetland resource. Some 29% of these Canadian wetlands are under direct federal jurisdiction, mainly in the northern territories, with the remainder under provincial government, non-government, or private landowner tenure. They provide a major portion of the nation's freshwater supply, significant pollution sinks, interaction with groundwater supplies, as well as watershed flood protection, water quality enhancement, and wildlife habitat.

Canada's wetland resources also provide a significant contribution to the national economy. It is estimated that their total economic value to Canadians readily exceeds CA$10 billion each year (Rubec *et al.* 1988). Some of the economic sectors that benefit greatly by the presence and ecological functions of wetlands are:

- non-consumptive recreation (photography, hiking, birdwatching);
- recreational and commercial hunting and trapping;
- forest, peat, wild rice and hay harvesting;
- water quality and flood control enhancement;
- market gardening;
- shoreline protection.

The wise application of sustainable development principles to wetland conservation will benefit Canadians in many ways (Rubec & McKechnie 1989). These benefits include:

- augmentation of waterfowl populations and improvement in wetland habitat quality for wildlife;

- promotion of soil and water conservation leading to reduced soil erosion, improved quality of groundwater and less degradation of the national agricultural base;
- reduction of shoreline storm damage and watershed flood impacts;
- buffering of the effects of drought and long-term climate change;
- improvement in coastal and estuarine shellfish and fish habitats and harvests;
- protection of the continental freshwater supply;
- improvement in the quality and availability of urban recreational lands;
- reduction in the impacts of non-point source pollution and acid rain.

The problem

The loss of Canadian wetlands

Current trends and results of monitoring studies indicate Canada has experienced a major loss of wetlands. In total, over one seventh (20 million hectares) of the original wetland area of Canada is estimated to have been converted to other land uses.

The most severe losses of wetlands are coincident with areas of major urban concentration and extensive agricultural development. Since settlement in Canada, up to 65% of coastal saltmarshes in the Atlantic region, 68% of all wetlands in southern Ontario (Canada's most populated area), and 70% of wetlands in prairie agricultural areas and Pacific estuaries have been drained or converted to other uses. Wetland loss in the vicinity of major Canadian cities is as high as 80 to 98% (Environment Canada 1986).

The factors causing wetland decline are many and vary in intensity and geographical focus. The majority (85%) of these losses have been attributed to drainage for agriculture, ongoing since settlement times. Expansion of urban and industrial lands represents 9%, and the development of leisure and recreational properties represents another 2% of the national decline in wetland area. Flooding of large areas for reservoirs for hydro-electricity production and water level management in areas such as the Great Lakes shared with the United States are other important factors.

The approach

The challenge faced by Canadians

While wetland use and conversion have historically contributed to the socio-economic development of Canada, continuing wetland degradation and loss are reaching critical levels in some areas. The challenge is to ensure that Canada's remaining wetlands are conserved and utilized in a sustainable manner and that actions are taken to restore and rehabilitate those critical habitats already affected by human activities.

Federal and provincial governments and the private sector have been working to develop effective wetland conservation policies, as well as supportive actions through conservation strategies across the nation. Rubec and McKechnie (1989) have noted that during the 1987 to 2001 period, over CA$1.07 billion will to be spent on wetland conservation programmes in Canada, a yearly average in that period of CA$77 million. This demonstrates significant commitment by both the public and private sector.

Development of a federal wetland policy

At the federal level, in order to ensure efficient use of public natural resources, greater coordination and guidance among departments was needed. In early 1987, Environment Canada sponsored a Non-Government Organizations Workshop on Wetland Conservation Policy. This workshop developed a series of recommendations directed to all governments in Canada concerning the need for a wetland policy. These recommendations were sent to all Environment and Natural Resource Ministers across the country. In June 1987, the Federal-Provincial Committee on Land Use produced a report entitled 'A Framework for Wetland Policy in Canada'. This report was endorsed by the full committee and members agreed to encourage use of this framework, as appropriate, in their own jurisdictions. Also in early 1987, the Federal Interdepartmental Committee on Land identified the need to develop a wetland policy statement to supplement the 'wise land use' provisions of the Federal Policy on Land Use. The Federal Water Policy adopted in 1987 also identified wetland conservation as a significant water resource issue.

A major national policy conference, the Sustaining Wetlands Forum (1990), produced recommendations for action on wetland conservation and management, including a call for all jurisdictions in Canada to adopt mutually supporting wetland conservation and management policies. This conference included a keynote address by the Prime Minister of Canada who called for urgent action to conserve the nation's wetland resources. Subsequently, the Green Plan announced the Federal Government's commitment to adopting a Federal Policy on Wetland Conservation (Government of Canada 1990).

One of the original considerations in the development of a federal wetland policy was that it should be crafted to deliver, wherever possible, Canadian commitments to the Ramsar Convention on Wetlands of International Importance. It was also apparent that greater influence on land use decisions by federal departments and agencies would assist in meeting Canada's commitments under the North American Waterfowl Management Plan (NAWMP). More recently, following Canada's ratification of the Convention on Biological Diversity, Canada expects that its federal wetland policy will form a portion of the implementation initiatives for this important and far-reaching international agreement.

The Federal Policy on Wetland Conservation

The Federal Policy on Wetland Conservation (FPWC) announced by the Government of Canada on 9 March 1992 is one of the first of its kind by a national government. The FPWC focuses on the sustainable wise use of wetlands in Canada, consistent with the wise use concept developed by the Ramsar Convention (Government of Canada 1991).

The stated objective of the Government of Canada, as articulated in this new policy, with respect to wetland conservation is: "to promote the conservation of Canada's wetlands to sustain their ecological and socio-economic functions, now and in the future".

In support of the above objective, the Federal Government of Canada, in cooperation with the governments of its ten provinces and two territories, as well as the Canadian public, will strive to achieve the following goals:

- **maintenance** of the functions and values derived from wetlands throughout Canada;
- **no net loss** of wetland functions on federal lands and waters;
- **enhancement and rehabilitation** of wetlands in areas where the continuing loss or degradation of wetlands or their functions have reached critical levels;
- **recognition** of wetland functions in resource planning, management and economic decision-making with regard to all federal programmes, policies and activities;

- **securement** of wetlands of significance to Canadians;
- **recognition of sound, sustainable management practices** in sectors such as forestry and agriculture that make a positive contribution to wetland conservation while also achieving wise use of wetland resources;
- **utilization** of wetlands in a manner that enhances prospects.

The FPWC is focused on areas of federal jurisdiction and management of wetlands under direct federal authority. As Canada is a federal state, wetlands in its ten provinces are generally under provincial regulation except on federal lands such as national parks. However, in its two northern territories, most wetlands are under federal management. Hence, while the policy will apply directly to an estimated 29% of Canada's wetland base (its federally managed wetlands), it also will touch on how the Federal Government affects other wetlands through its federal programmes, policies and shared fiscal programmes with the provinces and territories.

Federal policy strategies for wetland conservation

The Federal Policy on Wetland Conservation outlines seven strategies to provide for the wise use and management of wetlands so that they can continue to provide a broad range of functions on a sustainable basis. These strategies are aimed at building on past achievements and working in concert with ongoing initiatives for wetland conservation, in particular the North American Waterfowl Management Plan. The policy promotes a non-regulatory, cooperative approach. The policy strategies set out the direction to put the federal house in order, to manage federal wetlands, and to ensure delivery of effective wetland science and public awareness actions both nationally and internationally. The seven strategies are focused on:

1. Developing public awareness.
2. Managing wetlands on federal lands and waters and in other federal programmes.
3. Promoting wetland conservation in federal protected areas.
4. Enhancing cooperation with federal, provincial, territorial and non-government partners.
5. Conserving wetlands of significance to Canadians.
6. Ensuring a sound scientific basis for policy.
7. Promoting international actions.

The policy will affect all Federal Government programmes and institutions in Canada. Implementation guidelines are to be developed in consultation with affected individual departments and agencies. The lead agency with regard to the policy is the Canadian Wildlife Service, Environment Canada. A public report in both English and French is now available outlining the background to the development of the policy, the rationale for wetland conservation, and the full text of the policy and its seven strategies, as well a glossary of terms.

This wetland policy at the federal level provides:

- a signal of commitment to wetland conservation, for Canadians and the world community, and a catalyst for mutually supporting actions across the country;
- a heightened profile for the issue to call attention to wetland socio-economic and environmental benefits, and to ensure that wetlands receive adequate consideration throughout the Federal Government;

- direction and support for individual decision makers to ensure that opportunities for the sustained wise use of wetlands are realized, and to avoid or resolve wetland-related conflicts;
- clarification of specific federal responsibilities for wetlands, as well as a synthesis of existing legislation, policies and programmes which already contribute to wetland conservation;
- a consistent, coordinated approach among the many federal agencies which influence wetlands, aimed at adjusting activities which conflict with wetland conservation and ensuring progress towards specific objectives and goals.

'No net loss of wetland functions'

One of the goals of the FPWC is to ensure that its programmes, policies and expenditures do not result in a net loss of wetland functions. 'No net loss of functions' includes balancing unavoidable losses of wetlands with mitigatory action, such as replacement, so that further reductions to wetland functions may be prevented. In general, this means that, where development of particular wetlands in critical areas must proceed, wetland loss must be mitigated by replacement of wetland functions in close proximity. In developing this concept in Canada, guidelines must be developed and will call on the expertise and experience developed in 'no net loss of habitat' applications in other jurisdictions. To this end the Federal Government, in cooperation with the North American Wetlands Conservation Council (Canada), has recently published a report synthesizing North American experience and recommendations for implementing 'no net loss' in Canada (Lynch-Stewart 1992).

How will we conserve wetlands of significance to Canadians?

To date, many individual wetlands have been acquired for conservation objectives across Canada by various levels of government and the public, including landowners, non-government organizations and the private sector. However, these efforts, when considered collectively, fall short of comprehensive protection of the widespread interest in wetlands across Canada. A more systematic approach is required.

One strategy in the FPWC is securement of a 'network of wetlands of significance to Canadians' which would involve governments, non-government agencies, the private sector and individual landowners. The network would include:

1. Exemplary wetlands – those characteristic of both the common and the rare types of wetlands in each wetland region of Canada;
2. Strategic wetlands – those essential to meeting a goal or objective specific to a wide spectrum of ecological, social and economic values associated with wetland function.

Establishment of this network will require an assessment of those wetlands in Canada that are already secured and a systematic identification of those wetlands of significance to Canadians which should be secured. This identification of sites would then be considered by the many government and non-government parties which already participate in wetland conservation across Canada. The parties will be encouraged to use this list of candidate sites for setting priorities on their own agendas. In this way, the emphasis could be on establishing a systematic, coordinated approach to 'filling in the gaps' of a truly cooperative Canadian network of secured wetlands – which exemplifies all the wetland regions of Canada and conserves the full range of functions which wetlands strategically support.

Such a network is essential to ensure the maintenance of Canada's diverse wetland heritage, to exemplify sustainable use of wetlands, and for genetic conservation, research and educational purposes. These wetlands could serve as benchmark sites for monitoring long-term changes to ecosystems and for assessing the effectiveness of impact mitigation actions. Such a network has been proposed in the United States and exists in other countries such as Finland and Norway.

Achievements

National

To promote wetland programme coordination in Canada, the Federal Minister of the Environment created the North American Wetland Conservation Council (Canada) in April 1990. This Council, working closely with a parallel council in the United States and provincial and non-government partners, acts as the senior Canadian body for coordinating implementation of the North American Waterfowl Management Plan. It has also established a national secretariat and is publishing a new report series, entitled 'Sustaining Wetlands Issues Papers', on wetland science, management and policy topics of national interest.

Development of provincial wetland conservation and management policies are under way in several provinces, including Alberta and Saskatchewan. The Government of Ontario announced a provincial wetland policy in June 1992, focusing on implementation through its Planning Act. In the long term, mutually compatible wetland policies across Canada by all provincial and territorial governments as well as the Federal Government are a national ideal. Hence, it is critical that these provincial wetland policy processes are complementary to the federal initiative. The concepts of no net loss of wetland functions and recognition of sustainable wise use of wetland resources, as well as definition of key wetland areas for protection, are common themes across Canada. The creation of the Canadian Wetlands Conservation Task Force in March 1991 has also resulted in a tracking and delivery mechanism for wetland conservation and policy initiatives across Canada.

To date, governments and non-government groups have promoted a non-regulatory approach in most jurisdictions. In this regard, the introduction of non-regulatory wetland management and conservation policies is proceeding. Each of the provincial governments has developed a public review or consultation process for their wetland conservation strategies or policies. In two provinces, Prince Edward Island and New Brunswick, complementary regulatory procedures that result in protection of wetlands through environmental assessment of wetland development proposals are now in use.

An essential element in wetland management is the need for a nationally standardized approach to wetland site evaluation for planning and decision-making regarding the use of these wetlands. In 1988, Environment Canada and Wildlife Habitat Canada initiated a joint research project called 'Wetlands Are Not Wastelands'. The final report of this project, 'Wetlands Evaluation Guide' (Bond *et al.* 1992), provides a new planning tool in Canada for step-by-step analysis of wetland values and development decision-making.

International

One of the major considerations in developing the Federal Policy on Wetland Conservation was that it should deliver Canadian commitments to the Ramsar Convention on Wetlands of International Importance wherever possible. Few other nations have developed national wetland policy strategies. The FPWC in Canada focuses on the sustainable wise use of wetlands in Canada, consistent with the Wise Use concept developed by the Ramsar Convention. The Canadian policy may become a model for other governments internationally. Several countries have already utilized key elements from the draft versions of the Canadian policy in the development of national wetland strategies and policies. Others have expressed interest in modelling elements of the Canadian policy experience.

Canada is a world leader in the Ramsar Convention, having designated 30 sites as of 1992, covering in excess of 13,000,000 hectares of internationally significant wetlands (Gillespie *et al.* 1991). Canada has a special contribution to play in global wetland conservation, with the longest coastline of any nation in the world, 9% of the world's freshwater, 24% of the world's wetlands located within its borders, and the second largest peatland resource base of any nation in the world. In particular, Canada is ensuring the continued availability of wetland habitat to sustain Canadian migratory bird species along the western hemisphere flyways, improve the management of transboundary resources such as water, and contribute to the maintenance of the global environment.

To date, numerous valuable international precedents have been set. The 75th Anniversary of the Convention for the Protection of Migratory Birds between the United States and Canada was marked in July 1992. Implementation of this Convention has allowed a recovery of depleted waterfowl populations to a level that now generates several billions of dollars annually to North American economies. However, large-scale alterations of the wetland and grassland habitat base by agriculture, urbanization and industrial activities have affected the distribution and abundance of several important duck populations.

Significant for its migratory geese and shorebirds, this Manitoba wetland, a Ramsar site, also attracts several thousand tourists and local visitors. Photo: Jane Claricoates/WWT

The North American Waterfowl Management Plan has been developed jointly between Canada, the United States and Mexico since 1986 to reverse or modify activities that destroy or degrade waterfowl habitat, primarily wetlands. This multilateral initiative proposes to invest over US$1.5 billion in wetland conservation and management. The plan recognizes that, in the face of major alterations to the landscape by man, the continued maintenance and restoration of wetlands will be necessary to provide suitable habitat for waterfowl and many other wildlife species. To date, over 730,000 hectares of wetlands have been secured and/or enhanced under NAWMP for waterfowl production across Canada (North American Wetlands Conservation Council (Canada) 1991, 1992).

The 1978 agreement between the United States and Canada on Great Lakes Water Quality was amended in 1987 to include specific reference to wetlands and development of ecosystem health indicators for the Great Lakes. A memorandum of understanding was also signed by Canada, the United States and Mexico for the conservation of migratory birds and their habitats. This initiative expands the Canadian Wildlife Service's Latin American Programme which has several other components related to Neotropical wetlands. Among these, Canadian participation in the Western Hemisphere Shorebird Reserve Network (recently renamed 'Wetlands for the Americas'), embracing shorebird habitats in North and South America, promises to enhance wetland conservation internationally.

In June 1992, Canada was one of the first nations to join the Convention on Biological Diversity. This agreement will involve a strong commitment to wildlife and habitat conservation initiatives in Canada, particularly in high risk areas where many of its most threatened wetlands are found.

Implementation

Wetlands have become an important component in the development of conservation strategies across Canada. Through the preparation of provincial, territorial and federal conservation strategies and wetland policies, a common focus on the global themes of sustainable development and partnerships has emerged.

The Federal Government has stated that it views its role in wetland conservation as a full partner with other governments and the private sector; as a leader by example; and as a catalyst, stimulating and enabling Canadians to participate in a collective effort. The Federal Government has a particular stake in wetland conservation. Wetlands are critical to federal responsibilities for stimulating sustainable economic development; maintaining the quality of the environment, migratory bird populations, and inland and ocean fisheries; and managing international or transboundary resources such as water. The Federal Government is also responsible for the impact of its policies, programmes and federal land management on all wetlands in Canada. To date, the federal role has emphasized a cooperative approach with the provinces and territories, native groups and non-government organizations in conserving wetland ecosystems. The implementation of successful efforts towards wetland and habitat conservation in Canada have displayed a national focus on cooperation and partnerships.

It must be recognized that wetland conservation is closely linked to other natural resource sectors, particularly land and water use and management. Hence, respect for the jurisdiction of the provinces and territories and the rights of landowners is inherent in this federal initiative. Jurisdiction over wetlands in Canada is spread among federal, provincial, territorial and municipal governments, and among different government departments and agencies. No one element of this myriad of departments and agencies is completely responsible for wetlands management, conservation and sustainable use. The need is to stress better communications and consistent policy for all.

The Federal Government has also addressed wetland conservation within the context of other policies. The Federal Water Policy, approved in 1987, includes a statement on wetlands among its 25 water concerns. The Department of Fisheries and Oceans 1986 Policy for the Management of Fish Habitat addresses the conservation of many coastal wetlands for their commercial fish and shellfish habitat values, and establishes an objective of 'net gain' of the productive capacity of habitat. The Federal Policy on Land Use, approved in 1981, addresses federal activities with respect to land in general. The Canadian Parks Service 1979 Policy provides the framework for resource protection, including wetlands, within the National Parks System. Each of these policies affects wetland conservation, but wetlands have particular conservation requirements, integrating land and water considerations and relating to a wide range of sector interests. The Federal Government's commitment in the Green Plan was for a stand-alone policy with tailor-made objectives, principles and strategies for wetlands. The Federal Policy on Wetland Conservation will ensure efficient delivery of the substantial environmental, social and economic benefits of wetlands to all Canadians.

Lessons learned

Canada has established many commitments to wetland conservation that are far-reaching nationally and internationally. The Federal Policy on Wetland Conservation is but one example of the Federal Government's visible interest in wetlands. The Government of Canada is also committed to furthering the strong cooperation inherent in the North American Waterfowl Management Plan with the United States and Mexico. On the global scene, Canada's long-standing support and interest in the Ramsar Convention and the principles of wise use have been well recognized. Canada will continue to be a major proponent for the conservation of the wetland resources so important to our nation.

Wetland and waterbird conservation are inextricably linked at the international, national, regional and local levels. In Canada, these linkages are achieved through the multitude of agreements and partnerships that complement jurisdictional arrangements and achieve cooperation in conservation. A recent addition to such arrangements has been Canada's Federal Policy on Wetland Conservation; a policy that recognizes the serious plight of our wetlands and promotes action and leadership at the federal level. As a model for national-level conservation, it is too soon to evaluate the achievements of this new policy. Only time and effort will demonstrate its achievements and offer the opportunity to evaluate the success of this particular effort in cooperative conservation.

Clayton D.A. Rubec, Secretariat, North American Wetlands Conservation Council (Canada), Suite 200, 1750 Courtwood Crescent, Ottawa, Ontario K2C 2B5, Canada.

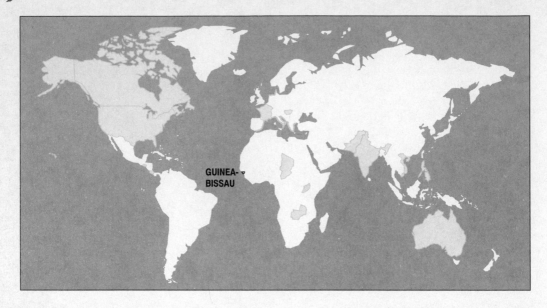

Coastal wetland planning and management in Guinea-Bissau

Pierre Campredon

Introduction

Though one of the smallest countries in Africa, Guinea-Bissau possesses one of the most important coastal wetland systems on the continent. For centuries the relative isolation of much of this system has inhibited major human activity and prevented major alteration. However, with rising population, growing demand for food self-sufficiency and modernization of the economy, there is increasing pressure upon these resources. Indeed, unless urgent action is taken, the coastal resources of Guinea-Bissau are likely to suffer irreparable damage before the end of the century.

In recognition of the importance of the coastal resources and the pressures upon them, the Ministry of Rural Development and Agriculture initiated a Coastal Zone Management Programme in 1988, and in 1990 joined the Ramsar Convention. At the same time the Government initiated a national conservation strategy process within which the Coastal Zone Management Programme forms a major pilot exercise to implement the principles of the National Conservation Strategy on the ground. This case study shows how the Government of Guinea-Bissau has approached the issue of planning and management of one particular group of wetland resources which dominate the national landscape.

The problem

The coastal zone of Guinea-Bissau makes up approximately half of the national territory. Its size and specific characteristics distinguish it from the rest of the country and allow it to be considered as a reasonably coherent functional unit. The contribution of this unit to the national economy is extremely important, in particular in the following sectors.

Fisheries

Overall, fisheries provide 30-35% of the country's foreign exchange earnings. While the greater part of this income is obtained from commercial fishing licences, the coastal zone plays an essential part in supporting this resource since the coastal wetlands, in particular the mangroves, provide breeding and nursery areas for fish and crustaceans. It is widely recognized that this nursery role also benefits other countries, such as Senegal and Guinea-Conakry, so giving Guinea-Bissau an international responsibility for which it does not, at present, have the financial resources to assume. In addition, it is from these coastal wetlands that the great majority of the human population obtains its daily protein intake in the form of molluscs and/or fish.

Agriculture

Although there has been a reduction in the size of the agricultural sector, from 89% in 1979 to 75% in 1992, this remains the dominant activity. Here again, the coastal zone makes a central contribution, notably through irrigated rice culture, fruit trees and the exploitation of palm groves.

Tourism

The coastal zone has the greatest tourism potential. Projects currently under development show clearly that the two areas of most interest are the Bijagos Archipelago and the beach of Varela near the Senegalese border. Mistakes made in establishing the latter, and which have led to substantial coastal erosion, demonstrate the fragility of these resources and the need for careful planning. Problems of erosion, the presence of mangroves and the relatively muddy waters of the coastal zone should be set against the region's spectacular scenery and rich cultural and natural heritage and should determine the form of tourism that is carried out in the region.

Industrial and commercial potential

The limited development of road transport in the country and the extensive coastal zone has made sea-going transport of critical importance and has influenced the location of centres of secondary and tertiary activities. While the creation of a tax free zone, possibly located in the Bijagos Archipelago, may bring substantial benefits for Guinea-Bissau, experience elsewhere has shown that unless this is very carefully planned it can lead to substantial costs.

Biological diversity

The last remnants of primary tropical forest in Guinea-Bissau are located in the coastal zone, on the border of the Rio Caine. At a regional level, one of the highest priorities for the conservation of biological diversity is the Bijagos Archipelago which has an abundance of rare or endangered species, notably four species of marine turtle, Manatees *Trichechus manatus,* Crocodiles *Crocodylus niloticus,* Hippopotamuses *Hippopotamus amphibius,* over 500,000 wintering shorebirds and a wealth of marine fish.

Ethnic Diversity

More than 30 different ethnic groups live within the coastal zone. Some have a long history of coastal resource use. The efficiency of the hydraulic structures established by the Balanta and the Feloupe for the cultivation of rice in saline areas, unequalled by modern methods, is a particularly instructive example.

Pressures on the coastal zone

The decision taken in 1983 to liberalize the economy in conjunction with the first phase of a structural adjustment programme has provoked significant changes within the social and economic climate of Guinea-Bissau. Of particular significance to the present study, liberalization has had a direct impact upon the natural resources which constitute the basis of the national economy.

The opening up of agriculture to foreign investment has led to the distribution of land concessions to private producers ('Ponteiros') who, in general, seek maximum short-term economic return from the land, rather than sustainable long-term management. This new occupation of the land, at present covering some 45% of the national territory, has led to conflict with local villagers who have traditionally exploited different ecosystems within a radius of up to 15 km from their villages. This process is likely to lead to the rapid destruction of the old village system, a change which will have substantial social and environmental costs.

At the same time, exploitation of the fishery resources is being encouraged and generates an important source of revenue; e.g. US\$12 million from 250 licences issued in 1989. A large commercial fishing fleet now fishes in an exclusive economic zone where the capacity of the fishery resource has not been evaluated and where there is no effective control measures. Stocks of several species of fish and shrimp are already showing signs of over-exploitation. Artisanal fishing, practised mainly by Senegalese, has also increased rapidly in recent years. The absence of management of the fishery resources and their exploitation by foreign interests runs the risk of compromising, in the long-term, not only the revenue that the Government might obtain, but also the living conditions of the coastal populations for whom fish and shellfish constitute an essential part of the daily diet.

Forest exploitation is also determined largely by a desire to obtain foreign exchange. In the absence of rational forest management, the current pressures upon it (conversion for agriculture, fuelwood and export of charcoal to Senegal, bush fires and exploitation of timber) are leading to a situation of diminishing resources in an area where the rural population is still dependent upon forest products, e.g. fuel and food, for their subsistence.

Rice growing is an important agricultural activity in the coastal wetlands of Guinea-Bissau.

The development of tourism is also placing considerable pressure upon the natural resources in the coastal zone. Foreign operators, in particular French and Portuguese, are seeking to obtain the best sites before the development of legislation obliges them to consider a range of aspects, such as the origin of the construction materials, the potential of the aquifer, the problems of waste water and domestic waste, and the social and cultural implications for the local people. Here again the emphasis is on short-term benefits and the investments being made are limited to the economic life of the project.

These pressures have a number of common elements. Essentially, the natural resources belong to the State, which possesses neither the technical expertise to manage them in a rational fashion, nor the legal instruments to protect them. Liberalization of the economy has allowed foreign interests to benefit from this situation and pursue short-term profit. This has led to unplanned and non-sustainable use of the resources by individuals who do not own the resource. While such economic development may be necessary in Guinea-Bissau, and there is a need for foreign exchange, the resources which form the basis for this development are renewable and it is essential that their exploitation is planned and executed carefully if the country is to maintain at least a minimum level of resources to allow regeneration.

Concurrent with the economic activities described, international aid agencies and NGOs have invested substantially in the country in recent years. However, there is a lack of trained Government personnel, and staff in general, to handle the massive amount of aid being provided to Guinea-Bissau. Ministries have few resources of their own and see in projects the possibility to procure a major part of their functioning costs. In consequence, there is a tendency for projects to dictate national policies, rather than the contrary, while ministries compete with each other for projects and associated funds. This competition is in clear conflict with the inter-ministerial approach essential for management of the environment.

The approach

By addressing management of the coastal wetland resources, the project described here not only addresses some of the most important natural resources in the country, but also the central problems of sustainable economic development, seeking to do so by acting as a catalyst. In addressing these problems in a country whose economy is dependent upon renewable natural resources, the project not only seeks to address critical technical issues, but also to build understanding within Government Ministries of the ways through which environmental issues need to be considered. At present there is still only limited understanding of the long-term environmental, social and economic consequences of over-exploitation of the country's fisheries, forest and agricultural resources, largely because these consequences are felt only in the medium term, and tend to affect the communities living nearest to the resources, rather than those living in the capital.

The project has pursued this work through four major activities: coastal zone planning, an integrated development plan for the Bijagos Archipelago, the creation of protected areas, and eco-development projects.

Coastal zone planning

The planning process has sought to identify land use options for the coastal zone, paying specific attention to the potential of the coastal system and the specific aptitudes of the human inhabitants.

Seven principles have guided this process:

1. The potential for regeneration of natural resources, including both aquatic and terrestrial resources;
2. Satisfying the fundamental needs of local people;
3. Efficient investment in labour and energy;
4. The harmonious pursuit of complementary activities, such as commercial fishing, artisanal fishing, agriculture, forestry, artisanal production, tourism etc;
5. Scientific monitoring of the impact of these activities on the environment;
6. The effective participation of people in planning decisions and development activities;
7. The definition of conservation zones for the maintenance of biological diversity and the productivity of natural habitats.

An interdisciplinary team covering socio-economic, biophysical and institutional aspects worked in the 24 administrative sectors of the coastal zone. A questionnaire was formulated and all levels of society were consulted, with the majority of discussions carried out at the level of individual families and through group meetings in villages. At the regional level, interviews were held with the 'Président de Région' (President of the Region), 'les Ministres résidents' (Resident Ministers), development projects, regional representatives of Central Government Ministries, and economic enterprises.

The biophysical analysis sought to describe the principal environmental units of the coastal zone by assessing their potential and examining their current use. The dynamics of the coastal zone were also analysed, paying particular attention to the processes of erosion and sedimentation. This was complemented by a series of studies of existing information, including preparation of a bibliography of work on the coastal zone; identification of socio-economic criteria for the rehabilitation of mangrove soils for rice culture; pedological criteria for soil use; viability of the different mangrove areas for rice culture; biological potential of different parts of the coastal zone; economic evaluation of the region; and analyses of the results obtained by different oceanographic missions.

On the basis of this work a preliminary proposal for coastal land use was prepared and distributed widely to all of the institutions which participated in the work. Simultaneously, a series of consultative meetings were held to discuss the report with all major ministries, notably those of Rural Development and Agriculture, Fisheries, Commerce and Tourism, Justice, Education, Health, Women, and International Cooperation. Senior officials, notably Directors, four State Secretaries and six Ministers, were directly involved. Following this process a workshop was held in Bissau to discuss the report in further detail. The workshop was covered by the press and television and provided an important demonstration of the involvement of local people. On the basis of this work the planning framework was substantially revised and a final framework document prepared.

In early 1991 a series of local events helped to build awareness among the local communities of the coastal zone planning process. The first of these was an all day festival on the coastal zone held in one of the regional capitals (Buba). Similarly, in order to explain the objectives of this exercise in the most simple terms, a series of seven radio programmes described the principal themes of the coastal zone planning process.

Despite the success of this exercise, it is clear that the planning exercise must be seen as a process. Rather than view establishment of wise use as being an exercise which can be prepared over one or two years and then adopted by the Council of Ministers, it needs to be seen as a progressive exercise designed to build understanding of the issues among technical staff, and define mechanisms for consultation with people and between the different ministries concerned.

In Guinea-Bissau this work is being carried out in conjunction with the complementary initiative to prepare a National Conservation Strategy and establish a National Commission on the Environment. This exercise emphasizes the same Inter-Ministerial and interdisciplinary collaboration that has been a feature of the coastal planning exercise.

An integrated development plan for the Bijagos Archipelago

In collaboration with the United Nations Development Programme (UNDP) and the 'Centre Canadienne d'étude et de Coopération International' (CECI), a study similar to that carried out for the continental part of the coastal zone has been carried out in the Bijagos Archipelago. This has included a socio-economic analysis of the populations on the 19 inhabited islands, and an analysis of the conservation status of the natural resources. This work began in February 1989 and has resulted in the production of an integrated development plan for the Archipelago. This document defines the land uses which are possible on the different islands, notably agriculture, tourism, forestry and conservation of biodiversity, and proposes regulation of artisanal fishing in order to preserve the nursery role of the Archipelago. The plan provides a framework for future investment in resource management, giving full consideration to local people. At the same time more detailed studies of the fishery resources within the Archipelago are being initiated by the International Centre for Ocean Development (ICOD).

Protected Areas

In order to preserve a representative sample of the natural habitats of Guinea-Bissau, protect those where biological diversity is especially high, and maintain critical ecological and hydrological processes, the coastal plan has identified four priority areas:

1. Cantanhès forest; the last of the country's sub-tropical forests;
2. The Laguna de Cufada; the country's first Ramsar site;
3. The mangrove of the Rio Cacheu; one of the most extensive and best conserved in the country and thought to be especially important for the reproduction of fish, molluscs and crustaceans;
4. The complex of islands in the Orango region of the Bijagos Archipelago; this has the highest diversity of aquatic fauna in West Africa with Manatees, Hippopotamuses, marine turtles and Crocodiles, as well as African and palearctic migratory birds.

The establishment of these conservation areas will require the development and enforcement of regulations, many of which could lead to conflict with local people. It is therefore essential that these regulations are studied in considerable detail, discussed widely, and ways sought to provide compensation where necessary. This, of course, is a complex process and, though already under way, it may take several years for solutions to be identified and elaborated. However time-consuming this may be, it is the only way to gain the support and participation of the people who, in the long term, will manage the resource most effectively.

Eco-development projects

In conjunction with the activities described above, it was felt essential that specific efforts be carried out to demonstrate to the human population the benefits obtainable from the rational management of natural resources. Nevertheless, eco-development projects, even though important, will not by themselves resolve the problems of degradation of the environment. It is the current system of exploitation of the resources which is causing most of the problems and which threatens the sustainable use of resources. Also, while the importance of developing practical examples of how conservation and development can be integrated is recognized, it must be understood that in Guinea-Bissau, where there is tremendous economic pressure, the economic operators are as far removed from conservation as the rural populations are from development. Within this context the utility of demonstration projects is limited, unless they are accompanied by a series of other measures designed to address the economic pressures which are currently undermining the resource base. Thus, the project is currently pursuing small-scale eco-development projects, which seek to improve management of natural resources within conservation areas, and rural development projects, which seek to develop alternative forms of economic development, thus reducing the dangers brought about through the pursuit of short-term profits.

An example of this approach is provided in the Ria Grande de Buba, one of the most important areas of reproduction for many species of fish, notably Barracuda *Sphyraena* spp.. The productivity of the estuary and the concentrations of fish there at certain times of year attract international commercial fisherman who arrive when the fish populations are highest. Their activities are now threatening the resource base and, at the same time, the livelihood of the native subsistence fishermen further upstream. The area is of tremendous national and international importance, yet there is limited control of the fishery and the largest quantities of fish are taken by international fishermen for whom there is little incentive to manage the resource on a sustainable basis, especially for those who come purely in search of short-term gain.

The coastal zone plan recommends that the fisheries in the estuaries and the rivers be reserved for Guineans and that associations of local fishermen be established to exploit these resources. Such an appropriation of the estuarine fishery resource would stimulate better management and facilitate regulation, in particular of equipment, size of fish caught and commercialization.

In the medium term the project may also have an impact upon the management of the catchment, which plays a fundamental role in the ecology of the estuary and regulates the inflow of freshwater while also limiting erosion. However, exploitation of the surrounding forests has been severe and it is now difficult to find trees large enough to construct boats. As a result there is growing awareness of the impending crisis and a forest conservation scheme associated with the present project is under consideration.

Achievements

The economy of Guinea-Bissau is based upon the country's renewable natural resource base, yet current forms of exploitation threaten their long-term future and, in consequence, the quality of life of the human population that depends upon them. By addressing the sectors involved in resource management, notably agriculture, fisheries, tourism, forest and conservation, the project described here has had a central impact upon the national debate on the environment and development, while also providing a framework for wise use of the coastal resources. In this context the project has tried to respond to urgent issues and to convince the Government to nurture the remaining natural resources, not only for short-term human survival, but for long-term development potential. The coastal zone plan will be used as the basis for environmentally sound investment in the coastal zone by a growing number of Government agencies and by some of the bilateral international agencies.

Lessons learned

The principal lessons learned from this project are:

1. Rational management of natural resources by local people is brought about only if people perceive, and are able to obtain, an appropriate value from such a regime.
2. The project has influenced Government policy through its close involvement with the efforts to establish a National Commission on the Environment and to formulate the Guinean National Conservation Strategy (National Environmental Strategy).
3. By emphasizing linkages with Government departments and the many aid agencies involved in natural resource management, a harmonious approach has been developed. This has facilitated communication within Government, while the considerable efforts made to work with local communities have been instrumental in the formulation of a land use plan which has support at local level. Only through this approach has it been possible to implement such a plan.
4. Despite the successes, the activities described here need to be seen as but the initial stages of a long-term process which must be continued over the next decade if wise use of Guinea-Bissau's natural wetland resources are to achieved to their full potential.

Pierre Campredon, Bureau de l'UICN, BP23, 1031 Bissau-Codex, Guiné-Bissau.

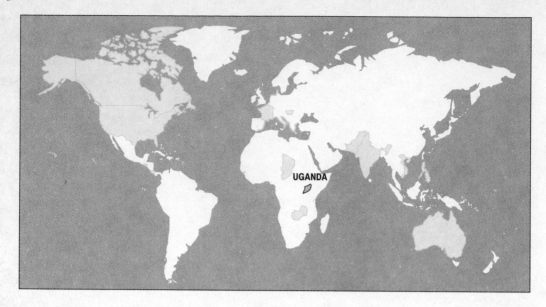

The National Wetlands Programme, Uganda

Paul Mafabi and A.R.D. Taylor

Introduction

Uganda is very well endowed with water resources, benefiting from both a high rainfall and from some of the largest lakes in the world, which feed the Nile river. On its way to the Nile, the water supports huge wetlands which occupy at least 10% of Uganda's land area of 205,333 km^2. These wetlands range in altitude from 1,134 m at Lake Victoria, to over 4,000 m in the Ruwenzori mountains.

Uganda's large wetland resource brings benefits to both rural and urban society, whilst playing a central role in the maintenance of biodiversity. At the same time, the relative accessibility and fertility of wetlands in a country with a rapidly rising population has placed these resources under increasing pressure. As wetlands have been lost, the close relationship between human society and wetlands has meant that both rural and urban communities have rapidly experienced the social and environmental consequences. As a result, Uganda has experienced rising community concern for the loss of wetlands and in 1986 this stimulated the newly created Ministry of Environment Protection (now the Ministry of Natural Resources) to take action, including imposing a ban on wetland drainage and initiating the development of a National Wetlands Programme. This case study describes the national approach to wise use of wetlands.

The problem

Uganda's wetlands form an extensive network covering 29,589 km^2, spread throughout the country. On the basis of current vegetation maps, 8,832 km^2 are swamp, 365 km^2 are swamp forest and 20,392 km^2 are wetland sites with impeded drainage.

While this mapping exercise can readily identify larger sites such as Lake Kyoga, and the fringing wetlands around Lake Victoria, many smaller sites are missed. Yet these small wetlands may be of great importance for the conservation of biological diversity. Indeed the interface between these wetlands and dry land is of special importance for conservation of biological diversity and use by human communities. These small wetlands are therefore deserving of high priority within a wise use programme.

Values and natural functions

Uganda's wetlands provide a wide range of inter-related functions, resources and products, ranging from groundwater recharge and discharge, to microclimate stabilization, and from forestry, wildlife, fishery, agriculture and water supply to recreation and tourism. While it is unlikely that any one wetland can supply all of these services, Uganda's wetlands clearly provide multiple benefits and any management of these wetlands should encourage multiple use.

Together with forests, Uganda's wetlands are responsible for the stabilization of the country's water supply and the conservation of its soils and nutrients. The following values are of special concern:

1. Hydrological values include the sponge-like nature of wetlands and their capacity to stabilize water availability, moderate floods and supply water during the dry season. Borehole and well recharge in some areas depend entirely upon wetlands.

2. Biological diversity is high in seasonal wetlands and low in swamps. However, the range in altitude of wetlands encompasses lowland tropical to Afro-Alpine, and less common plants (e.g. *Syzigium*) have important populations. Wetlands offer a refuge to fauna (e.g. Sitatunga *Tragelaphus spekei*) and a stable environment for many aquatic species, especially fish, for which wetland vegetation forms a vital feeding ground.

3. Biomass production is very high, especially of the swamp macrophytes such as papyrus, *Typha* spp., and *Phragmites* spp. These plants are largely responsible for the water retention properties of the wetland and also provide a large sink for atmospheric carbon. The ability of swamps to lock up this carbon in peat-like sediment may be very important in alleviating global warming. The wetland biomass also provides an essential foundation for numerous food webs which support a variety of plants and animals, both within Uganda's wetlands and remote from them.

4. Sediment, nutrient and toxin retention impedes the growth of wetland vegetation and the absorption and ion exchange capacity of the wetland substrate. Sediment carried in flood flows is stripped from the water. Similarly, dissolved nutrients and toxins are retained by the matrix of slowly decaying plant material and the substrate, thus stabilizing these components. Water leaving a wetland is thus of high quality.

Major economic uses

Biomass potential, especially of the macrophytes, papyrus, *Typha* spp. and *Phragmites* spp., is high; for example, papyrus can yield 25 tonnes of dry weight/ha/year. The high productivity of Uganda's wetlands provides essential building and thatching materials, important materials for carpet and screen-making enterprises, and the potential to provide a source of renewable energy through harvesting and briquetting, or through biogas plants.

Swamp fishing yields large catches of catfish *Clarias* spp. and lungfish *Protopterus* spp., as well as a very large supply of smaller *Haplochromids*. The fish occur throughout permanent wetlands as well as in seasonal floodplains and are caught using basket traps, hooks or gill nets.

Wetlands are vital for water supply and sewage treatment, and promise large financial savings in the design and construction of water and sewage treatment plants. For instance, the Nakivubo and Luzira swamps near Kampala remove pollutants from the almost raw sewage released from Kampala, thus protecting the nearby water supply intake. The water supply to Masaka is obtained entirely, and partly in the case of Bushenye, from a wetland, taking advantage of the filtering capacity of the swamp.

Agriculture in wetland margins and seasonal wetlands is common practice. There is huge potential for sustainable agriculture without drainage of the wetland, thus protecting soil formed under reducing conditions.

Threats to Uganda's wetlands

Despite the great importance of Uganda's wetland resources, the rising human population, together with the need for increased agricultural and industrial production, has led to substantial pressure upon these resources. Lowland valley and swamp forest wetlands are currently coming under the strongest pressure. However, this pressure has affected only a tiny proportion of the total wetland area.

It is the seasonal wetlands and smaller valley wetlands that are most closely associated with human activity and where a heavy toll on resources has resulted. Individually, these wetlands are of insignificant size, yet they have great significance both to people and wildlife conservation. They bridge the interface between dry land and water, often in narrow strips only 100 m wide.

Many current problems arise from past misuse of wetlands, while several present development proposals take little account of the importance of wetlands. Some problems and threats may arise as a result of neglect in enforcing existing legislation (e.g. on pollution and public health). Others arise due to a lack of intersectoral review of Government policy and implementation.

Large scale agricultural conversion

With funding from a number of external donors, notably the People's Republic of China, large scale agriculture has led to the loss of significant areas of wetland in eastern Uganda. However, returns from this investment have fallen short of expectation. For example, in the Kibimba rice scheme, yield which was estimated at 4.9 tonnes/ha/harvest in 1986 had fallen to 1.7 tonnes/ha by 1988.

Drainage

Small scale drainage activities in south-west Uganda have adversely affected most of the valley systems in that region. These valleys contained important papyrus resources but over the past 20 years much of this resource has been cleared for agriculture. In some areas where drainage commenced in the early 1970s, the majority of the papyrus has now been removed and the valleys are being used for grazing dairy cattle.

As a result of drainage and oxidation over the years, the peat substrate of many of these systems is eroding. Without careful management of the water level, continued dairy farming on these wetlands will not be sustainable. Drainage has also led to a reduction in access to the wetlands by smallholders and therefore precludes the multiple use of wetland resources.

Industrial pollution

Although Uganda does not have a strongly industrialized economy, there are a number of important industrial activities, several of which generate pollution which in turn impacts on wetlands. One of the most important cases is the wetland system of Lake George, Uganda's first Ramsar site. Several major rivers originating in the Ruwenzori mountains feed the northern side of the wetland across an alluvial plain. One of the rivers originates in the valley leading to the copper mining town of Kilembe. Here, the river waters have significant concentrations of dissolved copper, cobalt and iron, and it is possible that the copper inflow is responsible for changes in the vegetation of Lake George.

A second and more serious problem which originates from the Kilembe mines is an unstable stock of cobalt sulphide which, riverborne over a distance of 15 km, has contaminated the Queen Elizabeth National Park to the very edge of Lake George. There is concern that the lake's fisheries will be affected by the toxic effects of the cobalt on the algae which form the base of the lake's food chain.

Excessive harvesting of natural products

Over much of Uganda papyrus swamps are harvested intensively and some are showing signs of over-harvesting for specific purposes such as screen making. Only papyrus with a diameter of 2-3 cm is suitable for the production of mats and screens. Roadside traders display papyrus of uniform length and diameter in what is clearly a competitive market. To obtain such a uniform harvest, it is necessary first to burn an area of papyrus, then, after three months, to harvest the stems (culms). After a further three months the papyrus is again cut from the same site. Repeated harvesting in this way reduces the vitality of the plants and eventually leads to their demise. It is believed that the minimum harvest interval for sustainable yields is nine months. Unless the harvesting of culms is managed on a rotational basis, considerable pressure will be placed on the wetlands which supply the raw material for screens and mats.

Brick-making in Uganda's Mpigi district. Photo: Geoffrey Howard

The approach

The high level of Government awareness (from the President down) of the importance of Uganda's wetland resources and the threats to them led, in 1986, to an interim ban on all large-scale wetland drainage. Once the ban was in place, advice was sought on how a comprehensive approach to addressing the diverse issues might be initiated and the institutional capacity developed to manage the wetlands on a long-term basis. In 1989, a National Wetlands Conservation and Management Programme was initiated, based in the Department of Environment Protection (DEP). Funding was provided by the Norwegian Agency for Development, with technical assistance from IUCN. The programme was designed to assist the Ugandan Government to develop a National Policy for the Conservation and Management of Wetlands and to acquire the technical capacity necessary to implement this. The programme has seven major objectives:

1. To determine the location, biotic and physical characteristics of the major wetland systems.
2. To identify the values and services provided by wetlands, as well as current uses and the potential for further utilization.
3. To identify and quantify current and potential threats to wetlands.
4. To effect a detailed review of previous wetland development activities, identifying the short- and long-term costs and benefits of wetland loss.
5. To provide the DEP with the technical capacity to carry out environmental impact assessments (EIA) of proposed wetland development activities.
6. On the basis of the information collected in pursuit of the above objectives, to draw up a national policy for the conservation and sustainable utilization of wetlands.
7. Build governmental and public awareness of the importance of wetlands and of the economic and social benefits which can accrue from environmentally sound management of wetlands.

In pursuit of these objectives seven major activities have been pursued:

1. Inventory

A selective inventory of representative wetlands under stress is being carried out.

2. Identification of the values and services provided by wetlands

Four MSc students from the University of Makerere are carrying out studies of swamp fisheries, the social and cultural values of swamps, sustainable use of papyrus and the use of swamps as filters of pollutants. Specific work has also been carried out on the hydrological values of wetlands, the ornithological biodiversity and papyrus productivity. Substantial understanding of the functions and values of Uganda's wetlands has now been achieved, although some gaps, notably the long-term monitoring of the water balance of wetlands, need to be pursued.

3. Identification and quantification of threats to wetlands

In order to develop the country's capacity to monitor the threats to wetlands and effect detailed EIAs, a training link has been established between Makerere University's Institute of Environment and Natural Resources and a British university. An initial EIA training course took place, with special attention being given to the industrial pollution at Lake George.

4. Detailed review of previous wetland development activities

As part of the studies of swamp fisheries and the social and cultural values of swamps, the impact of wetland loss has been studied by means of questionnaires. Quantification of the economic impact of past development has been difficult to investigate, due to a large extent to the absence of Government records over the previous 20 years during which the country passed through a period of instability.

5. Provision of technical capacity at the Department of Environment Protection

From the outset special attention was given to training, with the Project Manager and associated staff in DEP and other ministries receiving training from technical consultants. In addition, by supporting and involving MSc students at Makerere, the project has increased the number of technical wetland specialists available in the country. Two of these students have now been incorporated into the wetlands unit within DEP as full-time staff.

6. Developing a national wetland policy

A fundamental premise of this work has been that wetlands comprise a broad range of land and water types and are therefore affected by almost all aspects of Government policy. A coordinated view of the impact these policies have upon wetland resources was therefore needed. To achieve this, an Inter-Ministerial Wetlands Committee, chaired by the Permanent Secretary of the Ministry of Natural Resources was established. Also represented are the Uganda Freshwater Fisheries Research Organization, Makerere University Institute of Environment and Natural Resources, Uganda National Parks Game Department, the Department of Meteorology, and the Veterinary Sciences Department.

One of the most encouraging features of the programme has been the willingness of the various ministries to work together on wetland issues. A particular success of this joint committee approach has been the direct communication which the Project Management Unit has had with the various ministries and departments. Of course, not all of the ministries are active in the programme's activities but all have responsibility for resources or processes which affect wetlands in some way.

The national wetlands policy was designed to provide a coherent framework for rational management of wetlands. At present, the only legal protection that wetlands have is that they are state owned and that all large-scale drainage activities have been suspended pending development of a national policy. The inception of the Inter-Ministerial Committee on wetlands has enabled much faster development of policy than anticipated. Following the first draft in December 1989, the policy has gone through five further drafts, incorporating many of the suggestions made in committee. Included in the policy is a section on 'Guidelines to Developers' which is intended to provide specific technical guidance to wetland users. The salient points of the policy and guidelines are provided in the Appendix to this paper.

The process of developing the policy includes consultation with selected District Development Committees (DDC). DDCs represent not only the district administration and the Government departments active in the district, but, most importantly, people at all levels – district, county, sub-county, parish and village – through Uganda's tiered system of resistance councils. This representation enables villagers to participate in the development of a national Government policy. Project personnel present the draft policy to full meetings of the DDCs and brief members on the contents. Feedback from the DDCs is used to amend the draft policy and result in one which is workable on the ground.

Considerable resources of manpower, experience and time are being devoted to this consultative aspect of development of the wetland policy, in the expectation that it will bring about a sensible white paper that will take into account the aspirations of all wetland users and result in a Wetland Management Act which will provide a model for wetland management in other countries and regions.

7. Governmental and public awareness

A public awareness programme consisting of two television films supplemented by posters and leaflets has been developed. Newspapers have also reproduced some of the materials, while Uganda radio has carried scripted programmes. Awareness within Government has developed at a faster rate however, with the Inter-Ministerial Committee ensuring that the various line ministries and departments are made increasingly aware of the importance of wetlands. However, further materials need to be produced and distributed within Government as well as at DDC level, where local administrators require resource materials for technical issues of wetland management. Seminars for DDC members are planned.

In February 1991 representatives of local communities and Government ministries and departments were involved in a two-day seminar on the formulation of the national wetland policy. The seminar enabled representatives from five DDCs to meet with wetland managers and planners. The DDC representatives came from districts where wetlands are especially important to the lives of people and where there are conflicts between current use and conservation of the wetlands. It was notable that DDC representatives were not prepared to make recommendations on behalf of their districts, insisting instead that they take the information from the seminar through the consultative process in their home areas. To enhance this part of policy formulation, technical staff of the National Wetlands Programme will visit the districts to assist with discussions on the wetland policy at district level and to provide information to wetland users.

Achievements

In contrast to most current approaches to wise use of wetlands, which focus upon individual sites, this initiative has sought to develop the capacity of national Government and local administrations to administer wise use of wetlands throughout the country. While this is a mammoth task, substantial progress has been achieved in strengthening the capacity of central Government to understand and address wetland issues, while at the same time providing technical assistance to local communities to improve the use of these resources such that the benefits can be obtained on a sustainable basis.

Such a long-term programme should ensure the survival of the country's wetlands, their functions and their biota, while encouraging wise use of these resources. At the same time, the programme, in particular through the Inter-Ministerial Committee, has facilitated cross-sectoral linkages, establishment of administrative structures and public awareness schemes that are necessary for the management of these national resources. In addition, by supporting research and the training of key personnel, the programme has begun to build the capacity to implement action to conserve and manage wetlands sustainably.

Lessons learned

Although the National Wetlands Programme is considered to be highly successful, it has highlighted the complexity of achieving wise use throughout the national landscape and emphasized the long-term nature of the work. Although initially a short-term initiative, the programme is now seen by the DEP as a long-term investment and as a clear demonstration of how the DEP can exercise its responsibilities for the management of the natural environment. Of great importance is the capacity of the Wetlands Programme to provide a framework for long-term cooperation between diverse authorities with influence over the wetland resources of Uganda. Accordingly, the Inter-Ministerial Committee on wetlands will remain a permanent feature of a long-term Wetlands Programme. The guiding principle of the DEP's chairmanship of the Committee is to ensure that coordination and sharing of information about wetlands is maintained, thus enabling the institutions with existing power over wetlands (Agriculture, Water Development, Health, Fisheries etc.) to use the resources wisely and enable them to provide sound and effective advice to the general public.

The need for the DEP to coordinate investigations, rather than to be the sole agency responsible for wetlands, was especially clear during the first two years of the project. It was therefore concluded that it was essential for other Government ministries and departments (Agriculture, Fisheries) to mount their own investigations of wetland issues with their own staff, but with DEP's guidance. In addition, it is clear that centrally performed research and investigation will not be capable of tackling the workload even if other ministries have assigned their staff to the task. An example of this is the processing of applications submitted by members of the public for the lease of state-owned wetlands. Each application is currently forwarded to the DEP, providing the applicant can persuade the district planning committee to do so. There are potentially very many of these applications to consider. An effective sustainable Wetlands Programme must therefore take this problem into account.

Uganda's wetlands consist mostly of permanent swamps and swamp forests, areas of impeded drainage. As such, there is little in the way of traditional wise use knowledge in Uganda compared to other parts of Africa which have floodplain areas and where the local communities have developed cultural traditions of interacting with wetlands. Wise use activity in Uganda therefore largely involves the modification of relatively modern farming practices.

The main conclusions arising from the development of Uganda's national wetland policy are:

1. The need for political will

The success in achieving a national wetland policy in Uganda was obtained because of political will at a national level. However, without the necessary will at all levels of government – central, district, and village administration – the process of formulating and implementing policy has been impeded. The Government ban on large scale drainage of wetlands in 1986 was not entirely successful because some District Administrations failed to follow up this issue seriously and drainage continued.

2. The need for a bottom-up approach

This is important because, until recently, decisions taken at the top for implementation lower down the scale have proved unsuccessful in terms of conservation. The Wetlands Programme recognizes this fact and the development of the national policy has thus involved the District Development Committees and people's committees (Resistance Councils) who have a stake in the decisions regarding natural resources in their areas.

3. Inter-sectoral approach

This has provided a holistic approach, especially given that wetland management in Uganda cuts across several departments and institutions. The Inter-Ministerial Committee has facilitated coordination and sharing of information, enabling influential institutions to use the wetland resource wisely.

4. Participatory awareness

District Development Committees have a key role in the development of a wetland policy. Since they implement decisions at the district level, there is a need to provide them with regularly updated information, documentation and field based advice on conservation and the sustainable use of wetlands. The DDCs also requested technical inputs from the Department of Environment Protection, and it is expected that these will be provided through the line ministries, based upon practical wetland interventions.

5. Effective demonstration of wise use

It is crucial that wise use activity and interventions are successful, otherwise rural communities are bound to be discouraged and may resort to traditional, unwise practices. A case in point occurred at Doho where the efforts of local people, encouraged to set up finger ponds at the edge of the wetland, were wasted because the source of water was not permanent and drought negated their hard work.

6. The need for an integrated wetland policy

Such a policy should outline the objectives for wetland conservation and the need for wise use.

7. Further Research

There is need for ongoing research to determine the actual potential of wetlands to perform the various functions. For instance, at Nakivubo swamp, which takes the sewage from Kampala city after secondary treatment, data is required on the wetland's hydrology, denitrification, removal of organic substances, and the oxygen regime.

8. Training

Training of personnel to translate the policy proposals and guidelines into practical actions.

9. Inventory

Inventory is crucial for proper management decision making. Experience with the Wetlands Programme shows that a nationwide inventory is expensive and requires much in the way of personnel, time and technical inputs. In addition it was found that policy should precede inventory, otherwise some wetlands will be lost before their values can be determined. The policy should therefore aim at curtailing significant loss of wetlands and call for an inventory.

An inventory of selected Ugandan wetlands is now being embarked upon. The approach will be to identify the controlling factors differentiating one wetland from another (e.g. slope, rainfall pattern, uses, natural vegetation types). The country map will be extrapolated from this exercise, then tested for accuracy at a range of locations.

10. Legislation

This is crucial to support the policy and ensure the principles enshrined in the policy are adhered to. Legislation is also important to control the activities of line ministries and influence their understanding of wetlands.

11. The catchment approach

There is need to emphasize effective management of areas, especially the control of erosion, use of agrochemicals and disposal of industrial waste, since these impact a great deal on wetlands. Many activities around, but not actually in, wetlands impinge upon wetlands, and it is impractical to place precise borders around them. The Wetlands Programme therefore recommends that wetlands should be considered as part of the total catchment area. There is, however, a need for caution since this approach can lead to problems where catchment boundaries do not coincide with civic boundaries; this is particularly the case in Uganda. It may be impossible for committees to arrive at an independent decision. However, consultation across administrative boundaries can, in principle, resolve these matters; the provision of technical information and public awareness is also important in this respect.

12. Management of populations

One crucial problem affecting wetlands is the ever increasing human population. Although this is not always the root cause of wetland drainage, it certainly is the case in Kabale and Bushenyi Districts. There is therefore need for a policy to manage the increasing population better, either through resettlement schemes or provision of alternatives to wetland drainage.

13. Socio-economic considerations

It is generally assumed that cash profits from rice growing benefit the local community as a whole. However, this is only the case where the profits are recycled, reinvested in the project, or spent on community amenities. Environmental development projects should incorporate culturally acceptable ways of ensuring increased standards of living, and opportunities for spin-off entrepreneurial activities. The Wetlands Programme recognizes this fact and has now embarked on a socio-economic assessment of rice growing in the Doho region.

In the long term, conservation and management of wetlands will be effective only if rural communities have a stake in the utilization of the wetland resource. Effective management will have to be demonstrated at local level without being controlled directly from Kampala, otherwise such pilot demonstrations will not be seen as relevant to the needs of rural people. The Wetlands Programme must strive, through the District Development Committees, to achieve a decision-making structure for wetland management, even though the DEP's own district level structure is incomplete. The Wetlands Programme already stands as a model of how other areas of environmentally sound management may be coordinated at district level and below.

Paul Mafabi , Ministry of Natural Resources, PO Box 9629, Kampala, Uganda.

A.R.D. Taylor, Somerset County Council, Department for the Environment, County Hall, Taunton, Somerset TA1 4DY, UK

Appendix

Summary of draft policy and guidelines for management

The most important product of Uganda's Wetlands Programme will be a policy on, and management of, wetlands, and a legislative package to assist the Department of Environment Protection in its role of ensuring that wetlands are managed on a sustainable basis.

The main goal of the wetland policy is to promote the conservation and management of Uganda's wetlands in order to sustain their ecological and socio-economic functions for the present and future well-being of the people.

The draft National Wetlands Policy:

- elucidates the wetland resource problems;
- sets goals for achieving sustainable development and optimum utilization of wetlands;
- outlines the principles on which the policy goals may be achieved;
- elaborates specifically targeted policy proposals.

The draft wetland policy is based on the following principles:

1. No drainage of wetlands;
2. Environmentally sound management;
3. Sustainable use;
4. Diversification of uses and users;
5. Environmental impact assessments for all developments planned in wetlands.

These principles will be brought to bear through some of the following strategies:

- no net drainage of wetlands unless more important environment management requirements arise;
- only environmentally sustainable activities to be permitted in wetlands; e.g. water supply, fisheries, grazing;
- protection of wetlands of high biological diversity, particularly from encroachment, drainage or modification;
- no leasing of wetlands to any person or institution at any given moment for whatever reason, with the exception that communal use and other uses should be permitted as long as the principles of environmentally sound management are adhered to. Government to issue permits to developers;
- rehabilitation or restoration of previously drained or modified wetlands, and, where necessary, cancellation of wetland leases, or eviction of users with no leases, on the basis of environmental impact assessments;
- promotion of Government and public awareness and understanding of wetland resource values and functions;
- carry out research and compile an inventory of wetlands in order to determine their capacity, as well as their location, characteristics and status;
- introduce laws, regulations and guidelines, and develop an appropriate institutional arrangement in order to implement the policy effectively.

Guidelines for developers

It is the intention to provide wetland developers with guidelines which will be based on the principles of the policy. Although currently limited, the guidclines will be produced for circulation with the policy, and will be updated at intervals through publication of supplements which will be distributed to the Districts.

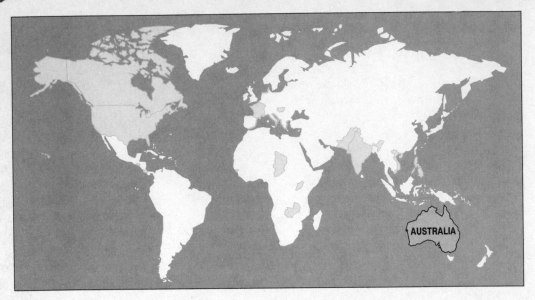

The Chowilla Resource Management Plan, Australia

Bill Phillips and Tony Sharley

Introduction

The Chowilla Anabranch is a tributary system of the River Murray within the Murray-Darling Drainage Basin which covers an area of 1,060,000 km^2, or approximately one seventh of the entire surface of Australia. The Chowilla lies some 100 km downstream of the confluence of the Murray and Darling rivers and its floodplain straddles the State borders of South Australia and New South Wales, extending approximately 25 km from east to west and up to 10 km north of the Murray. The floodplain covers some 177 km^2 and is dissected by numerous channels and creeks which flow permanently and feed several large ephemeral lakes when flows in the River Murray exceed 50,000 ml/day. Abandoned river loops have formed oxbow lakes and there are intermittent lakes and swamps around the margins of the floodplains.

In November 1987, the 'Riverland' Wetland, comprising approximately 30,600 ha of River Murray floodplain and including part of the South Australian portion of the Chowilla Anabranch system, was added to the Ramsar List of Wetlands of International Importance. It was the fourth South Australian, and 29th Australian wetland, to be included in the List.

The problem

Climate and hydrology

The local climate is semi-arid with an average annual rainfall of 221 mm and an average annual maximum temperature of 24.2°C (hottest month January). Rainfall is higher in the cooler months of the year, i.e. May-October inclusive, and the average annual minimum temperature is 10.8°C (coolest month July). Hence, the Chowilla floodplain is a wetland oasis in an arid environment; rainfall and run-off in the immediate vicinity are negligible by comparison with the volumes of river water which flow through the area and periodically overflow onto the floodplain.

Before the River Murray was regulated by weirs and dams, the flow regime was more variable. In spring and early summer the river was generally high and fast-flowing, gradually changing to low and slow-moving towards the end of summer. Lower-lying areas of the floodplain were inundated, on average, every two years, while the higher areas were flooded every three to seven years. Since regulation, these flooding frequencies have been reduced to once every three years, and once every 5-35 years, respectively. Although the river acted as a drain, by intercepting regional saline groundwater, at times it receded to little more than a series of saline waterholes. Prior to the construction of Lock 6 (see Figure 1) on the Murray, flow in the creeks of the Chowilla Anabranch occurred only during periods of high river or flood. · The Chowilla now flows continuously and regional saline groundwater now flows into the Anabranch creeks because the artificially high level of the Murray above Lock 6 has caused the elevation of floodplain groundwater levels.

Salinity

The Chowilla Anabranch has been a natural discharge site for salt, via naturally saline aquifers beneath the floodplain, since before regulation of the River Murray began in 1922. The construction of a lock on the River Murray adjacent to the Chowilla Anabranch in 1930 worsened the salinity problem by elevating the level of groundwater under the floodplain.

River Murray salinity first emerged as an issue of public concern during the dry years of the mid 1960s when the quality of water supplies for human consumption and irrigation declined alarmingly. For instance, at the township of Morgan in South Australia, salinities approached an annual average of 480 mg/L with peak readings of 840 mg/L.

In a normal year, the total salt flow to South Australia from the Murray-Darling Basin (as measured at Lock 6) is estimated to be about 1,100,000 tonnes, consisting of 600,000 tonnes from tributary and mainstream inflows, about 260,000 tonnes from drainage inflows and about 250,000 tonnes from groundwater inflows.

The groundwater in the sub-surface aquifers beneath Chowilla is as saline as seawater, some 35,000 mg/L. Water of this salinity extends for at least 100 km in all directions from Chowilla. As indicated above, the construction of Lock 6 resulted in elevated river levels which in turn resulted in higher water tables beneath the Chowilla floodplain. This brought saline water from the underlying permeable Monoman formation into the overlying Coonabidgal clays which are approximately 5-10 m thick. This process has been assisted by capillary action in the finer surface soils. The end result is that trees, mainly Black Box *Eucalyptus largiflorens* and River Red Gum *E. camaldulensis*, are now dying in increasing numbers in many areas.

In the Chowilla Anabranch, salt enters the creeks from the groundwater system and is carried to the main river through Chowilla Creek. Most of this salt enters the river during and following floods. It has been estimated that 50-100 million tonnes of salt are stored in the sands beneath the thin clay soils of the Chowilla floodplain.

Salt is also continually being brought to the floodplain surface, including the lakes and billabongs, from where it is washed into the river when floods occur. While the river is in flood there is ample water to dilute the salt, but as soon as river levels drop, salinity increases dramatically. A post flood salinity surge can continue for up to a year or more, as the water table gradually drops to a steady level. Salt loads have averaged 700 tonnes/day immediately following a major flood. Saline inflows gradually return to a base flow of 43 tonnes/day about two years after a flood.

The post flood surge in salinity is the major concern in water quality management for the Chowilla Anabranch as it occurs at a time of low river levels, and often in summer when water use is at a maximum, especially for irrigation.

The construction of Lock 6 has also exerted a major influence over the hydrology of the Anabranch creeks. The lock created a three-metre increase in river level on the upstream side, resulting in all the Anabranch creeks flowing continuously, even during periods of low river flow. Another effect of locking is that the higher river upstream began to push freshwater into the shallow aquifer beneath the floodplain, displacing the existing groundwater ahead of it as it travelled across to the creeks and creating a narrow 'flushed zone' adjacent to the river. Groundwater moves very slowly, usually only a few metres per year, so the flushing process is still continuing today, some 50 years after the lock was built. In the flushed areas, groundwater salinity is very low (less than 3,000 mg/L) and trees are healthy because ample freshwater is available from the water table.

It is estimated that a 1.5 mg/L increase in the salinity of the River Murray would cost water users in South Australia between AUS$80,000 and AUS$100,000 per year (domestic use 62%, industry 5%, agriculture 33%). When it is considered that post-flood salinity levels can be as much as 40 times the average level, the economic impact of the salt problem becomes more apparent.

Effects of salinity and river regulation on plants and animals

Many factors interact to determine the health of plants on the floodplain. These include soil moisture store, soil salinity, groundwater depth, flood level, flood frequency and duration, and

Figure 1. The Chowilla floodplain.

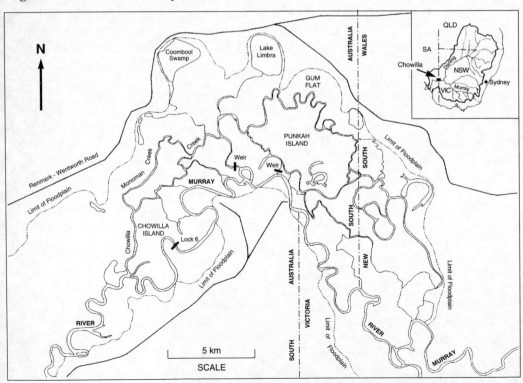

run-off. Before the river's flow was regulated, most of these factors varied within ranges which the biota of the Chowilla Anabranch could tolerate. However, since regulation, plant species have been exposed to highly variable flooding regimes and increasing salinity. For example, River Red Gum and Black Box are tolerant of saline conditions and can grow in salinities of 20,000 mg/L and 35,000 mg/L respectively. However, vigour decreases at even moderate salinities, especially where the water table is high, leaving only a shallow zone of aerated soil. River Red Gum can tolerate quite shallow water tables, as occurs adjacent to the main river, because freshwater enters the root zone from the water table by capillary action.

Trees are continuing to die in a number of areas on the Chowilla floodplain, due to salinity effects. In the long term this will serve to accelerate soil erosion.

Changes to flood regimes seriously affect the health and regeneration of many plant species. River Red Gum seedlings will not establish unless the forest floods at least every second year in winter and spring. Young seedlings suffer from both desiccation and lengthy flooding, so that changes from the 'natural' flooding regime are important.

Likewise, waterbird and fish breeding are closely linked with the timing and duration of flooding, and declines in both these faunal groups can be partly attributed to river regulation. In addition, declining vegetation cover from salinization effects is also likely to have contributed to the reductions in the abundances of fish and waterbirds.

Human factors

Europeans introduced exotic plants and animals and have cleared, tilled and burned the landscape to varying degrees. In addition, river management has elevated water tables, increased salinity and caused deterioration of soils. Suitable areas of the floodplain are farmed, principally for sheep grazing. There are commercial fishing operations, as well as numerous recreational pursuits such as canoeing, fishing, waterbird hunting, houseboating and general sightseeing and tourism.

Introduced species

Rabbits, sheep, cattle and feral goats browse and trample plants, affect the regeneration of trees and alter the composition of ground and shrub flora. (Kangaroos can also impact on native vegetation when populations increase periodically.) Unpalatable plant species increase at the expense of more palatable species. They become more vigorous and limit soil moisture for other plants, thereby hindering regeneration even when stocking pressure is reduced. Grazing depletes bank vegetation, increases siltation and, by depletion of vegetation everywhere, contributes to soil salinization and erosion.

Grazing has reduced the habitat value of specific plant associations, altered the species composition of plant communities and prevented regeneration of most perennial plant species, including River Red Gum, Black Box and chenopod species.

The mammals of the area have been greatly affected by European settlement. The introduction of foxes and rabbits and grazing livestock has led to the dramatic reduction of most ground-living, medium-sized mammals, and several species which are believed to have existed in the general region of Chowilla are no longer found there.

The introduced European Carp *Cyprinus carpio* is widespread in permanent wetlands and also exploits temporary wetlands. It eats zoo-plankton and, in the process, destroys the aquatic vegetation.

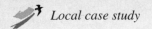
Pastoralism

Although several adjoining areas are under conservation management as nature reserves and national parks, the Chowilla floodplain is used by pastoralists under leasehold agreements with the relevant State Governments. Land north of the River Murray is used almost exclusively for sheep grazing; away from the river valley, carrying capacity is relatively low at just over 1 sheep/10 ha, while the floodplain carries up to 1 sheep/2 ha. A few small areas of irrigated perennial pasture (including lucerne and clover) have been established in order to supplement natural forage in the dry season.

The Chowilla Anabranch system is vital to sheep graziers in several ways:

- water is pumped from the creeks to tanks and dams in the back country; several stations would not be viable without water from the creeks;
- grazing is better in areas subject to winter/spring flooding;
- sheep can drink directly from the creeks in the floodplain;
- the creeks act as fences;
- water from the creeks is used to irrigate pastures for stock feed on one of the stations.

Commercial fishery

Since the 1950s, there has been a significant decline in the total commercial fish catch. Although changes such as the construction of locks and weirs, removal of obstacles in the river, extensive land clearance, introduction of exotic fish species and greatly increased recreational fishing have all had an impact, the main cause of the decline appears to be linked with the increase in the water storage capacity of the upper Murray-Darling Basin. This has reduced the regularity of small to medium floods and appears to have reduced the breeding success of commercially important species.

River Red Gum (Eucalyptus camaldulensis) has a high water requirement and grows on river and creek margins in the Chowilla floodplain.

Although the Chowilla Anabranch system is a relatively small part of the River Murray floodplain ecosystem as a whole, it has provided 15% of the South Australian commercial catch from rivers during the past decade. In 1988-89, it was estimated that the area's commercial catch yielded 14 tonnes of native fish and nine tonnes of lower value fish, or about 3% of the totals for the entire Murray-Darling Basin.

Tourism and recreational activities

The Chowilla Anabranch system provides an exceptional location for a range of water-based recreational activities, including canoeing, houseboating, fishing, hunting, camping and general boating. A report commissioned by the Murray-Darling Basin Commission (M-DBC) (Social and Ecological Assessment *et al.* 1989) reports that there are approximately 15,000 visitor-nights spent in the area each year; about 75% of these are spent by visitors from outside the Riverland region.

However, it is thought that the economic value of tourism contributes relatively little to the area's economy – perhaps as little as AUS$10/day/visitor – as there is a high level of visitation for educational reasons and the nature of many of the recreational activities (e.g. houseboating) means that most visitors are relatively self-sufficient.

It is estimated that almost 300,000 South Australians participate in some form of fishing activity every year and the River Murray is an important recreational fishing area even though catches are limited. The impact of recreational fishing on the Chowilla system is not known.

The Chowilla area is the most favoured destination for canoeists in South Australia. Secondary schools, tertiary institutions, outdoor educational organizations, as well as the general public appreciate its many qualities, including fast- and slow-flowing water, a range of routes, interesting scenery and remoteness.

The Murray River above Renmark is a popular location for houseboat use. About 60% of all houseboats in South Australia are in the Riverland Region. In 1985-86 there were 180 commercial houseboats licensed in the State, with a 58% occupancy rate. By 1986-87 this had increased to 213, although the occupancy rate had fallen to 48.5%. Most houseboating is done in the main channel of the river, and although it is possible for houseboats to leave the river at Chowilla Creek, Ral Ral Creek and Rufus River, travelling distance is limited because of narrow channel width, obstructions and shallow depth. Houseboat operations are important economically to the Riverland region.

Protection status

The Chowilla Anabranch is not protected within any type of conservation reserve or national park. Although suitable areas of the floodplain are farmed by private landowners, principally for sheep grazing, a majority of the land is held under leasehold agreements with the relevant State Governments.

The approach

A major objective in developing the Chowilla Resource Management Plan was to involve the community in the development of an integrated resource management plan sympathetic to the requirements of commercial and recreational users and to protect and/or restore the natural ecological features of the Chowilla Anabranch system.

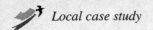

Management framework

In November 1985, the Murray-Darling Basin Ministerial Council was formed to promote and coordinate effective planning and management for the sustainable, equitable and efficient use of the water, land and environmental resources of the Murray-Darling Basin.

In 1988, the Murray-Darling Basin Commission (M-DBC) superseded the River Murray Commission (itself formed in 1915) to advise the Ministerial Council on land and environmental matters in the Basin in addition to its traditional role of managing and distributing the waters of the River Murray.

Consideration of options for integrated management

In 1989 the Ministerial Council released its Salinity and Drainage Strategy which consisted of several salt interception schemes in the catchment. One of these schemes was proposed for the Chowilla Anabranch.

1988 draft Environmental Impact Statement

Prior to the release of the Salinity and Drainage Strategy, the South Australian Engineering and Water Supply Department (SAEWS) released a draft Environmental Impact Statement (EIS) describing several salinity mitigation options for the Chowilla area being considered for incorporation into the Strategy. The salinity mitigation strategies examined in the EIS included:

- interception of groundwater;
- lowering the pool level of Lock 6;
- raising the level of creek entrances;
- isolating the Anabranch from the river using banks;
- selectively managing surface flows through the Anabranch by various combinations of weirs and banks.

The option preferred by SAEWS was a strategy that regulated the surface flows through 50% of the Anabranch area and disposed of the impounded salty water to an evaporation basin away from the river. An estimated 60% of the salt entering the Anabranch would have been intercepted by this option. The affected creeks would have dried up at times of low to moderate river flows and would have been flooded under high river flows (exceeding 35,000 ml/day) every two to five years. The remainder of the Anabranch would have been unaffected.

The community rejected the surface water regulation proposal in the EIS. Fifty-six submissions and two petitions were generated by the public and interested organizations. Criticisms of this option included reduction in fish habitat, no benefits for already degraded vegetation, interference with paddock boundaries, reduced recreational opportunities and reduced access to water for stock.

Community consultation process

Following the public reaction to the draft EIS, the M-DBC agreed to fund several studies to gain a better understanding of the consequences of the proposed salinity mitigation proposals on the Chowilla Anabranch. In August 1990, the Ministerial Council agreed to implement a community consultation programme to develop an integrated management plan for Chowilla.

The M-DBC appointed a Chowilla Working Group, with representatives from the relevant State Government agencies and the Commission itself to oversee these initiatives.

Table 1. Options for natural resource management at Chowilla.

Salinity management

1. Groundwater interception by tubewells

Land management

2. Revegetation of degraded areas of floodplain, upland rise, and highland.
3. Wind and water erosion control works (excluding revegetation) to stabilize and protect sensitive areas.
4. Controlled releases from Lake Victoria.
5. Management strategies for domestic stock, rabbits, kangaroos and other fauna.

Wetlands management

6. Flow control structures at Lakes Littra and Limbra.
7. Reintroduce a wetting and drying cycle at Pilby Creek.
8. Re-establish flow through the banked off creeks above Lock 6 on Chowilla Island.

Recreation/People management

9. Development of access, recreation and information facilities.

Land tenure

10. Establishment of a Regional Reserve on the South Australian portion of Chowilla floodplain.
11. Land swap between Calperum Station and Chowilla Station to bring all of the floodplain in SA under Regional Reserve.
12. Purchase of Kulcurna Station and establishment as a Crown Lands Reserve.
13. Land swap between Kulcurna Station and Noola/Tareena Station to bring all of the floodplain in NSW into Crown Lands Reserve, facilitating contiguous cross-border management.

The implementation of the Chowilla Community Consultation Programme (CCCP) was delegated to the South Australian Department of Environment and Planning which, in turn, appointed two consultants to assist in implementing the programme; one to advise on the process for the programme and the other its implementation.

A series of factsheets were produced to provide the community with the technical information derived from the studies. The factsheets also contained information on the original EIS and information resulting from an earlier biological study of the area by the Nature Conservation Society of South Australia. This information was used as the basis for discussions at two public meetings held in October 1990.

On the recommendation of the Chowilla Working Group, the M-DBC responded to the public concerns by funding studies into the hydro-geology, soils and vegetation, fish habitat value and recreational uses of the area (Clark & Lowe 1990; Collingham 1990a,b,c; Hollingsworth 1989; O'Malley & Sheldon 1991; Pierce 1990; SEAP *et al.* 1989; Waterhouse 1989).

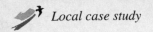

Public information days

At the first of two public meetings (termed 'information days') in October 1990, representatives of the Government departments which undertook studies presented information on the key issues. A 'national park' in the Chowilla area was regarded as undesirable by a large portion of the community and there was a general view that hunting and fishing should not be further restricted. At the second meeting, one week later, members of the public formed discussion groups to express their views on key issues and suggested various options for managing the area.

Engineering solutions were favoured for managing salinity with preference for groundwater interception schemes. There was little support for surface water regulation schemes. Rabbit and other pest animal control measures were supported, along with flood regime management to encourage recovery of floodplain vegetation. Ongoing fishery research, maintenance of water flow through the backwaters, and development of uniform fishing regulations between States were recommended.

Following on from the public meetings, a newsletter was produced at regular intervals to inform the public of progress with the CCC Programme.

At the conclusion of the public information meetings the community was invited to make submissions until the end of January 1991, and expressions of interest were sought from persons wishing to serve on a Community Reference Group to assist the Chowilla Working Group with development and evaluation of the options proposed. The Chowilla Working Group agreed that the Reference Group should reflect widespread community views and that, apart from the secretary, Government officers should be excluded.

The two groups met independently on several occasions during 1991 to develop and evaluate options and ideas for integrated management of the Chowilla floodplain. In October 1991 agreement was reached between the two groups on the appropriate management options for Chowilla. The Chowilla Working Group made several recommendations to the Murray-Darling Basin Commission (Table 1). Significantly, the recommendation relating to salinity mitigation proposed the use of a network of 15 tubewells spread across the northernmost parts of the floodplain where salinity effects are greatest. This was proposed as the most environmentally benign method of salt interception.

Decisions of the Ministerial Council

The Murray-Darling Basin Ministerial Council considered advice on integrated management at Chowilla in May 1992. The Council agreed to:

- adopt the option for salinity mitigation by tubewells as the favoured method of environmentally sound salt interception;
- defer consideration of construction of a tubewells scheme until 1997;
- negotiate for the purchase of Kulcurna Station and to restructure adjoining properties;
- establish a Management Group to implement an integrated management plan for Chowilla;
- fund partial rehabilitation of Chowilla through the Natural Resources Management Strategy Interstate Programme (at an estimated cost over four years of AUS$1 million excluding the purchase of Kulcurna) under a detailed programme to be developed by the Management Group;
- release a progress report to the community outlining these decisions.

The total cost of these initiatives, excluding the tubewells proposal, is estimated at around AUS$2 million. If the full tubewells proposal were to be implemented at Chowilla, the establishment cost (at November 1992 values) would be approximately AUS$18 million, with annual maintenance and running costs of nearly AUS$1 million.

Lessons learned

The development of the Chowilla Resource Management Plan has demonstrated that where there is multiple use of a resource with high conservation value, thorough consultation with community and interest groups is an essential part of developing an integrated management plan. This is the only approach that gives the community ownership of the plan and therefore ensures sustainable resource use.

In this case the community's response to the draft EIS catalysed the consultation process, in turn ensuring that, in developing an integrated resource management plan, Government agencies took account of a wide range of interests and concerns. Ongoing consultation throughout the development phase also served to satisfy the community's desire to make a valuable contribution to the management strategies ultimately endorsed. While the process has not been without difficulties, it has allowed for constructive discussion and negotiation between the community and Government agencies, which, it is hoped, will continue as management action is taken at Chowilla.

Although there is no simple formula for community consultation, the Chowilla experience is likely to serve as a model for such undertakings in Australia in the future. The key elements of this community consultation process have been to meet with the community on site, and to be responsive to their requests for more information or clearer explanations of what is already known. Another key element is the establishment of a Government-based working group to ensure regular dialogue between relevant agencies, and a community-based reference group to allow open discussion of concerns. A link between these two groups is essential, and, as occurred with the Chowilla case, a skilled facilitator is needed to provide feedback between the community and Government groups.

Both Government and community groups participating in the process have learned and benefited from the exercise. What is clear is that, in the future, Government agencies with different management responsibilities must be able to communicate and consult effectively between themselves before consulting with the community on issues relating to integrated resource management.

Dr Bill Phillips, Landscape Conservation Unit, Australian Nature Conservation Agency, GPO Box 636, Canberra ACT 2601, Australia.

Tony Sharley, Murray-Darling Basin Commission, Canberra ACT 2601, Australia.

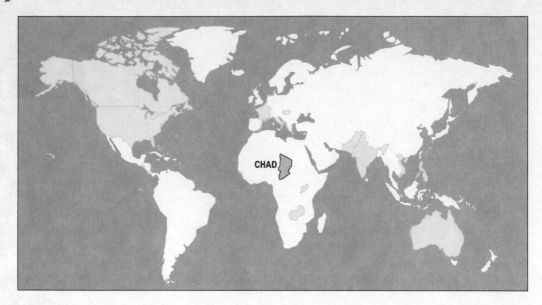

Traditional management systems and integration of small scale interventions in the Logone floodplains of Chad

Klamadja Kodi Dadnadji and Jeroen C.J. van Wetten

Introduction

About 7.8% of the surface of Chad consists of wetlands, covering some 100,600 km². While many river floodplain systems in the Sahel-Sudan zone are prone to large scale hydrological interventions (Drijver & van Wetten 1992), in Chad, the upper and middle sections of the Chari and the Logone rivers are largely intact. Although 114,940 km² of land are protected, the National Park of Zakouma (3,000 km²) is the only area in which a substantial wetland ecosystem is part of a protected site. In addition to Lakes Chad and Fitri (together covering some 15,000 km²), the other main wetland areas in Chad lie along the rivers Logone (covering approximately 15,625 km²) and Chari (approximately 62,500 km²), both situated in the Lake Chad Basin. Approximately 40% of the Sudan zone in Chad consists of inundation flats, river floodplains, marshes or smaller lakes.

The Logone river originates in the humid eastern part of North Cameroon and leaves the Sudan zone shortly before its confluence with the Chari. Droughts have affected the frequency and magnitude of river inundations, as well as seriously constraining rain-fed agriculture. Nevertheless, the natural characteristics of this part of the river remain unchanged, and traditional natural resource use and management systems still exist. To avoid the dangers of drought and unpredictable inundations, small interventions, originating from local and outside initiatives, have been carried out.

This case study looks at the positive role traditional systems and small interventions can play in supporting sustainable use of wetland resources and in improving sustainable development in rural wetland areas, in particular in the middle valley of the Logone between Eré and Lai.

The approach

The socio-economic context

Apart from pastoralism and fisheries at Lakes Chad and Fitri, the northern part of Chad lacks any substantial productive sector. In contrast, the southern Sudan zone is the main food and cash-crop production sector of the country, producing a surplus of cereals and fish. Sufficient rains and inundation by the two main rivers, Chari and Logone, make this part of southern Chad suitable for a wide variety of crops and land use systems. For centuries the productive and fertile floodplains of the Logone have attracted invading tribes. In recent years, an increasing number of nomadic pastoralists, Fulbe and Shoa-Arabs, have moved into the region and become permanent residents in the face of deteriorating conditions for their animals in the Sahel zone.

Eré, with 2,955 inhabitants can be considered a typical village. The village leadership is hereditary and the 'Chef de Village' acts as the legal representative of the village. Rice and taro (a large tropical plant cultivated for its edible tubers) growing and fisheries are the main activities, followed by vegetables, millet and sorghum. The region has almost a monopoly on taro production in Chad. Compared to Chad's average annual income of US$80 per capita, the region has a relatively high income of US$360.

Rain-fed rice was introduced at the beginning of this century, followed in the mid 1970s by the introduction of irrigated rice. Foreign non-government organizations (NGOs) are active in the region with small scale projects. Since 1987, a local NGO, Association d'Appui aux Initiatives Locales de Développement (ASSAILD), has supported local activities by facilitating credits, education, training and technical assistance.

Government policies on rural development and natural wetland resources

Under the 'Plan Directeur de Lutte Contre la Desertification' (Desertification Control Action Plan), the Government of Chad expressed its desire for sustainable use to be made of natural resources. One of the main thrusts of this national strategy is the protection and regeneration of forests, pastures, fish and wildlife. In the Logone and Chari basins, flooding and inundation are highly important for the production of cereals, fish, rice and meat. While the potential of the area for rice irrigation is recognized, flood-dependent activities have a higher priority.

The Lake Chad Basin Commission regards water allocation as the essential issue for the sustainable resource utilization of the whole Lake Chad basin. The growing demand for water for rice irrigation and other requirements will create problems for the water levels of Lake Chad. The fragility of the existing ecosystems and the growing scarcity of water need to be taken into account when new projects and activities are being planned.

In the 'Plan Intérimaire 1986-1988', socio-ecological balance is given as the basis for sound development. Active cooperation and consultation with the local population are considered to be essential for restoration and development activities (SNV-Tchad 1989). Foreign and local NGOs are widely accepted by Government as the main source of development interventions. During times of political turmoil, civil war and lack of a strong administration, the power of NGOs has grown, such that they are highly influential in the development and implementation of policies. NGO-led programmes have also stimulated participation by local people. The existing tendency for people to be organized into groups at the village and village sector ('quartier') level has given rise to a situation in which many of these groups have connections with, or are supported by, NGOs.

The cycle of life

Rain and floodwater inundations determine people's activities in the floodplains between Eré and Lai. The first rains come in April and reach a peak in June, July and August. The dry season extends from November until the end of March. Mean precipitation in the region around Eré and Lai is about 1,000 mm/year. Rivers begin to rise after the first rains and reach peak levels at the beginning of August, eventually breaking their banks and inundating the floodplains from the second half of August through to November.

Villagers on the riverbanks and in the floodplains are mainly occupied with fishing and floodplain agriculture, utilizing higher ground for rain-fed rice agriculture. Settlements on the outer edges of the floodplains are mainly occupied with rain-fed agriculture, cattle-rearing and some fishery.

When looking at the diversity of land use, it can be seen that various crops and activities are adapted to aspects of the physical environment, including topography, soil, hydrology and climate. The use of crop species best adapted to the environmental conditions, tied to the yearly influx of rainwater, floodwater and soil fertilization, has led to a land use system characterized by low external input and low external dependency. At the same time, this risk-spreading strategy enables the villagers to use different resources from the same ecosystem, thereby avoiding the risk of too high a dependency on one single resource.

Before the floods arrive, long strips of floodplain vegetation are cleared and burned and the resulting ashes put on the ridges on which the taro is planted and later harvested as the flood recedes. At the onset of the rains, hard labour is required to prepare and cultivate the rain-fed rice fields. Rain-fed rice fields are surrounded by small dikes which retain run-off rainwater and moisten the soils, while also protecting the ripening crops against excessive river inundations. Rice is the main crop but some villagers cultivate millet on the light clay and sandy soils which are rarely inundated.

When migratory fish arrive and begin their reproductive cycle, men are occupied with fishing activities. During the fishing season, in November and December, the women and youngsters mainly tend the crops and will only join in the fishing activity when all hands are needed. The constant availability of nearby water makes the riverbanks highly suitable for the cultivation of vegetables; this is carried out mostly by the women and children. Cattle breeding and dairy activities are of minor importance in these villages. Nomadic pastoralists often keep one or two cows owned by village people. Cattle migrations are limited in scale. Only during the high floods are they moved to dry areas some 25-50 km away, returning as early as the beginning of December. In very dry years, when the pastures in the Sahel zone are too poor, nomadic pastoralists from northern Cameroon, Niger or Nigeria may enter this region, some having travelled more than 200 km.

In the mid 1970s, irrigated rice was introduced along the banks of the Logone. After extensive and costly construction work, financed by relief agencies, irrigation of rice fields became an increasingly important activity. The long period of drought through the 1970s and the first half of the 1980s accelerated the acceptance of irrigated rice production. The need for double rotation of the labour force in the irrigated rice fields interfered to a high extent with other activities. However, the increased staple food security provided by the irrigation method brought a willingness to invest in the high labour costs involved. Although irrigated rice has a higher output in tonnes/ha, people continue to invest in rain-fed or floodplain agriculture and fishing. Only floating rice agriculture has gradually disappeared. The substantial amount of protein resulting from the fishing and agricultural activities, and the cash income from rice and taro, has meant that the villagers have tried to combine the land use forms described. Irrigated rice agriculture has been introduced at a slow rate and on a small scale, enabling villagers to gradually adapt and integrate this new activity into their lifestyles.

Traditional resource management systems

Hunting

Before colonial- or central-governmental laws came into being, hunting in the floodplains of Eré was controlled by the 'Chef de Terre'. While one or more lesser Chefs governed game hunting activities in and around the villages, his authority extended over other land tenure rights and every kind of hunting without his permission was forbidden. Where crops were damaged by wild animals only the Chef de Terre could approve a hunt. In years of abundant game he would declare a collective hunt by all villagers, and he decided when and how many wild animals should be killed. A mutual responsibility for sustainable killing existed, and the villagers, by way of their game revenues, and the Chef, by way of his share, both profited from this system.

Governmental laws, first introduced by colonial powers, abolished the authority of the Chef de Terre, and his regulating function and decision-making role disappeared. Lack of governmental control on the implementation of these new regulations and the loss of the authority of the Chef gave rise to unsustainable exploitation of game animals in the floodplains, leading to the eventual extinction of many animals.

Taro and pasture

To enable the floodplain to recover after a taro crop has been harvested, the cultivated land lies fallow for two to three years. The taro fields are owned by the different sectors of the village and it is the elders in each sector who decide which areas will be farmed out for taro and which will be used as pasture. The fallow fields provide grazing for goats from the village and the cattle of nomadic pastoralists. In times of flood, the regenerating vegetation serves as a breeding area for fish, while in the second and third years following the taro harvest, a tall herb, *Sesbania* sp., emerges. Its wood-like stem serves as the main fuel resource in the village and is also important in the construction of fish traps and cages.

Marigot fisheries

Around Eré, the floodplain is dotted with a dozen or so marshes, each between 1 and 5 km^2. These 'marigots' are old stream beds of the Logone and each is owned by a 'Chef de Marigot', closely allied to a number of families or village sector. During the floods, the marigots are too deep and the open water area is too extensive to allow any concentrated fishing activity to take place. As the floodwaters recede, small drainage channels, both natural and man-made, are used as fish traps. Ownership of the channels also lies with the Chefs de Marigot and people can hire a fishing site, paying a percentage of the catch to the Chefs. The abundant fish stocks ensure a high yield, amply paying back the investment made by the fishermen in fish trap construction and channel digging.

From December onwards, all fishing in the marigots is banned, enabling the remaining fish stocks to recover. Only in exceptional cases, when the marigots dry out, is permission given for villagers to harvest what would otherwise be a lost protein resource. At the start of the rainy season, when fish stocks in the marigots are at their height, villagers are invited by the Chef to join in collective fishing in the marigots; a small proportion of the catch is donated to the Chef. By monitoring yields and fish stocks, the Chef can decide whether to invite further collective fishing parties. When the floods return, there are enough fish remaining in the marigots to allow a second cycle of reproduction and growth.

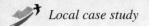

At the onset of the floods, the natural drainage channels between the river and the marigots are used to catch fish moving from the river to the marigots and the adjacent floodplains. Here again the Chef de Marigot will ban the placing of traps on a number of the inlets to the marigots, enabling migratory fish to enter and spawn, thus ensuring a plentiful supply of fish for subsequent marigot fishing seasons.

Riverine fisheries

The Chefs de Marigot protect the marigot fish stocks during the dry season by banning all fishing from December until the beginning of April. This system of resource management in the Logone river ensures a continuing supply of fish through to the end of the dry season, by which time stocks normally become exhausted.

The Chef de Village and the Chefs de Pêche, the latter having jurisdiction over a section of river belonging to a village sector, enforce a ban on fisheries in certain stretches of the river from December until the end of March. During this period, each sector builds cage-like structures in the shallow parts of the river. Each cage consists of poles, intertwined with branches, stuck in the river bed. Dead animals, household rubbish and handfuls of rice and other grain are regularly thrown into the cages. The cages provide a variety of fish species with food, shelter and a safe place to breed at a time when conditions are normally unfavourable. At the same time, migrating fish, originating from Lake Chad, find a suitable habitat in which to await the floods which will enable them to enter the floodplains and spawn.

At the end of March, after a successful sample catch, the Chef de Village and the Chefs de Pêche will invite villagers and inhabitants from surrounding settlements to join in the collective fishing. Villagers pay 10% of their revenues to the Chefs. Under this system of fishery control, overfishing of migratory and non-migratory species is prevented. By maintaining the ban in certain parts of the river until water levels start to rise in April, the presence of spawning fish at the beginning of the flood period is ensured, thus guaranteeing the annual influx of fish to the floodplains.

Dry season fishing in the Logone river near Eré. Photo: J.C.J. van Wetten/CML

Local interventions in resource management systems

The climatic and hydrological conditions in the middle valley of the Logone offer good opportunities for both rain-dependent and irrigated agriculture. The severe droughts of the 1970s and 1980s have shown that rainfall and floods can reach dangerously low levels. To counter the adverse effects of late or marginal rains and limited flooding, local interventions are undertaken. Three examples are given here, for the area between Lai and Eré.

Dam construction

In an attempt to catch run-off rainwater and retain floodwater, a small dam was constructed in the Logone floodplain. Initiated by four villages, the scheme was supported by a credit from a local Chadian NGO. Total costs were approximately US$2,700 (ASSAILD 1990, 1991). An earth dam, 125 m long, now influences some 91 km^2 of upstream floodplain adjacent to its natural drainage canal, the Criel. In years of poor rainfall and flooding, water can be retained in the basin behind the dam, providing about seven villages along the Criel with an extended period of inundation. This inundation influences the water table in the surrounding area, improving vegetation growth and stimulating regeneration. Villagers use the ponded water for fishing and for irrigating gardens and rice fields.

Canal construction

The second example involves the construction of a canal system, undertaken by a group of 55 people from the village of Nergue, also situated close to the Criel. As in most villages, rice is sown when the first rains fall in May. After inundation by rain or floodwater, it is harvested after the floods in November each year. Some 24 ha of rice fields were surrounded with small dikes, and canals were constructed to provide transportation. A small canal, 1.5 km long, was dug by hand through elevated ancient riverbanks in order to provide an easy and early flow of water from the Criel to the rice fields. The scheme cost US$2,400. Rice production in 1990 reached some 4.5-6.0 tonnes/ha of rice paddy, compared to 2.0 tonnes/ha prior to the scheme.

Dike construction

In order to optimize fish production and the efficiency of floodplain fisheries, villagers have modified, to a large extent, the hydrological characteristics of the plains (Blache 1964; Blache *et al.* 1962). By digging canals through riverbanks, inundation during periods of low flooding is enhanced and the passage of fish into the plains is more or less secured. The construction of numerous 30-50 cm high semi-circular dikes on the plains obstructs floodwater run-off and retains rainwater, extending the period of inundation. At the end of the rain and flood season, the small reservoirs behind the dikes are drained by small outlets. These outlets are excellent places to gather escaping fish. Construction and maintenance of the dikes is done by hand and forms an integral part of the farming activity.

In each of these projects, the practical work was carried out by local people. Outside assistance came in the form of credits provided by the local NGO, which also helped groups to organize themselves so that they were able to generate income to pay back the credits. It was the local people themselves who determined the actions or interventions which were needed to improve the productivity of their land use systems.

External interventions

As a result of the droughts in the mid 1970s and 1980s, irrigated rice production was introduced in the floodplains between Lai and Bongor, initiated by Catholic organizations. In the mid 1980s, the NGOs CARE-Chad and Association Rurale pour la Promotion Economique et Sociale (ARPES) took over most of the assistance provided for rice irrigation. In five villages, small (25-100 ha) irrigation schemes were created, each divided into quarter-hectare lots. Each lot is owned by a member of the village group which manages the scheme. Under these schemes, like the one at Eré, as much as 8 tonnes of grained rice/ha were obtained annually.

Local NGOs gave technical and financial assistance for the installation of simple water pumps, which enabled women to create small gardens on the riverbanks. These gardens are especially important to the daily family diet. Any surplus of vegetables is sold at the local village market, providing most of the village with a considerable amount of fresh produce. The initiative to establish these gardens originated from the women's groups, the members of which also manage and carry out the physical work. The groups also provide the finance to maintain these gardens through fund-raising and membership fees. Although income is minimal compared to other, more extensive land use forms, for the women they are a highly important and independent source of income.

The introduction of fertilizers for both rain-fed and irrigated rice culture has improved the yields per ha by 150%. The state organization, Office de Mise en Valeur de Satégui-Déressia (OMVSD), has played an important role in the introduction and distribution of fertilizers, as well as in their use. The production per cycle of irrigated rice is comparable to rain-fed rice culture, but the lower cost of rain-fed rice production, combined with its reasonable yields, explains why this method remains an important activity for farmers.

While the interventions described here are small in scale, and have involved considerable participation by local inhabitants, they have not interfered with or obstructed other existing and profitable land use forms. Conflict between the inundation of taro plots and the new rice irrigation scheme has been avoided by the careful selection of plots. The new activities have become integrated into the more traditional lifestyles, have increased the food supply and, in some cases, have brought economic development. The decentralized nature of these interventions and the practical involvement of the local people in all aspects of the various schemes have brought a high measure of success and acceptance for them amongst the communities involved.

Constraints

While management of the natural resources has proved successful, there are still many problems. One of the main problems is outbreaks of fire in the floodplain vegetation during the dry season. The encroachment and higher density of pastoralists in the floodplains has led to a greater number of fires being lit by these land users. The fires propagate an early growth of fresh grass for cattle grazing during the dry season. Fire is also used to capture small rodents. Degradation of the grasslands is now occurring. The lack of an effective authority over the use of these 'free' resources, has led to uncontrolled exploitation and unsustainable practices. There is no dialogue between the villages and the pastoralists over vegetation management, and hence no mechanism which could bring about a means of controlling the fires. Pastoralists themselves still regard the grassland resource as free and do not accept any regulation on its use.

Through the OMVSD, irrigated rice production was propounded as a way to overcome the shortage of cereals during droughts. However, in years of sufficient rains and floods, the labour requirements for double-cycle irrigation interfere with other activities. As taro, fishery and rain-fed rice production are also highly productive activities, villagers who own irrigated fields face a dilemma when they try to combine them; for example, the start of the rain-fed rice cycle coincides with the harvesting of irrigated rice. To date, the OMVSD has only supported rice producing activities; taro, millet, sorghum and fisheries, all productive and income generating activities, are all unsupported.

Poor transportation facilities make it difficult to get fish to the markets, with the result that the fisheries play only a limited role as an income-generating activity. With sufficient funds, motorized boats could easily bring large loads of fish to urban centres such as N'Djamena.

Lessons learned

The land use and management systems in the floodplains of the Logone, combined with development initiatives, form a basis for sustainable use of the floodplain wetland. Interventions to increase rice production have not damaged or interfered with the natural hydrological system of river- and rain-water inundation, and the annual regeneration and productivity of the natural resources provide the basis for sustainable use. However, serious constraints exist. The lack of a substantial game population, the ongoing process of vegetation degeneration through fires and overgrazing, and the pressures placed on the resources by a growing human population could, ultimately, destroy the present balance. Additional activities or alternatives within traditional lifestyles are necessary in order to cater for the needs of future generations.

Three main lessons can be learned from this case study:

1. In an unchanging environment, people are capable of managing the natural resources around them through the maintenance of traditional practices combined with new technology. Within limits, the productivity of the natural resources is guaranteed and optimized. The embodiment of these systems into the social and hierarchical structure of the community is essential if they are to be effective; this is especially so when the authority of governmental institutions over resources is limited or weak.

2. Responsibility for, or ownership of, resources, and the right to use and profit from them, forms a better basis for sustainable use than free use open to everybody. Not all traditional management systems are sustainable; e.g. the over-exploitation and degeneration of grassland vegetation by pastoralists.

3. Integrated small scale development and people participation are necessary to match growing demands and ensure the continuation of sustainable resource use. Droughts and other natural hazards are a threat to people's health and livelihoods. Years of poor productivity place the growing population at risk. Initiatives to optimize certain land use forms and to increase output are essential in order to cope with the growing demand for food, productivity and financial reward. Locally-based initiatives have proved to be successful. Not only have they improved the output of certain resources, but also people's awareness of the values of other resources. The role that local, decentralized NGOs can play must be regarded as highly important.

Klamadja Kodi Dadnadji, Direction des Parcs Nationaux et Réserves de Faune, Tchad.

Jeroen C.J. van Wetten, Center for Environmental Science (CML), Leiden University, Leiden, The Netherlands.

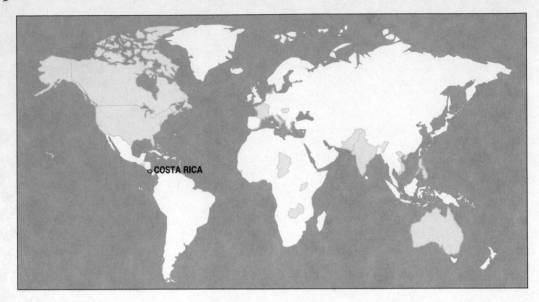

The mangrove forests of Sierpe, Costa Rica

Enrique Lahmann

Introduction

The Terraba-Sierpe Forest Reserve is located on the Pacific Coast of Costa Rica. It is the largest mangrove forest in the country with an estimated surface area of 16,700 ha. This forest reserve covers close to 40% of the total mangrove forest in Costa Rica.

Mangrove products have been extracted from the Terraba-Sierpe forest for many years without a major impact on the ecosystem. However, since 1984 pressure has increased substantially as the number of people exploiting the mangroves for subsistence purposes has increased. This is a direct result of the decline of the banana industry, the closure of the banana company in the Sierpe area, and the resulting unemployment. People have now turned to the mangrove resource as the most easily available source of income and food.

In Costa Rica mangroves are protected by law. All mangrove forests were declared forest reserves in 1977 (Executive Decree number 7210-A), under the jurisdiction of the Fisheries and Wildlife General Directorate. Two years later, in 1979, by Executive Decree number 10005-A all mangrove forests were placed under the jurisdiction of the Forestry General Directorate (Dirección General Forestal - DGF) which regulates the use of all forest reserves. In order to extract any forest product from a forest reserve legally, it is necessary to have a management plan approved by the DGF. Legally, the communities now using the mangrove must obtain such permits from the DGF.

In recent years two management plans have been prepared for Sierpe but, in the absence of funds and clear local support, neither has been implemented. In response to this situation action was taken in 1989 to work with local communities in managing Sierpe. The present case study describes this work.

The problem

The most important resources presently extracted from the Terraba-Sierpe Mangrove Forest Reserve are wood for charcoal production, bark for tannins, firewood, construction materials and molluscs. However, fisheries inside the mangroves are for subsistence only, since commercial and even artisanal fishery is presently forbidden inside the mangrove channels.

As in most other mangrove systems there is a close, direct relationship between the mangrove forest and commercial, sports and artisanal fishery. Some of the most important commercial shrimping grounds in Costa Rica are located in the Bahia de Coronado, offshore from the Terraba-Sierpe Mangrove Forest Reserve, while artisanal fishery could be an important source of food and income if managed in the correct fashion.

The potential shrimp fisheries associated with Terraba-Sierpe are estimated to be worth as much as US$29 million/year, in addition to the value of other fisheries. Close to five million individuals of the mollusc *Anadara* are extracted annually from this Mangrove Forest Reserve.

Indirect services are also provided by the Terraba-Sierpe mangroves. During the 1988 floods caused by Hurricane Joan, houses and property were spared greater damage from drifting wood and other debris by the natural barrier of fringing mangroves.

In terms of the potential value of forest products, it has been estimated that 1 ha of mangrove in this reserve can produce US$619.

People and the mangrove resource

There is a large number of small communities dispersed within and adjacent to the Terraba-Sierpe Mangrove Forest Reserve. The most important are Coronado (215 inhabitants), Tres Rios (205), San Marcos (200), Tortuga Arriba (113) and San Buenaventura (110) (Gonzales 1990). There are also several villages located at the mouths of the rivers Sierpe and Terraba, each with between 50 and 100 inhabitants. In total, there are close to 1,700 people living within the Terraba-Sierpe Mangrove Forest Reserve, each depending in one way or another on the natural resources provided by the Mangrove Forest Reserve.

Coronado is the largest community adjacent to the forest reserve and is located on the northern shore of the Rio Terraba. The economy of this community is based on the extraction of wood and bark from the mangrove forest and a cooperative called 'Coopemangle', a grassroots organization constituted of local people who make their living by extracting wood and bark from the mangroves, has been formed. Coopemangle is the only group legally authorized to extract forest products from a mangrove reserve in Costa Rica.

The approach

An analysis

Although the mangroves of Terraba-Sierpe are protected through the forest reserve, the increasing use being made of the mangroves by local people means that pressure will increase upon these resources in the long term. Therefore unless sustainable management systems are established, the forest is likely to be degraded and its benefits lost in the medium term. In order to establish forms of sustainable use, the precise reasons for the absence of proper utilization of the economic potential of the renewable natural resources of Sierpe needed to be determined. An analysis of the causes of the pressure upon the resources was therefore the first step in approaching the problem. This analysis identified five major problems facing the current use of the natural resources of the Terraba-Sierpe Mangrove Forest Reserve:

1. Absence of efficient techniques for the extraction and processing of charcoal and tannins

Although large amounts of charcoal are extracted, the method is extremely inefficient. The charcoal is produced by heating wood under conditions that carefully restrict the quantity of oxygen available for combustion. The higher the moisture content of the wood, the greater the heat needed to dry the wood. At present, mangrove wood used by Coopemangle does not receive any air-drying treatment and logs are usually wet when stockpiled in the earth kilns. As a result, a considerable amount of the energy that could be used for charcoal production is used during the drying phase in the kilns. Consequently, charcoal yields are lower and the impact on the forest is greater since more wood needs to be extracted to make up for the production deficit.

The traditional earth kilns are also very inefficient. The kilns consist of a pile of wood placed with the logs parallel to the ground. The pile is covered with fern leaves over which soil is laid. The uncontrolled air-flow results in over-burned charcoal, with a significant portion burned to ashes. This results in larger amounts of wood than necessary being extracted.

Mangrove bark is currently sold direct to the tanneries as raw material. Tannins are extracted in a very rudimentary way, with a very low efficiency rate. Because of the much longer periods needed to preserve leather using unprocessed mangrove bark, as compared to tannin extracts, demand for mangrove bark has decreased considerably. Currently, close to 75% of the mangrove logs used for charcoal production are not de-barked.

Hence, there is considerable post harvest loss from the mangrove resource. While considerable effort is put into harvesting the resource, the value that can be obtained from this raw material is not maximized.

2. Commercialization of mangrove products is not in the hands of the mangrove users

At present Coopemangle cannot sell its products, particularly charcoal, directly in markets because they lack the appropriate means of transportation. Consequently, they sell the charcoal to intermediaries. The selling price of charcoal is 100 colones (US$1.10) per sack in Coronado, while in Ciudad Cortes and Palmar, 20 km away, a sack will sell for 160 colones (US$1.75). In San José, the wholesale price is 350 colones (US$3.85). Good quality mangrove charcoal, properly marketed, could reach much higher prices in San José.

As a result of the low prices which Coopemangle obtains for its products, the impact on the forest is greater because the 'mangleros' (mangrove users) need to extract greater amounts of wood in order to obtain the same income.

3. Poor characterization of the resource and its potential

Use of the different mangrove species is governed to a large extent by tradition, and opportunities for greater economic return are, as a result, not fully exploited. For example, the mangrove species *Pelliciera* has been considered by many people, including Coopemangle, as a non-desirable species which should be eliminated. Previously considered as non-commercial forest, the wood of *Pelliciera* makes good quality timber for furniture and general construction purposes; under certain conditions it might even obtain a higher commercial value than *Rhizophora,* which is considered to be the primary species.

Similarly, eco-tourism is another activity whose potential has only recently begun to be explored in the reserve.

4. Illegal mangrove harvesting

While Coopemangle has purchased permits to operate within the Mangrove Forest Reserve, there are a number of illegal 'mangleros' without permits who live in the villages at the mouths of the rivers (the Bocas). The problem caused by these illegal mangrove harvesters is twofold. Firstly, since their activity is illegal, wood extraction is clandestine with the first concern being to avoid capture. As a result, the impact on the forest is greater, both in terms of damage and waste. Secondly, the illegally taken mangrove wood is sold at less than market value, creating a heavy burden not only on Coopemangle, but also on the illegal 'mangleros' who do not receive a fair price for their goods.

This situation is self-perpetuating because, in order to operate under the law, the illegal harvesters must obtain a permit from the DGF. However, to obtain this permit they need a management plan and the illegal harvesters have neither the financial resources nor the technical capability to formulate such a plan.

5. Shortage of manpower and resources

Financial constraints are limiting the effectiveness of the DGF's programmes. At present only one person is assigned to the whole Terraba-Sierpe Mangrove Forest Reserve and the situation is similar in other reserves. The difficulties facing the DGF are a lack of experience in management, protection and integrated use of mangrove resources, and insufficient funds, vehicles, boats and tools to undertake large-scale mangrove management activities.

The five factors outlined above combine to impact the mangroves in three principal ways:

i) Considerable wastage of resources. In spite of the good conditions which prevail for silviculture, it is estimated that present utilized yields are only 1-2 m^3/ha/year. As a result, a much larger forest area has to be impacted per unit time in order to satisfy the needs of the 'mangleros'.

ii) Poor economic return. Because the harvested timber is not utilized to maximum advantage, the economic return is well below its potential. This further encourages the 'mangleros' to exploit a larger area.

iii) Degradation of the mangrove forest as a result of these practices.

Until now the unsophisticated management practices carried out have not adversely affected the Terraba-Sierpe Mangrove Forest because the population density in the region is low. However, if the population density increases, as is likely in the near future, then pressure upon the mangrove resources will increase. Action must be taken now in order to promote the wise use of the natural resources of the Terraba-Sierpe Mangrove Forest Reserve.

The approach

In response to the problems facing the mangroves of Sierpe, a work programme has been initiated to promote the wise use of the natural resources of the Terraba-Sierpe Mangrove Forest Reserve and develop a series of management alternatives for neotropical mangroves. Four major objectives are being pursued:

1. To consolidate Coopemangle as a community organization capable of managing the mangrove resources in a sustainable fashion.

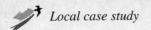

2. To implement *in situ* pilot projects which demonstrate the economic viability of using mangrove resources sustainably.
3. To disseminate, at the community, technical and decision-making levels, information on the potential of mangrove resources for rural development.
4. To strengthen the institutional capacity of the DGF as the government institution in charge of mangrove forest reserves.

The major activities being carried out in support of these objectives are:

Improvement in the extraction and processing of wood for charcoal production

Following analyses of the existing forms of charcoal production, and of the current extraction methods, four stages are now being pursued:

i)   Testing of different methods for extraction of wood from the forest, with emphasis on more efficient operation and less disturbance;
ii) Construction of two barges to enable transport of wood to the kilns in a more cost-effective manner;
iii) Construction of simple facilities to store sufficient logs for the air-drying of the wood prior to charcoal production. The amount of wood stored will be sufficient to allow sustained production;
iv) Reconstruction of three brick kilns in order to produce a higher quality charcoal and increase the efficiency of the process. Members of Coopemangle are being trained in the construction and management of brick kilns.

At the same time the results of work being undertaken in Nicaragua to improve the efficiency of tannin extraction from mangrove bark will be applied in Terraba-Sierpe, once these become available.

Better commercialization of mangrove products

A market study for mangrove charcoal and tannins, and timber from *Pelliciera*, is being carried out. A new truck will allow Coopemangle to take charcoal direct to market, while at the same time enabling them to bring other goods back to Coronado at a price cheaper than is currently the case.

Pilot project with 'Pelliciera'

Studies show that *Pelliciera* will make very good timber. Accordingly more detailed analyses of the mechanical properties of *Pelliciera*, and of the economic feasibility of its sustainable use, are being carried out. In addition, a portable saw-mill to process the timber is planned, together with a scheme to improve local housing using *Pelliciera* and other local resources.

Membership of Coopemangle

Coopemangle has agreed to accept illegal mangrove harvesters as members, thus extending the benefits derived from the project to other communities, while at the same time removing the negative impact of unregulated wood extraction. In the long term, other mangrove cooperatives may be established within the forest reserve, particularly in areas distant from Coronado. The activities currently under way will serve as a model for activities elsewhere.

Strengthening of the DGF

Two areas of action are being pursued: (i) the training of DGF staff in management, protection and integrated use of mangrove resources through seminars, workshops and field courses. In the medium term these training programmes will be extended to DGF staff in other mangrove forest reserves; and (ii) regular provision of technical assistance and documentation on mangrove management to DGF.

Biological and socio-economic studies

Underlining these management initiatives, a series of biological studies will map the areas where extraction activities have been carried out. These will quantify the extraction of charcoal, firewood, timber, bark, shrimp, shellfish and fish; quantify the growth rates of the mangrove species in the different areas of the forest reserve; compare the quality and quantity of regeneration under different management schemes, particularly clear-felling and selective extraction; identify critical areas requiring strict conservation; and establish non-consumptive use and preservation areas.

Concurrent with the biological studies, a detailed socio-economic study of the community using the mangrove resources is being undertaken. This will concentrate on quantifying the frequency of use of the mangrove resources, as well as the contribution these resources make to household and local economies. This will provide a baseline against which subsequent annual monitoring of key parameters can be measured, allowing the economic impact of the management plan to be studied. Corrective actions can then be taken where necessary.

Education and awareness

The DGF representative in Terraba-Sierpe has initiated a highly successful and innovative environmental education programme with the children of the elementary school in Coronado. This will be continued and expanded to incorporate other communities of the mangrove forestry reserve.

Costa Rican schoolchildren learn about the ecology of the Terraba-Sierpe mangroves.
Photo: WWF/Hervé Lethier

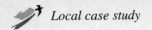

Achievements

While the problems of the mangrove reserve at Terraba-Sierpe have been analysed and approaches to addressing them have been identified, activities are only in their infancy. It is therefore too early to claim major success. Nevertheless, there is very strong local support for the approach described and a number of formerly illegal 'mangleros' have joined Coopemangle. Similarly, the first brick kiln is being tested by Coopemangle. In addition, a fund has been set up to provide basic financial support for improved extraction of wood, e.g. through the purchase of better saws and outboard motors for boats. The fund allows purchase of these materials with Coopemangle repaying the money from the increased profits obtained from improved extraction. To support education efforts, a mangrove festival was held in 1990 to help build wider community understanding of the value of the mangrove system.

Lessons learned

Although this work is still at an early stage of development, it provides a number of important lessons.

1. Although degradation of the mangrove resources of Terraba-Sierpe is not yet widely evident, the rising population is leading to increasing pressure upon these resources. The need for wise use of the resources and a clear management structure under which this can be carried forward is therefore urgently needed. It would be wrong to wait and allow pressure to reach unsustainable levels.
2. The existence of legislation enabling the creation of mangrove forest reserves provides a solid legal base upon which to proceed. Similarly, the issuing of permits by the DGF to Coopemangle to exploit the mangrove resource decentralizes day-to-day control over use of the reserve.
3. The stipulation that no extraction can take place in the absence of a management plan is an important step. While the existing management plans have weaknesses, this wise use project is designed to strengthen the management plans and make them more effective.
4. The existence and legal recognition of Coopemangle as a coherent, tightly-knit community with a specific interest in managing the mangrove resource provides a clear local institution with which central Government can both work and delegate responsibility.
5. Analysis of the socio-economic situation and the current management activities has allowed identification of the ways in which the mangrove can be managed more effectively, thus maximising the chances of success.
6. The associated education programme is critical in building awareness of the importance of the mangrove system and the need for controlling resource use.

   While the present case study points to a successful beginning in working with local communities to manage the mangrove resource, the long-term viability of the mangrove forest of Terraba-Sierpe will depend upon maintaining the ecological and hydrological integrity of the watershed. It is therefore important that the action taken by the Costa Rican authorities includes an all-encompassing, long-term plan for the management of these mangrove resources.

Enrique Lahmann, IUCN, PO Box 1161-2150, Moravia, Costa Rica.

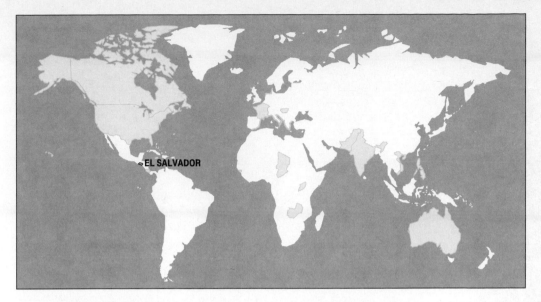

Wise use activity in Laguna El Jocotal, El Salvador

Manuel Benitez

Introduction

El Salvador is the smallest country in the American continent, with a land area of just 21,000 km². At the same time it has one of the highest population densities in the region (214 inhabitants/km²), and one of the highest population growth rates in the world (3.6% in 1985). Forestry Department statistics show that only 12% of the country's land surface is covered by trees, only 3% of which can be considered as natural woodland. Wetlands, especially mangroves, lagoons and floodplains, are under pressure from excessive felling, drainage, eutrophication and pollution. In the face of these pressures, wildlife populations have decreased dramatically. In recent years civil conflict has precluded large-scale management of the country's resources. Despite this, some notable conservation successes have been achieved. This case study describes one of these successes.

The problem

Laguna El Jocotal is located to the south of the San Miguel Volcano and is separated from the Pacific coast by the Cordillera de Jucuaran. The water inflow to the lagoon comes largely from the slopes of the volcano. The depth of the lagoon fluctuates from 1 m during the dry season to 3 m during the wet season.

El Jocotal was formerly floodplain forest which has been almost totally reclaimed as grazing land for cattle, for the cultivation of cotton and, more recently, melons. In areas adjacent to the San Miguel river, which supplies the lagoon during the rainy season, remnants of this woodland remain, still rich in wildlife.

The biological importance of Laguna El Jocotal attracted the attention of the National Parks and Wildlife Service in the 1970s. In particular, El Jocotal supports a large diversity of plants and animals and is the most important area of freshwater in El Salvador. As such, it provides a vital resting place for migrant birds from North America.

More than 60 species of aquatic plants and more than 130 species of aquatic birds have been recorded at the lake. Among the resident species are Fulvous Tree Duck *Dendrocygna autumnalis*, Black-bellied Tree Duck *Dendrocygna bicolor*, Muscovy Duck *Cairina moschata* and Masked Duck *Oxyura dominica*; the latter two species have almost disappeared in other areas of El Salvador. During the dry season, from November to March, large numbers of migratory birds visit the lake, including Blue-winged Teal *Anas discors* and Northern Shoveler *Anas clypeata*.

Although bird populations are rich, the terrestrial fauna is relatively poor. Hunting, combined with the loss of natural habitats, has placed enormous pressures on these fragile populations. However, a small population of Crocodiles *Crocodylus acutus* remain, and around the lagoon there are still Green Iguanas *Iguana iguana* and Boa Constrictors *Boa constrictor*.

Approximately 150,000 people live near El Jocotal, supplemented during the period of the cotton and melon harvest by migrant workers. These people live in conditions of extreme poverty. More than 65% of the population can neither read nor write, and there are limited facilities for health care and education. The absence of a water and sewage system forces people to use the lagoon and banks of the San Miguel river to wash their clothes, bathe, dispose of waste, and obtain drinking water.

These communities depend almost exclusively upon agriculture and fishing. Maize, sorghum, melons and cotton are the principle crops, while the main source of energy is firewood which is obtained from the few remaining trees. To complement these crops, fishing is carried out in the lagoon. During the dry season, El Jocotal supplies water for approximately 10,000 people in the surrounding region.

Wildlife is the principle source of animal protein and, with the population increasing, the demand for protein continues to rise. Malnutrition affects more than 65% of the children and the average consumption of meat is less than the minimum requirement set by the World Health Organization.

In addition to the problems of malnutrition, El Salvador suffers from high levels of illiteracy and an absence of basic services, in particular health and education. Added to this, the country has suffered continuing civil conflict over many years. All these problems affect the people who live in the region of El Jocotal.

The high demand for protein and economic well-being has placed considerable pressure on the lagoon's resources over many years. Most noticeably, wildlife populations have decreased substantially, while there is continuous pressure on the lake's shores for agricultural land.

The approach

The National Parks Service took over responsibility for Laguna El Jocotal in 1976. At this time the area was used by a tourist company as a hunting reserve catering for foreign hunters. With the establishment of a Wildlife Refuge, hunting and the cutting of trees were forbidden.

As a first step, the Wildlife Service established a small team of wildlife guards who were responsible for the protection of the lagoon and its resources. The guards were recruited from among the local population; many had worked in the past as guides for the foreign hunters. As a result of this first action, the incidence of illegal hunting declined significantly.

Upon establishment of the reserve, surveys carried out by the Wildlife Service confirmed the importance of the wildlife resources of the lagoon and their critical condition. In particular, many years of hunting had almost totally wiped out the populations of tree-nesting ducks. In 1977, it was estimated that only 500 ducks remained at El Jocotal. In addition, their nesting sites, natural tree-holes, had been almost totally lost as the tree cover declined. Accordingly, a decision was taken to establish a pilot project to provide nesting boxes for tree-nesting ducks.

The project began in 1977, and in the first year of the project the ducks utilized more than 50% (47 out of 80) of the boxes, producing more than 800 chicks. In the three subsequent years, more than 150 nestboxes were erected. At the end of the 1970s, analysis of the preliminary results revealed that birds were laying eggs in more than one nest and some nests held as many as 100 eggs, many of which could not be covered by the female and were lost. Accordingly, it was decided to offer these eggs for consumption by the local community. Duck eggs and duck meat have traditionally been a food source and by providing the eggs, the project sought to increase protein consumption by the community. It was also felt that this direct benefit from the project would increase support for the conservation of the lake by local people.

Between 1981 and 1985, 300 new nestboxes were established and from these more than 30,000 eggs were harvested and 12,000 chicks were hatched.

More than 80 people from the local community were contracted to carry out the work, including the harvesting of the eggs and maintaining the nestboxes. Several of these people have now built and erected nestboxes around their own homes.

Achievements

Throughout the project, the protein consumption by the community dependent on Laguna El Jocotal has increased. While the consumption of 30,000 eggs may appear to be a fairly modest contribution, for the desperately poor local communities of El Jocotal, this is far from being negligible.

The project has also been a significant ecological success, having resulted in the rapid restoration of a resident population of ducks which had previously been reduced to a low level through hunting and a lack of nesting sites. In addition, the simple technology used can be reproduced for other species and in other sites.

At the same time, the project has provided an excellent and almost unique opportunity to provide training for technical staff in El Salvador, which will be extremely valuable both at El Jocotal and in other parts of the country.

More than 80 inhabitants of the El Jocotal area have worked directly or indirectly for the project and many have established their own nestbox schemes. Overall, the project has contributed to a substantial increase in the awareness amongst the local community of the importance of the lagoon and the benefits that can be obtained from it, as well as to increased local support for protecting the lagoon from the pressures it faces.

The experience at El Jocotal has now been applied in two other areas with similar problems, and attempts are now being made to extend the technology used to encourage other species to nest.

Despite the success of the project, the activity has been very specific and has focused upon only one component of the ecosystem. A large number of problems remain. For example, during the dry season, as water levels fall, grazing land is exposed. Cattle ranchers have taken advantage of the situation to extend their land into the lagoon and have begun to drain these areas, placing yet more pressure upon the overall resource.

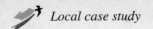

Elsewhere, the cultivation of cotton uses large quantities of pesticides which are transported into the lagoon by the San Miguel river. This threatens the long-term survival, not only of waterbird species, but of the local community which consumes food from the lake.

In addition, the area lies within that part of El Salvador which has been the scene of much military activity in recent years. This has precluded any concerted long-term programme from becoming established and building upon the fragile success so far obtained.

Lessons learned

This case study focuses upon a very specific initiative designed to rehabilitate one component of a complex ecosystem. However, in this it has been strikingly successful. The reasons for this are:

1. From the outset the project team has worked very closely with the local population; many local people have been involved directly in the project and this has generated substantial local support.

2. The project brought immediate benefits to the local community in the the form of employment and, subsequently, protein from the resulting food source.

3. The increased benefits provided by the lake have raised awareness in the community of the potential long-term value of its resources, as well as its fragility. This is an extremely important step in the long-term work that is clearly needed to improve and maintain the quality of the water entering the lagoon, and to ease the pressures upon it from agricultural activities.

Manuel Benitez, World Conservation Union, c/o Fundacion Friedrich Ebert, Cal. Nueva 2/No. 9, Col. Escalon, San Salvador, El Salvador.

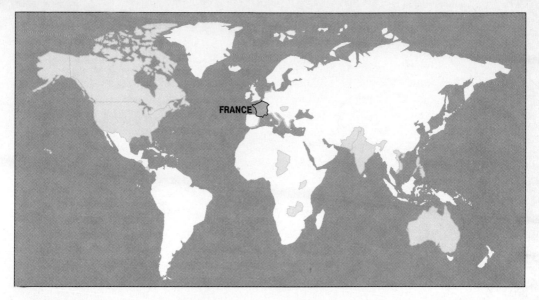

Developing a wise use strategy for the Cotentin and Bessin marshes, France

François Lorfeuvre

Introduction

The Cotentin and Bessin marsh complex straddles the boundary between the Calvados and Manche 'départements' on the north coast of France and covers approximately 25,000 ha. Of this area, 22,000 ha are inland marshes which correspond to the branching lower valleys of four important rivers – the Douve, Taute, Vire and Aure – which make the Cotentin region a peninsula. The condition of this natural heritage has been sustained across the centuries through a balance between human activities and the area's natural characteristics. This was threatened between 1960 and 1990 when changes in the socio-agricultural situation exposed the marshes to the risk of drainage and land reclamation. Today the area is threatened by the disruption of traditional agricultural management practices which could lead to the loss of the wetland's ecological importance.

A ten-year study, initiated in 1981, has provided a more optimistic outlook on the sustainability of the area's wetlands. The study involved decision-makers at every level (European, national, regional, departmental and local), including representatives of all those who use the area, sometimes for conflicting purposes.

The problem

It was not until the 18th century that tidal gates were installed in the estuary of the four rivers, in order to prevent saltwater from progressing upstream. The introduction of these gates resulted in temporary winter floods covering 14,000 ha, thus accounting for the importance of the area for migratory birds. At the confluence of the rivers, the Veys Bay has been empoldered over 3,200 ha, marking the transition with the sandy foreshore of the bay itself.

It is the diversity of the marshes' plant communities which gives the area its unique ecological character. The mosaic of wet biotopes found in the area (peatbog, heaths, open water) also makes it a valuable nesting site for several uncommon species, including Corncrake *Crex crex*, Common Snipe *Gallinago gallinago*, Montagu's Harrier *Circus pygargus*, Black-tailed Godwit *Limosa limosa* and Pintail *Anas acuta*. Moreover, the diversity, number and quality of the nesting bird species make this marsh complex one of the most important ornithological sites in France. Several species of migratory birds from northern Europe use the Cotentin and Bessin marshes, as well as the marshes of the west coast of the Cotentin, as a stopover en route from Veys Bay to the Mont Saint Michel Bay.

The most ecologically important areas of the Cotentin and Bessin marshes are:

1. Marais de la Sangsurière et de l'Adriennerie
2. Réserve de St Georges-de-Bohon et de la Plaine
3. Marais de la confluence Douves/Sèves
4. Marais de la Haute-Sèves
5a. Marais de Graignes/Montmartin-en-Graignes
5b. Marais de St Hilaire/St Pellerin
6. Réserve de Beauguillot/Ste Marie-du-Mont
7. Pointe de Brévands
8. Roselière de Marchésieux

Listed in the pre-inventory of specially protected areas, as defined in European Directive No.79-409, the lower Douve and Taute valleys were designated as an EC Special Protection Area in January 1990, and in July 1990 the Cotentin and Bessin marsh complex was added to the List of Wetlands of International Importance under the Ramsar Convention.

Today's landscape is the result of a gradual reclamation of land which occurred relatively late in comparison with marsh reclamation in other European countries. The land is used mostly for grazing and although, in winter, the marsh takes on the appearance of a huge fingered lake, the water subsides at the onset of spring, leaving meadows separated by ditches. Parts of the marsh complex are privately owned while the remainder is common land. Where the marsh is in private ownership, most often in plots situated along the edge of the valleys, relatively intensive agriculture takes place. Where the marsh is communal, use is extensive.

In 1979, there was a tendency to privatize communal marshes, leasing the land out to farmers, and to modify farming practices, introducing drainage and the use of fertilizers.

The first conflicts between agriculture and the environment arose in the Gorget valley (Sangsurière and Adriennerie marshes). For two years, alternate drainage projects and nature reserve plans opposed each other. The opponents were always the same: farmers, nature conservationists, hunters, local council offices and local authorities.

The ecological importance of land areas is closely linked to rural activity. If agricultural activities cease, the environment evolves naturally towards afforestation, and the herbaceous wet meadows become peat moors and then peat woods, resulting in a decrease in biological diversity. Hence, the retention of the Cotentin and Bessin marshes as a diverse biological ecosystem can only be achieved through a management system which involves farmers, fishermen, hunters, nature conservation interests and all other users of the area.

The introduction of measures to cut milk production in 1984 only succeeded in changing the nature of the problem without providing solutions, even from a strictly ecological point of view. It is against this general background that steps were taken to create a dialogue and a partnership which resulted first in a 'Wetlands Charter' and later in the creation of the Cotentin and Bessin Marshes Regional Natural Park.

The approach

Under the aegis of the Government, a working group composed of individuals involved at several levels was formed in 1981 in order to find solutions to the problems faced. Based on an initial series of pedological, agricultural, faunistic and floristic inventories, the resulting study reports served as a basis for negotiations to develop a programme for the implementation of a Wetlands Charter: a document stating the commitments of each sector and based on a global approach to agricultural and environmental problems.

The programme, consisting of complementary studies, experiments and fieldwork, was carried out between February 1983 and June 1989, with financial assistance from the European Community. This led to the drawing up, in 1989, of the Wetlands Charter, which was approved by the State, represented by the Administrator and Council of the Department of Manche.

The charter included a number of regulatory measures, such as the establishment of nature reserves (as at the Sangsurière and Adriennerie marshes which were designated in March 1991), and 'contractual' measures, such as the agreement by the Manche Department to stop subsidizing drainage projects in the lower Douve and Taute valleys.

The most important of these 'contractual' measures was the launching by the Lower Normandy Region, at the request of the Manche Department, of the Cotentin and Bessin Marshes Regional Natural Park project. Following work carried out by Government and technical agencies between 1981 and 1989, the association responsible for the creation of the Park was set up in May 1989 and included representatives of all sectoral interests. Such was the success of this move that the objectives of the association were broadened to consider not only the wetlands, but also the surrounding woodland as well as higher and lower areas utilized for agriculture. Hence, the future of the marshes would be considered in a global rural development context.

Winter inundation of the Cotentin and Bessin marshes. Photo: François Lorfeuvre

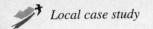

The association had two main objectives:

1. To define a framework of actions designed to bring about economic development based on an appreciation of the area's natural landscape, and cultural and historical heritage; and
2. To involve the communities in the fulfilment of its goals.

Working committees (on which each commune was represented by its mayor or a deputy town councillor) were set up. Each action theme, whether agriculture, tourism or the environment, was discussed. Information meetings and the relaying of information by the local press enabled a fervour for development to be kindled across an area of 120,000 ha.

This phase lasted two years and eventually bore fruit in June 1991 with the creation of the Cotentin and Bessin Marshes Regional Natural Park, following the passing of a decree by the Minister of the Environment. This ministerial order is partially an acknowledgement by the French Government of the importance of the obligations mutually incurred by the various interest groups concerned (communes, departments and regions).

Effectively, 109 communes, representing a population of approximately 57,000 inhabitants, the Manche and Calvados Department Councils and the Lower Normandy Regional Council came together to form a joint syndicate: the Cotentin and Bessin Marshes Regional Natural Park. These were joined by a number of specialized associations: the Chambers of Agriculture, of Commerce and Industry, and of Trade, tourist offices, Conservatoire de l'Espace Littoral, Office National des Forêts, and Pays d'Accueil du Bessin. Local communities are represented by Lower Normandy trade unions, fishing or hunting federations, nature conservation associations, development organizations and others.

The establishment of working committees and the creation of a specialist group will help to focus the expertise of the various interest groups, coordinate their initiatives and carry out actions according to the framework laid down in the charter which established the Park.

The Park Programme

The Park Programme, financed by these interest groups and by the State, is the logical follow-up to the Wetlands Charter and enables areas that fall within the jurisdiction of the communes to be taken into consideration. This aspect is fundamental since the regulatory approach applies only to limited areas. For example, out of a total of 25,000 ha of wetland, only some 1,500 ha enjoy statutory protection (as wildlife reserve, area under public ownership), leaving 23,500 ha to be managed. Only through awareness and by incentives can this be achieved. Such a campaign was launched by the Park and the agricultural organizations in autumn 1991. Aimed at farmers working the most fragile areas, the scheme offers contracts under which farmers undertake to adopt particular management practices. In return, the Ministry of Agriculture and the EC pay compensation which corresponds to the farmer's loss of income. By the beginning of 1992, 104 farmers and 10 communes, working an area of approximately 3,000 ha, had joined the scheme. In this way, the Park Programme has significantly increased wetland conservation and will continue to encourage sensitive management of the Cotentin and Bessin marshes, as well as the surrounding woodland.

Themes for action

The plan for the Cotentin and Bessin Marshes Regional Natural Park contains three central themes. An environmental theme links all the actions, while those of agriculture and tourism serve as extensions.

Environment

Three lines of action specifically related to the environmental approach are:

i)   Natural resource management: development of an action programme aimed at maintaining surface water and, indirectly, groundwater quality; promotion of stream maintenance systems; management and improvement of fishery resources; water management in the main rivers; equipping ecologically important sites so that they may be opened to the public, with the frequency of visits to these areas controlled;
ii) Species management: establishment of a waterfowl monitoring network; setting-up of a fish monitoring system; support for wild stork populations;
iii) Awareness and discovery: introduction to the environment and awareness-building among schoolchildren and the general public (in conjunction with appropriate organizations); provision of educational materials; maintenance of the inventory of natural riches.

Agriculture

Four lines of action have been established:

i)   Continuation of existing agricultural management;
ii) Promotion of agricultural diversification to provide additional income;
iii) Sound management of rural areas (in particular by amalgamating land and developing land-use plans);
iv) Training and information.

These actions apply not only to marshland but also to wooded and coastal areas in the Park; for example, measures to develop the Park's hedgerows and the shellfish resource.

To achieve this, a joint effort is being sought through which action could take the form of management agreements; e.g. where communes have communal marshes, the focus could be on developing income from the marshes' natural resources (agricultural produce, reeds, eels, pike, etc.) and promoting their sale through a Regional Natural Park trademark.

Tourism

The attraction of the Cotentin and Bessin marshes as a tourist site is linked to its landscape, people, history, geology and its rich flora and fauna. Up to now the area has not been fully exposed to tourism and does not offer adequate accommodation facilities.

To develop this natural heritage, the region's image must first be developed and promoted, e.g. through the creation of a logo, advertising and the production of relevant publications.

The aim should be to draw tourists into the area along specific routes – main highways and roads – plus the western coast road (already used by tourists visiting the coastal departments). This could be achieved by developing major tourist attractions along the key routes, from which tourists may reach the interior along clearly signposted secondary routes. Here, smaller, dispersed tourist facilities, such as walks, bicycle hire, horse riding, fishing and sailing, could be developed.

A complementary objective should be to increase the amount of tourist accommodation: rural lodgings, guest houses, holiday villages.

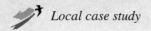
Achievements

It is difficult to evaluate the results of this ten-year effort, in that concrete steps are only just being taken. However, it is worth emphasizing the importance of the preliminary dialogue which took place between 1983 and 1989, leading to the creation of the Park, and which continues today. This dialogue involved all the 'users' of the wetland area: farmers, communes, hunters, fishermen, visitors, scientists and Government.

Lessons learned

It is too early yet to draw final conclusions from this case study. However, the period of research leading up to the creation of the Cotentin and Bessin Regional Natural Park was relatively short (20 months) because the preparatory stage which preceded it lasted several years.

The future of the marshes cannot be guaranteed until all managers learn to accept multiple use of the area and incorporate into their practices the constraints brought about by the activities of the other users. Because a consensus of sorts was reached during the dialogue, it has been possible to find solutions to overcome conflicts which have arisen from the multiple use of the area.

By bringing together the various interest groups, including 'institutional' regional development bodies, each was able to increase their knowledge and understanding of wetland management, and of each other. The creation of different working groups and a scientific committee also helped considerably and brought the various parties closer together.

François Lorfeuvre, Parc Naturel Régionel des marais du Cotentin et du Bessin, Maison du Département, Rond-Point de la Liberté, 50008 St Lô Cedex, France.

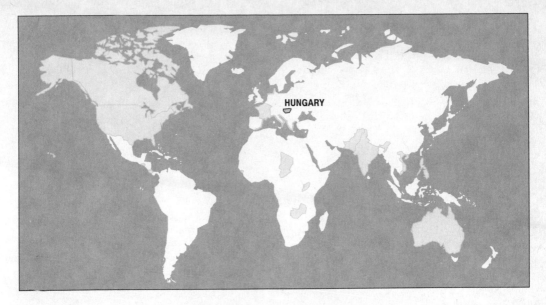

Wetland conservation in Hortobágy National Park, Hungary

Mihály Végh

Introduction

In Hungary, protected areas are designated at a national or local level according to the level of their importance. Those of national and international importance are either national parks, landscape protection areas or nature conservation areas. Hortobágy National Park was established in January 1973 as the first, and largest, Hungarian National Park. The Park is located in north-east Hungary and takes in part of two counties, Hajdu-Bihar and Jasznagykun-Szolnok, including three towns and ten villages. The Park covers an area of 69,766 ha, of which 55,300 ha form the core or central area while the remainder are 'connected areas'. Some 55,713 ha form part of the UNESCO Man and Biosphere Programme reserve, while 20,574 ha are designated for the List of Wetlands of International Importance under the Ramsar Convention.

The problem

Within the core area of Hortobágy National Park, 4,179 ha – less than 10% of the total protected area – are owned by the Park authority. Other areas, among them Biosphere core areas and the Ramsar site, are owned by state farms, cooperative farms, city and village councils, private owners, and other state-owned authorities such as Water Management Directorates.

The following management activities are carried out in the Park:

- grazing on 4,179 ha of Park Authority owned land, where optimal conditions are provided for Hungarian Grey Cattle, Hungarian Racka Sheep and Water Buffalo, all ancient Hungarian domestic animals;

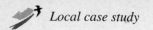

- coordination and control of pastoral and rural activities such as culling of game, fishing, forestry and reed-cutting;
- control of other forms of land use;
- maintenance of the three existing water supply systems of Fekete-ret, Kunkápolnás and Nagyret swamps;
- control of tourism to protect natural features;
- creation and maintenance of semi-arid biotopes with shallow waters to re-establish habitats which have disappeared during the last 50 years;
- monitoring of the populations of valuable species and of habitats;
- conservation activities for Great Bustards *Otis tarda* and Lesser White-fronted Goose *Anser erythropus;*
- coordination of scientific research activities.

The landscape is an almost perfect plain with height variations between 86 and 92 m above sea-level. The most striking features of the plain are tumuli, small hills between 3-10 m in height and 50-60 m in diameter. The area slopes from north to south and is bordered by higher areas which slope towards the Hortobágy river which forms the region's hydrographic axis.

Present day conservation problems stem from the succession of different development stages:

Original Holocene forest steppe

The Hortobágy plain, part of an extended floodplain of the Tisza river, was probably a forested steppe before the introduction of agriculture. Alkaline grasslands existed in places and salinization probably occurred in semi-arid continental climatic phases. In prehistoric times such plains were probably frequented by seasonally migrating large ungulates.

Freely flooded grasslands

With the expansion of agriculture, the floodplain forests were felled, with the exception of some isolated patches. At this time the area was freely flooded for long periods by the Tisza river. The formation of alkaline soils was limited, as was local run-off, and the area consisted of temporary and permanent marshes. Grazing was intensive in summer and kept the grasslands short.

Local run-off and intensive grazing (until World War II)

After the regulation of the Tisza river, inundation of the plain ceased, the marshes partially dried up and solonetz soils with salt accumulation at the surface developed more extensively. Grazing remained intense. The combination of intensive grazing and increasing alkalinity of the soil led to a mosaic of vegetation types and barren surfaces. Local run-off waters accumulated in the former depressions and river beds, and temporary swamps formed, although much smaller than the original floodplain marshes.

Reduction of local catchment areas

In the 1950s, various agricultural and aquacultural projects were implemented. These projects seriously decreased the local catchment areas, leading to a further reduction in the already limited marsh areas.

Reduction in grazing

Since the mid 1940s, the number of cattle, sheep and horses grazing the area has declined, allowing longer grass to cover formerly barren surfaces and causing areas of short grassland to disappear.

Drought

The latest change, since the 1980s, has come about as a result of a prolonged dry period, with rainfall being on average 10% less than before. Remaining areas of marsh have gradually reduced or disappeared altogether, except for those that are artificially supplied.

Conservation values

The Hortobágy plain is a truly unique combination of biotopes. The Southern Grasslands represent the largest remaining 'puszta' in Europe, abounding with endemic relict plant species and rare animals. The marshes, whether of a permanent or seasonal nature, support large numbers of birds and amphibians, many of which are endangered species.

Hortobágy's vegetation consists mainly of species that are widely distributed in the Eurasian temperate zone, but a great number of Pontian and Ponto-Mediterranean species are also present. Many of the plants are listed in the IUCN Red Data Book or the Hungarian Red Data Book.

The rich insect fauna, especially Orthoptera, reflects the varied vegetation cover, while more than 300 species of birds have been recorded, of which 140 species have nested. The area is especially important as a breeding, moulting and migratory site for Central European waterfowl.

Noteworthy breeding species are Red-necked Grebe *Podiceps grisegena,* Little Egret *Egretta garzetta,* Great White Heron *Egretta alba,* Squacco Heron *Ardeola ralloides,* Night Heron *Nycticorax nycticorax,* White Stork *Ciconia ciconia,* Spoonbill *Platalea leucorodia,* 180-200 Great Bustard *Otis tarda,* Baillon's Crake *Porzana pusilla,* Kentish Plover *Charadrius alexandrinus,* Avocet *Recurvirostra avosetta,* Black-winged Stilt *Himantopus himantopus,* Stone Curlew *Burhinus oedicnemus,* Common Pratincole *Glareola pratincola,* White-winged Black Tern *Chlidonias leucopterus,* Short-eared Owl *Asio flammeus,* Moustached Warbler *Acrocephalus melanopogon,* Aquatic Warbler *Acrocephalus paludicola,* Bluethroat *Luscinia svecica* and Bearded Tit *Panurus biarmicus.*

More than 100,000 migratory geese include White-fronted *Anser albifrons,* Bean *A. fabalis* and Lesser White-fronted Geese *A. erythropus,* together with 100,000 ducks, as well as several Black Stork *Ciconia nigra* and more than 40,000 Common Crane *Grus grus,* a significant part of the Central and East European population. In recent years a few of the now endangered Slender-billed Curlew *Numenius tenuirostris* have passed through and, among several species of rare birds of prey, about 30 White-tailed Eagles *Haliaeetus albicilla* regularly winter.

Notable mammals are Otter *Lutra lutra,* Steppe Polecat *Mustela eversmanni* and Stoat *Mustela erminea.* The National Park is also home to a number of ancient Hungarian domestic animals, such as Grey Cattle *Bos primigenius f. domestica,* Hungarian Merino and the Hungarian Racka (a subspecies of sheep) *Ovis strepticeros hortobagyiensis.*

Benefits

In spite of its National Park status, which determines the forms of land-use, a whole range of activities are allowed. The Park has more than 2,000 ha of extensively used, artificial fishponds; huge reedbeds are harvested during the winter; hay production, mainly in wet meadows, is a significant source of winter fodder for domestic animals; and a small amount of arable farming is also carried out. The most important benefit provided by the Park is grazing. Large pastures for domestic animals produce high yields of meat and also help to ensure maintenance of the gene-pool of ancient Hungarian domestic animals. Tourism and forestry are other important activities in the Park.

Threats

The greatest threat to the area is the loss of wetlands, which has a knock-on effect for conservation and grazing. The construction, in the 1950s, of rice fields, fishponds and irrigation systems for pasture have reduced local catchment areas and run-off, and have blocked natural flow paths.

The number of grazing animals has decreased considerably and this has altered the vegetation structure. Over an area of some 24,000 ha, where, in the 1930s, there were 35,000 summer grazing cattle, over 40,000 sheep and 15,000 horses, there are now 3,300 cattle, 13,700 sheep and 27 horses.

The response of the vegetation to light grazing, or an absence of grazing altogether, is the development of a coarser structure and a change in its composition. In the long term, this process might accelerate and, with a build up of litter, will encourage larger plants. Bare patches, important for certain breeding birds, have already disappeared.

It is clear that heavy seasonal grazing by cattle, sheep and horses is responsible for the puszta ecosystem, and that intensive grazing is crucial for its survival.

Other problems have been over-intensive grazing in fenced-in areas, leading to degradation of the alkali-micro-topography and a loss of the more vulnerable grasslands; damage to the original micro-topography of the puszta by vehicle tracks; disturbance and damage in areas freely accessible to tourists; and loss of wetland biotopes as a result of long dry periods.

The new ownership structure under Hungary's new political system might also prove to be a threat in protected areas.

The approach

To deal with the threats facing Hortobágy National Park, the Park Authority, in conjunction with the National Authority, decided on two courses of action: to draw up a feasibility study for the restoration of wetlands and grasslands; and to ensure the status of the protected areas by the introduction of new laws. For the feasibility study, the National Park Directorate contracted a firm of consultants from the Netherlands, with assistance from the European Community's PHARE Programme.

Some wetland reconstruction, mainly for water supply, had taken place in the Park during the 1980s but lack of an overall coordinated plan for the work meant that the restored sites were isolated and did not form a compact system. As the last of this work was being carried out, a long-term process of scientific research and monitoring began. It took around ten years to gather all the necessary data before a more complex programme could begin. The southern part of the National Park was chosen for this process because it forms a distinct unit, not least in terms of its hydrology and management.

By this time, the political changes in Hungary had taken place and the first phase of the EC's PHARE Programme had just begun. The National Park Directorate, together with the

National Authority, recognizing the importance of wetlands and their surrounding areas, sought funding for a feasibility study for the restoration of wetlands and grasslands in the southern part of Hortobágy. The application was successful, Dutch contractors were appointed and, in 1991, work began at the site.

At the same time, significant new legislation was being prepared by the National Authority. The first step was to set up a priority list of sites and to determine their role within the restoration work.

High priority tasks

The Southern Grasslands are the catchment areas for the National Park's wetlands. They are characterized by a mosaic of diverse grassland vegetation types which reflect the variety of the soils and drainage of the terrain. The ecological functions within the grasslands vary considerably depending on the season; e.g. dry grasslands may function as wetlands during the spring. To prevent the loss of grassland variation due to the decrease in grazing pressure, medium to heavy grazing pressure will be restored on the grasslands by creating new economic conditions for livestock grazing, and by introducing a gene-pool of Hungarian Grey Cattle. An EC export quota has been requested for 'nature conservation beef'. If this cannot be obtained, contingency measures have been prepared to conserve at least a small gene-pool through management by the Park authorities. Meanwhile, other Hungarian national parks, and nature conservation organizations, have also obtained stocks of ancient Hungarian domestic animals. The National Authority have asked the Ministry of Agriculture whether nature conservation interests might supervise gene-pool activity for the whole country.

Kunkápolnás swamp, one of the largest alkaline marshes of Central Europe – every plant species found in the Hortobágy swamps occurs here.

Kunkápolnás swamp, one of the largest alkaline marshes of Central Europe, is part of the Biosphere Reserve and lies within the Ramsar site. Every plant species found in the Hortobágy swamps occurs in this swamp and the diversity of wildlife is considerable. The objective here is to maintain the semi-static swamp conditions by managing the water regime, e.g. through periodic inundation and reed-cutting, creating relatively large open water areas in some areas, and opening up channels for boats.

Zám Puszta is also part of the Biosphere Reserve and Ramsar site. Its largest area of swamp is intact and in good condition. The catchment is partly covered by unique halophytic plant communities and the entire area is highly sensitive to disturbance, due to particular pedological circumstances, as well as to the movement of surface and ground water. The aim here is to re-create the water movement characteristic of the pre-Tisza regulation flooding regime. Such management action will provide more effective protection for the area against human activities in adjacent, unprotected areas, e.g. adverse discharges from fishponds. Grazing is also of special importance in managing the periphery. Reconstruction will take place over an area of 200 ha, within which 6 ha will be open water.

The Angyalháza swamp project will see the enlargement of an existing water supply for a semi-static wetland system, with the addition of a further 80 ha and the renewal of engineering structures. Again, the site falls within the Biosphere Reserve and Ramsar site. A number of channels and rice fields, established in the 1950s, prevent the water flow in a north-south direction. The restoration project, which covers 210 ha, has two aims: to increase the size of the catchment, and to restore the natural connections between the deepest areas of swamp.

Medium priority tasks

The loss of alkaline shallow water and shoreline in the transitory wetlands of Anagyalháza has resulted in a serious decline in the populations of many important bird species, especially spring migrating shorebirds. The conversion of abandoned rice fields back to shallow water and shoreline requires relatively little investment and results in highly valuable biotopes. Work here, over an area of 20 ha, will concentrate on re-creating shallow water areas with a mosaic of small bare mudflats.

Low priority tasks

The project at Kunmadaras Nagyret (meadow) involves increasing the existing water supply to 60 ha of shallow, inundated wetlands used by migratory birds in the autumn. Ancient alkaline water biotopes formerly encircled extensive grasslands. Management of the site will involve inundation of the area with shallow water, without disturbing the dry habitats and their valuable plant communities.

Water payment

With the exception of the Southern Grasslands and transitory wetlands at Angyalháza, new or improved water supply systems – the basis of the proposed management regimes – are planned at all the project sites. The qualitative and quantitative aspects of the water supply are equally as important as the period of actual flooding of the wetland areas. For this reason a monthly study was made of the quality of the floodwaters.

In Hungary, fees are levied against water used. The yearly cost of water taken for Hortobágy National Park would be around 4,000,000 forints (US$50,000). To avoid having to pay such high costs, the National Park Directorate, in 1991, agreed a fixed price for a variable amount of water for the park with the Water Management Directorate. In 1992, the National Authority opened negotiations with the Ministry for Traffic Communications and Water Management to stop paying fees altogether, arguing on the basis of ecological needs.

Livestock breeding

In the Southern Grasslands a study on livestock breeding showed that should Hungary succeed in obtaining the extra EC quota for 'nature conservation beef', the result would be higher prices and a small profit. Against this, should the quota not be won, the study showed that the activity would be uneconomic. The first option would obviously be more beneficial for nature conservation, the profits being utilized for development. However, since conservation of the grasslands requires preservation of the native cattle, the second option is also acceptable. The difference is that the latter would require Governmental aid.

However, both solutions rely ultimately on the participation of local people. While the National Park would manage the grazing regime, by offering free grazing rights and reduced taxes, and by employing herdsmen, livestock breeding can be made attractive for the local community.

The political changes wrought in Hungary brought changes in the structure of ownership. Where important protected areas fall under private ownership, or are in shared ownership, opportunities for even adequate management are reduced. Recognizing this, the National Authority initiated a process of legislative work. This resulted in three significant Acts passed by the Hungarian Parliament. Nature conservation benefits under the new laws in that National Parks, or land for which protection is planned, cannot fall under private ownership; neither can citizens of another country buy protected areas.

Further laws to strengthen the conservation of nature are in preparation, drawing on the experiences of the projects and activities described in this paper.

Achievements

The Hortobágy project is multi-faceted and has demonstrated and found solutions to many problems.

During the project's planning stage, data which had existed for years were finally used to good effect. For the first time an entire ecosystem, rather than parts of one, was the subject for restoration. Not only has this approach produced better results, it has proved to be a more cost-effective way of carrying out habitat restoration.

The programme for Hortobágy also produced a highly detailed management plan for its National Park Officers to operate, providing solutions for each individual site, as well as for the whole of the Southern Grasslands. New methods, e.g. the use of aerial photographs, were introduced, and much was learned from the contract Dutch consultants.

Costs were minimized in a number of ways, e.g. by using natural gravitational flow to supply water, using excavated materials for the creation of artificial islands, and using animals to control vegetation in important grassland areas.

The involvement of governmental bodies in such work also proved beneficial, ensuring finance for the longer-term implementation of management practices and creating special funds for nature conservation.

A particular achievement was the legislative work connected to the development project. It was clear that the best results could only be achieved in areas wholly owned by nature conservation interests. In Hungary, where there is a shortage of public funds for land purchase, land ownership within protected areas can only be assured through legislation. In so doing it was important not to conflict with private landowners, so land of equivalent value away from state-owned, protected areas had to be found. All of these issues were covered in the Acts approved by the Hungarian Parliament in 1991-1992.

The project also seems to have solved the problem of preserving the ancient Hungarian domestic animals. This success was closely connected with grassland management and with the livelihood of the people who live in or near the National Park.

Overall, the success of the project will result in an increase in the biodiversity of Hortobágy National Park and its surrounding areas.

Lessons learned

The main lessons learned from the Hortobágy National Park project, and which can be applied to future projects, are:

1. Where there is a shortage of funds, restoration work has to be planned on sites where minimum investment can achieve maximum results, thereby achieving the highest possible efficiency in terms of economy and ecology.

2. Local and national objectives must be in harmony.

3. Legislative processes are essential.

4. All available data should be incorporated into such projects.

5. Survey work should be undertaken on restored areas and on those where restoration work has yet to be carried out, and should be continued after work has been completed.

6. Adequate nature conservation management cannot be achieved without the involvement of local people, who must also benefit from the process.

Mihály Végh, National Authority for Nature Conservation, Kolto u 21, 1121 Budapest, Hungary.

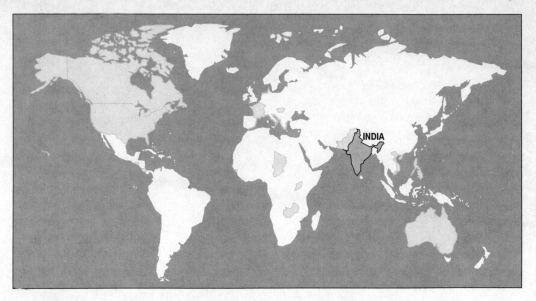

Towards sustainable development of the Calcutta wetlands, India

Dhrubajyoti Ghosh

Introduction

The practice of urban agriculture and fisheries in the wetland fringe of Calcutta has been a matter of considerable discussion in relation to the future development of the city. Any development scheme in this region, over and above its obligation to accommodate settlement extensions, should recognize that:

a) The wetland region to the east of Calcutta is no longer a natural choice for urban expansion;
b) Planning which takes no account of ecology can bring disastrous consequences;
c) The interests of a few sections of society need not necessarily coincide with the welfare and survival of the whole;
d) Urban expansion in the wetland region will involve very high development costs.

This paper considers the pressures and development options in the wetland region to the east of Calcutta. It looks particularly at the problems and prospects of redeveloping urban agriculture and fisheries for waste water treatment and resource recovery.

The problem

It is possible to distinguish four different perspectives on the options for developing the wetlands to the east of Calcutta: those of the private developer; the 'old-school'; the environmental stance; and the global overview.

Private developers are in the most advantageous position in having a market which works entirely in their favour. The method is simple. The broker or land speculator negotiates a price with the seller, e.g. the owner of a fishery relative to the declining profitability of the fishery. After the transfer of the land title, the purchaser moves in, carries out whatever work is required (e.g. building a house) and then sells the land for as much as ten to twelve times the buying price. Such profit margins are a clear indication of the strength of the private developers and the influence they have on the city and its surrounding environment. Unregulated, such land speculation can only serve to worsen the state of the environment, in particular the wetlands.

The 'old-school' perspective considers the city's outlying areas and wetlands as 'ripe' for development. A number of planning exercises have been attempted on the wetlands to the east of the city. Applications have to date been submitted for a truck terminus, a railway loop, and residential blocks.

The environmental standpoint emerged in the mid 1980s. In short, it supports retention of the wetlands as a means of providing food, sanitation, additional employment, and open spaces:

- 'garbage gardens' provide an average 150 tonnes of fresh vegetables daily for the city of Calcutta, while the fisheries provide 8,000 tonnes of fish per year. Better management systems would see this figure rise to about 16,000 tonnes/year.
- the city's sewage output amounts to some 680 million litres per day. At present, no more than a third of this reaches the fishponds which help to treat the sewage and act as stabilization tanks. A new treatment plant for the city would cost about US$4.5 million.
- the wetland region provides year-round employment at the rate of two people/ha. Any plan to establish an alternative land use in the region would have to include relocation of approximately 20,000 families.

Beyond the regional significance of these wetlands, a number of unique features make it an internationally important wetland:

- the wetlands sustain the world's largest and oldest integrated resource recovery system, in which both agriculture and aquaculture use waste water nutrients.
- the resource recovery system is one of the foremost examples of an alternative, viable, self-regulating option for the disposal of waste.

A proper planning approach should take into account all the above inter-related aspects, some of which are harmonious and some of which conflict with each other.

The approach

Although settlement stresses on the city's fringe present a very difficult challenge to finding an appropriate wise use model for these wetlands, it is essential that a solution is found if a balance between conflicting demands is to be made.

The task of wise use planning will require a clear delimitation of the city's growth to enable the remaining wetland area to be properly developed as a sanitation and resource recovery ecosystem, centering around the existing urban agriculture and fishery practices. In efforts to restrict urban sprawl, attempts will have to be made to accommodate as many settlement projects as possible, at the same time retaining a minimum area of fishponds sufficient to treat the city's sewage whilst maintaining safe conditions for fish production.

Between the present edge of the city and the proposed boundary of the resource recovery region a buffer zone should be created. This will have a mixed land use system, including housing schemes, institutional uses and industrial installations, recycling as much of the waste materials as possible. Industrial effluent must not be allowed to contaminate waste water channels leading to fishery and agriculture areas. A provisional concept plan, incorporating the different sectoral interests, has been worked out on the basis of extensive field surveys. An unavoidable problem with the plan is its inability to adopt the Calcutta Metropolitan Area boundary as the territorial limit of its operation. A new authority will be required to run the resource recovery region.

Engineering aspects

Although adjacent to one another, there has been little, if any, interaction between those involved in agriculture and fishery activities in the waste recycling areas. In historical terms, each has grown independently of the other, responding to different pressures. Initially, this will present practical problems to the redevelopment of the urban agricultural and fishery areas.

The 'garbage' farms present three difficulties:

1. The availability of garbage. Until the late 1960s, garbage was distributed via a light rail system, but, since the discontinuation of this service, getting the garbage out to the agricultural plots has been difficult. A network of roads, re-establishment of the light rail system, or some other efficient means of transporting waste to the farmers will have to be introduced.
2. Yields and storage. In spite of a reasonably efficient cropping intensity, the cropping pattern can be adjusted for certain crops in order to provide a greater economic return. At present the uncertainty of the land tenure acts as a disincentive for farmers to improve yields by adjusting the cropping regime. A lack of good storage facilities is another problem for farmers and, when buyers for their produce cannot be found, produce is wasted.

Bunded fishponds in the Calcutta wetlands. Photo: Dhrubajyoti Ghosh

3. Irrigation. Out of 400 ha of land under urban agriculture, about 120 ha are retained as waterbodies or 'jhil'. At one time these waterbodies were interconnected and obtained municipal sewage from drainage outfall channels. Now largely destroyed, these interconnections will need restoring to their former condition.

Technical barriers to redevelopment of fishponds using sewage are:

i) Waste water diversion and drainage. The sewage from Calcutta currently flows 28 km down the outfall channels into the Kulti estuary. Fishponds to the north of the outfall channels are fed by a fishery feeding channel which starts in Bantala, whereas the fishponds to the south of the outfall channels are fed by three siphon structures. In addition, a number of private channels carry sewage to various fishponds. Overall, this system of diverting the city sewage to the fishponds is inadequate and needs a thorough overhaul.

Each fishpond needs a drainage connection to dispose of the clear water effluent. (Better situated fishponds have separate channels for waste water loading and clear water disposal, the latter ideally released by gravity.) The existing drainage network, a large part of which is privately owned, falls well short of this requirement. In many cases, managers of smaller fishponds are at the mercy of the bigger fishponds for the closing or opening of drainage channels for intake or release of water. Moreover, unplanned bed levels of channel branches and lateral drains does not permit timely release of fishpond effluents.

ii) Desilting the channels and fishponds. A major task of redevelopment will be the desilting of fishponds and drainage channels. Over the last 40 years very few fishponds have been desilted; the rate of silt deposition is about half a metre/year. Today, most of the ponds are shallow and are in need of a comprehensive desilting programme, both to improve their productivity and to upgrade water quality.

iii) Incomplete integration of resource recovery practices. The absence of forestry, horticulture, dike farming and the use of non-conventional energy technologies has prevented creative development of the overall system. Integration of these activities into the existing resource system will pay large dividends within a short time.

iv) Economic inefficiency of pond sizes. The economics of any production system are likely to be related to its scale of functioning. A majority of the 168 fishponds in the east Calcutta wetlands are less than ten ha in size (66 are under five ha and another 36 are under ten ha) and could be classed as less efficient in terms of productivity. However, reliable data on determining efficient pond size are not available.

Health risks

Calcutta's storm-water drainage system was redesigned by the World Health Organization (WHO) in the late 1960s and assumed a two-month frequency of flooding. The system has succeeded in striking a balance between the health requirements of the community and the locations of the various activities in the Calcutta wetlands. It provides an example of a rational approach to risk assessment where human health is associated with sewage-grown fish or garbage-grown vegetables.

In assessing risks to health, it is important to establish the 'relative' risk of contamination as against 'absolute' risk. For example, in South Korea or Japan, where people are used to eating raw fish, a count of 10 coliforms per 100 litres of water in fishponds is permissible. However, the same standard does not apply in India, where fish are invariably deep-fried before consumption, and the relative risk is therefore much lower.

Risks to health from eating sewage-grown fish and garbage-grown vegetables cannot be properly understood without a comparative assessment against all the major food items commonly consumed by the target community. This is certainly a requirement and any resulting matrix of risk values against all the major food items will indicate the level of risk associated with a particular item of food, relative to other contaminants.

Non-availability of information

Information on traditional resource recovery practices is scarce and, particularly in the Calcutta wetlands, is available in oral form only. As this heritage has become increasingly endangered, so knowledge of traditional skills has dwindled. In 1986, over 300 farmers formed an informal cooperative and took possession of 65 ha of land to run a waste water aquaculture complex. This fishpond area had been lying derelict for some time because of a protracted legal battle over ownership of the land. Although the cooperative obtained prime land rent free, with an adequate supply of sewage, the cooperative incurred an annual loss of Rs.10 lakhs (in excess of US$38,000). A poor understanding of traditional management practices was one of the main reasons for this failure.

Even modern management procedures, to be successful, require data on loading rate, quality of waste water, the abundance of plankton, the degree of water quality improvement through fishponds, stocking density and types of fish stocked, micro-climate of the region and information on the hydraulic regime. It is important that a systematic method of record-keeping is developed in the region. A good example is provided by the Mudialy Fishermen's Cooperative Society of Calcutta. The Society has transformed an area of about 70 ha of waterlogged land into an urban fishery ecosystem. In these ponds about 25 million litres of waste water is treated daily up to secondary treatment plant effluent quality. Not only financially successful – the annual revenue from this activity is more than Rs.50 lakhs (US$19,000) – the model sets a new trend in municipal sanitation.

Before the urban agriculture and fishery practices of Calcutta's wetlands can be upgraded, the information gap will have to be bridged if a comprehensive and successful development plan is to emerge. What information is available, even though fragmentary, should be good enough for experimental design and information recording systems to be carried forward.

Lessons learned

It is anticipated that 54% of Third World populations will be living in cities by 2025. Conserving wetlands on fringes of large centres of population will present many problems, particularly when they perform many functions, not least as drainage basins, employment centres and open spaces for recreation. Planners will be hard pressed to balance the needs of the many sectors dependent on the wetlands for their various activities.

The agriculture and fishery activities in the Calcutta wetlands provide the city with two outstanding urban facilities: treatment of the city's sewage, and nutrient recovery from which an abundant supply of fish and vegetables is the end product.

Calcutta has no sewage treatment plant for its daily output of 680 million litres of waste water. A viable and efficient sanitation system for a city like Calcutta is difficult to conceptualize. The cost of setting up and maintaining a conventional sewage treatment plant is extremely high. In addition, the reliability of such a system must be considered as doubtful. Nevertheless, to proceed without any formal provision for waste water treatment for a city the size of Calcutta would be a totally unacceptable situation. The integrated resource recovery system provided by the agriculture and fishery activities, making use of city waste, provides a comprehensive answer to the city's sanitation and resource recovery needs. With just a little effort at upgrading the existing resource recovery practices, the task of turning municipal sanitation into a revenue earning project can be achieved. No urban development plan, anywhere in the world, can afford to ignore the value of wetland ecosystems until there are other, technological, low cost options as reliable and as efficient.

With careful planning, incorporating the needs of every sector and activity in the Calcutta wetlands with improved structures for resource recovery, it is entirely possible to delineate a 'wise use' map of this vast wetland area which, invaluable for its unique environmental attributes, will sustain the wetland into the future.

Dr Dhrubajyoti Ghosh, Calcutta Metrop. Water & Sanitation, 32 BBD Bag (South), 100001 Calcutta, India.

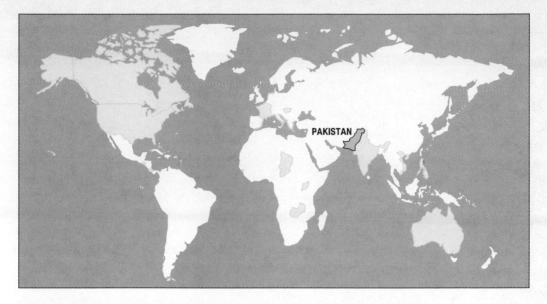

Sustainable management of mangroves in the Indus Delta, Pakistan

Peter John Meynell and M. Tahir Qureshi

Introduction

The Indus Delta is about 200 km long and 50 km wide and extends over an area of some 600,000 ha on the border between Pakistan and India. It is a typical fan-shaped delta built up by the discharge of large quantities of silt washed down the Indus river from the Karakoram and Himalayan mountain ranges. It consists of about seventeen major creeks and extensive mudflats; recent satellite imagery indicates that about 160,000 ha of the delta are covered with mangroves. The Indus Delta mangroves are perhaps unique in being the largest area of arid climate mangroves in the world. They are almost wholly dependent upon the freshwater discharges from the River Indus and a small quantity of freshwater from run-off and discharge from domestic and industrial effluent from Karachi. Average annual rainfall is very low at 221 mm and in some years virtually no rain falls during the monsoon season (April-September).

The problem

The Indus Delta mangrove ecosystem is dominated by a single species *Avicennia marina* (over 95% of the trees), although a few stands of *Ceriops tagal, Bruguiera conjugata* and *Aegiceras corniculatum* exist. Previously, *Rhizophora mucronata* used to grow in the delta but it is thought to have died out due to selective over-exploitation and degrading conditions.

Human benefits and stresses on the mangrove ecosystem

Perhaps the greatest direct economic importance of the mangroves comes from the fisheries which they harbour. The creeks and mangroves provide excellent nursery areas for young fish, especially shrimps. Shrimps are a major export commodity, making up 68% of the US$100 million which Pakistan earns in foreign exchange from fishery exports. A large proportion of the fish caught in Pakistan's coastal waters spend at least part of their life cycle in the mangroves, or depend on food webs originating there. Whilst there is apparently room for expansion of some parts of the fishery, shrimps, the most valuable species, are seriously overfished and have begun to decline following several years in which the estimated maximum sustainable yield has been exceeded.

The mangroves are also used by coastal villagers for fuelwood and fodder for domestic animals. Although *Avicennia* does not make such good fuelwood as the other mangrove species, e.g. *Rhizophora,* it is still used extensively by local people. It is rarely sold outside the coastal areas. Nevertheless, within the project area along the northern edge of the Indus Delta there are about 100,000 people who take a total of about 18,000 tonnes of mangrove firewood each year.

However, *Avicennia* leaves make excellent fodder for animals and are collected regularly by villagers. In addition to cattle, sheep and goats kept in the villages, it has been estimated that at certain times of year about 16,000 camels are herded into the mangroves. This activity places considerable pressure on the stands of mangroves nearest the villages, to such an extent that many mature stands are stunted from overgrazing, browsing and lopping.

One of the most important benefits of the mangrove ecosystem is the protection they afford the coastline from wind and ocean currents. The Indus Delta is low-lying and bears the full force of the south-west monsoon. The natural protection provided by the mangroves is shown by the siting of Port Qasim, Pakistan's second largest port, some 30 km within the Korangi-Phitti Creek system. Without the mangroves, it is unlikely that Port Qasim would have been located there in the first place, for the engineering measures necessary to protect the coast and port would have been prohibitive.

Mangroves also assist maintenance of the port by reducing dredging needs. Since the port was built in 1977, no further maintenance dredging has been required within the creeks, although some is carried out each year in the approach channels outside the mangrove areas.

Environmental stresses on the mangrove ecosystem

The severest environmental stress which the mangroves face results from the reduction in freshwater flows down the Indus, and the reduced loads of silt and nutrients. Whilst mangroves, especially *Avicennia,* are able to survive in saltwater without regular freshwater input, it is unlikely that they will thrive indefinitely.

The estimated available freshwater flow of the Indus is about 180 billion m^3 per year, carrying with it some 400 million tonnes of silt. Over the last 60 years man has built dams, barrages and irrigation schemes to such an extent that the annual flow reaching the delta is now less than 43 billion m^3. Further development proposals indicate that the flow may be further reduced to about 12 billion m^3. The quantities of silt discharged are now estimated to be 100 million tonnes/year, reducing to about 30 million tonnes (IUCN 1991a).

The reduced flows in the Indus mean that the already high salinity of the creek and soil pore waters will increase. It is not unusual to find salinity in excess of 40-45 parts/thousand in some areas, well above normal saltwater. This tends to have a stunting effect upon the growth of both trees and animal life. It will also have a significant impact upon the mangrove forests, and already there are signs of poor recruitment in some areas. What little rainfall there is takes on even greater significance in this context. It appears that the mangroves take advantage –

through increased growth rate and seed setting – of years in which rainfall is high, and just survive in years of low rainfall.

The reduction in silt flows takes on an even greater significance when sea-level rise as a result of global warming is considered. It has been estimated that mangroves with significant land discharge can maintain themselves by accumulating deposited silt when sea-level is rising at rates as high as 2.5 mm/year. Without significant land discharge, mangroves will have difficulty in maintaining themselves above sea-level rises of 1.2 mm/year. It is probable that the Indus Delta may be moving from the former position to the latter. Over the last 100 years the sea-level near Karachi has been rising at a rate of 1.1 mm/year and this may increase in the future. In the short to medium term, however, it is probable that sea-level rises will enhance mangrove survival by increasing the tidal area available for mangrove colonization (IUCN 1991b).

Apart from these longer-term threats to the survival of the mangroves, there are pressures from overgrazing and lopping for fuelwood and fodder which result in stunted trees. Within the vicinity of Karachi there are other pressures resulting from the steady growth of a major industrial city of over ten million people. Apart from untreated domestic sewage which flows into the rivers, streams and creeks, there are significant industrial discharges from major industries such as steel mills, refineries and power stations, as well as from tanneries and textile mills. Tanneries represent perhaps the most immediate source of pollution, since the waste has a high heavy metal content and comes from a number of different sources which are less easy to control (IUCN 1987a).

The effects of pollution on the mangroves themselves are probably slight; they are able to survive and may even flourish in the localized discharges of freshwater and high nutrient wastes, as is shown by the apparently healthy growth of mangroves within Karachi harbour, the most grossly polluted body of water along the coast. However, many of the faunal populations will be seriously affected and contaminated. This may have an indirect effect

Camels, which swim across the creeks to browse the mangroves, are one of the pressures on mangroves in the Indus Delta. Photo: Peter John Meynell

upon the mangroves in reducing the efficiency of breakdown of mangrove leaf litter and changing the character of the soils. Such pollution also introduces contaminants into the food chain when fish and crustacea are caught from the creeks for human and animal consumption. The high nutrient content of these waters has caused eutrophication in some creeks, resulting in excessive growth of algae which can smother the young mangrove seedlings.

In 1977, Pakistan's second-largest port, Port Qasim, was built, capable of taking ships up to 50,000 tonnes. It is principally a bulk cargo port for grains and molasses, with plans for an oil terminal and expansion to take ships up to 75,000 tonnes. The area surrounding Port Qasim is being developed as an industrial area, at present dominated by a vast complex of steel mills and a thermal power station.

Before the end of the century it is expected that major new developments in the recreation and tourism sector will have opened up in the areas adjacent to, and including, the mangrove areas. The creeks represent an important resource for recreation, water sports and eco-tourism for a city which has relatively few such resources nearby. Such development will change the relationship between the local people and the mangroves, and will add to the existing stresses on the environment unless developments are planned sensitively. Preservation of the area for viewing wildlife, such as migrating waterfowl, dolphins and mangrove jackals, is being discussed to some extent, as is the idea of a mangrove protected area.

The approach

The Korangi Ecosystem Project was set up to develop a management plan for the two major creeks adjacent to Karachi, to be used as a model for sustainable management in the Indus Delta as a whole. The approach is multi-sectoral with a focus upon the mangrove forestry which characterizes the whole ecosystem. The entire project area (one tenth of the total area) has been mapped by satellite imagery at a scale of 1:50,000, with the aim of identifying zones for different uses, e.g. local management for fuelwood, fodder and browsing, protected areas for wildlife and a possible national park, and for fishing.

The first phase of the project began in 1987 with a series of studies designed to assess the levels and impacts of pollution in the two northernmost creeks of the Indus Delta, the Korangi and Phitti Creeks, those nearest to Karachi. These studies included a rapid assessment of the industrial wastes entering the creeks, a marine pollution survey and a baseline survey of the social and public health conditions in the coastal villages. The conclusions of these studies indicated that industries such as tanneries, which discharge untreated wastes into the storm drains, were perhaps the most damaging. They were also more difficult to control than the large single industries such as refineries, steel mills and power stations because of the large number of small units (IUCN 1987a).

The marine pollution study showed that Karachi Harbour was very polluted with oils, organic matter and heavy metals, but that levels of pollutants decreased with distance from shore. Thus, more southerly creeks are relatively unpolluted and it would seem that Korangi Creek effectively acts as a buffer against pollution for the rest of the creek system. Analysis of the fish and molluscs caught in the area showed that levels of persistent organochlorines and heavy metals were slightly higher than normal, but were not worryingly high (IUCN 1987b).

The sociological survey of the coastal villages showed that over 50% of the population were involved in the fishing industry and that a large proportion of the villagers depended upon the mangrove trees for fuelwood and fodder for their animals. Freshwater supply, sanitation and education were highlighted as the major needs of these villages. The survey also provided insight into the attitudes of the villagers to the natural resources on which they depend. They did not, for instance, recognize the threats to the mangrove ecosystem, considering that they were "God-given" and would always be there, even though signs of ecosystem degradation were evident to them. The survey showed that the reasons for the poor response to a two-month shrimp trawling ban were primarily due to lack of alternative income opportunities during that time, and a poor appreciation of the need for such a ban to protect stocks. The public health survey showed the usual diseases due to inadequate water supply and sanitation, but nothing unusual such as heavy metal poisoning which they might get from regularly eating contaminated fish (IUCN 1987c).

Developing the coastal management plan

Following these studies, the second phase of the project started in 1991 and aimed to develop a working plan for sustainable management of the mangroves in the Korangi-Phitti Creek. The term 'creek' is misleading. At its mouth, Phitti Creek is several kilometres wide and, for about 30 km up to Port Qasim, is navigable by ships of up to 50,000 tonnes. The area was chosen partly because it is the most extensively studied area in the Indus Delta, and partly because it represents a microcosm of the whole delta, with the combination of environmental stresses and opportunities. The Korangi-Phitti Creeks cover about 60,000 ha and have some of the densest growths of mangroves near the largest concentrations of people (100,000) living along the northern edge of the delta.

The project's Coastal Management Plan could only be drawn up through an understanding of the stresses upon the mangroves and how to manage them sustainably. Since these stresses and opportunities cut across many different aspects, the project's approach has been multi-sectoral.

The Space and Upper Atmosphere Research Organization (SUPARCO) prepared maps of the area at a scale of 1:50,000, based on satellite imagery. These show the creeks, mudflats and sandbanks, and the distribution of dense, normal and sparse mangrove stands. They are the base maps on which management plans are being plotted. Overlays showing the environmental constraints and opportunities are being prepared. These include pollution sources, pressure from browsing and lopping, areas protected by the presence of Port Qasim, fishing grounds, and proposed industrial and tourist developments. The maps will be used to suggest zones for different uses, such as forest management for fuelwood and fodder production, browsing areas, recreational areas and wildlife protection areas.

The maps will also provide the information required for the selection of protected areas. A mangrove National Park has been proposed but, because of the multiple uses already going on in the area, such as wood gathering and grazing, as well as port and industrial developments, this may not provide the right structure to protect the mangroves adequately.

Mangrove forestry

The project's principal partner is the Sindh Forest Department (SFD) which is replanting barren areas in the northern part of the delta with mangrove species, especially *Rhizophora mucronata*. This is an attempt to increase the ecological stability and biodiversity of the area by reintroducing an indigenous species from stock taken from the Makran Coast to the west of Karachi. Trial plantations carried out under a previous UNESCO project showed that the *Rhizophora* stock can thrive in the Indus Delta conditions, producing flowers and propagules after about five years.

In conjunction with the replanting of other species, including *Avicennia marina*, SFD are studying the problem of seedling survival, which appears to be very patchy. *Avicennia*, with

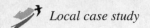

its radiating root structure and numerous pneumatophores (aerial roots) protruding from the mud, is most useful for stabilising the soil and encouraging accumulation of sediments. In places where *Avicennia* has been clear-felled, soils have become harder and less amenable to mangrove recolonization. Mixed stands of *Avicennia* and *Rhizophora* will be maintained because of the different soil stabilization characteristics of their root structures (pneumatophores and prop roots respectively).

A continuing decrease in the discharges of freshwater and silt down the River Indus, due in part to freshwater abstraction to meet the demands of a rapidly increasing population, will result in higher soil and water salinity in many parts of the delta. This will cause the young mangroves to be less dense and more stunted than before. For successful management of the mangrove resource, it is therefore important to identify those sites which receive inputs of freshwater and nutrients (e.g. from irrigation drains, domestic and industrial effluents); even though they may be polluted, these areas can act as nodes of more profuse growth and can be actively planted.

The third component of the forestry programme is social forestry. This has the objective of taking pressure off the mangroves by providing alternative trees for fruit, fodder and fuelwood for local villagers. However, in coastal villages where the soils are rather saline, production of fuelwood and fodder from mangroves may be higher than from alternative trees; this is especially relevant since villagers claim not to have enough freshwater for themselves, let alone for watering seedlings. Hence, the social forestry programme will also encourage management of village mangrove plantations: *Avicennia* for fodder and *Rhizophora* for fuelwood. This is a new venture in Pakistan and a number of factors need to be addressed beforehand, e.g. security of access to the resources (which lie on Government-owned land), management control of the mangroves by the villagers, and training in all aspects of mangrove management.

The convoluted trunks of 'Avicennia marina' in the Indus Delta. Photo: Peter John Meynell

Back-up studies

The forestry programme is backed up by studies designed to improve knowledge of the mangrove ecosystem. The World Conservation Union (IUCN) has a role in identifying the gaps, commissioning the various studies and coordinating their implementation by Government and non-government agencies.

The Botany and Geology Departments of the University of Karachi are assessing mangrove biomass and soil conditions in stands of mangroves exposed to different environmental stresses – exposure to winds and currents, areas with higher soil salinity, exposure to pollution and pressure from lopping and browsing. At the same time the Zoological Survey of Pakistan is surveying the distribution of benthic organisms associated with these different mangrove stands, and the distribution of bird populations (IUCN 1992 a,b).

The full importance of mangroves to Pakistan's fisheries is unknown. It is assumed that because they are nursery areas to many commercial species, these species will decline if the mangroves disappear. Various means of controlling fishing have been attempted – e.g. a two-month ban on shrimp trawling, and increased mesh sizes – but all have proved ineffective. The project is developing a study on the value of the mangroves to the fishing industry as a means of increasing awareness of the problem, and preparing a fisheries management plan. Vested interests in the fishing are so high industry that it may be difficult to achieve very much. However, since very little is known about where fish breed and whether there are areas in special need of protection, it is important that such investigations are carried out and these are planned for 1993-94.

As fish catches decrease, so fishermen will seek other means of income, initially from fishing and secondly from employment close to home. Shrimp aquaculture in the mangroves offers some possibilities but the shortage of freshwater may be a limiting factor. Elsewhere in the world, shrimp farms have created enormous environmental problems in mangrove areas, but a simple approach, which uses mangrove trees to stabilize pond banks at the back of the fringing mangroves, may be more environmentally sound. The falling mangrove leaves would be used to feed the shrimps. The project will link in with the present Asian Development Bank Aquaculture Development Project to explore these possibilities, within the context of sustainable use of the mangroves.

Shirkat Gah, the NGO which carried out the original social studies, has recently finished a resource use study asking detailed questions of particular groups making use of the ecosystem's resources – fishermen, fuelwood collectors and sellers, fodder collectors and camel herdsmen. This has produced some fascinating information about the patterns of use and insights which will become important as the community programme develops (IUCN 1992c). For instance, there appears to be circumstantial evidence of the importance of mangroves to fisheries, since the preferred creeks for fishing are those with the highest density of mangrove cover.

Coastal community development

Any sustainable ecosystem management initiative must have the support of the local population which depends upon the resource. Alongside the forestry programme, therefore, a community development programme is being set up as part of the Korangi Ecosystem Project.

The prevailing attitude towards the mangroves has been rather fatalistic even though there are clear signs of degradation of the environment. Changing community awareness about such problems is difficult without establishing the confidence of the local people. First steps are geared towards addressing pressing environmental needs close to home; for example, water supply and sanitation.

Once the confidence of the local communities has been gained, proposals concerning the sustainable management of the mangrove ecosystem can be introduced. It is important that such proposals are socially and economically attractive to the villagers. One example, which the project is currently testing, is the production of mangrove honey. If honey production in the mangroves is viable during the flowering season, which occurs at the same time as the slack fishing season, an alternative source of income can be promoted. This will have two benefits: (a) it will increase the awareness of the usefulness of the mangroves, and (b) pressure on fish stocks may be reduced.

Changing awareness requires a subtle approach through both formal and informal education, so care will be taken over the introduction of scientific information confirming the degradation of the mangrove environment. The project will provide basic environmental training to some of the teachers in the villages. It has also commissioned the development of an environmental street theatre to prepare and perform a play about the coastal environment.

Pollution control

Domestic and industrial wastes from Karachi are discharged untreated into the creeks around the city. Pollution control is very expensive and is beyond the scope of the Korangi Ecosystem Project. However, the role of the project in this area is to act as a catalyst for action, to provide objective information and to advise on the technical and institutional means of achieving pollution control. It can even bring together polluting industries and the international donors who can assist with the financing. With the help of the Embassy of the Netherlands, the project has been able to begin this process by holding a consultative workshop on the treatment of tannery wastes. Such workshops, newspaper articles and assistance promotes public awareness and increases the demand for action (IUCN 1992d).

Since prevention is better than the cure, the project is engaged in carrying out an environmental review of the activities in Port Qasim, such as dredging, berthing arrangements, loading and unloading, as well as its accident and oil spill contingency plans. Future developments near the port include a major industrial area, and the review will suggest environmental protection byelaws which the Port, as the landowner, can impose on incoming industries. This will have the advantage of setting standards of environment protection which are not yet legally enforceable in Pakistan. Similarly, guidelines and byelaws will be suggested for tourism developments in the area controlled by the port.

Freshwater, silt, nutrients and sea-level rise

Early on it became clear that the fundamental issue about the long-term survival of the mangroves in the Indus Delta is the availability of freshwater, silt and nutrients from the River Indus. At about the same time the Government announced the Indus Water Accord, which apportioned the use of the Indus waters between the four provinces of Pakistan. While this accord recognized for the first time the need to allow some freshwater discharge into the delta to safeguard the ecosystem, it set a minimum of 12 billion m^3, which many consider too low. In accordance with its aim of increasing awareness at different levels, the project published an issues paper highlighting the problem and the importance of the mangroves in a national and provincial context (IUCN 1991a).

As a follow-up to this, the project is developing a study to investigate freshwater balances in several different creek areas in the Delta and to compare mangrove cover and density. This may help to answer the fundamental question of how much freshwater the mangroves need.

A study has been carried out on the related issue of the impact of sea-level rise upon the mangroves in the Indus Delta. The management plan should incorporate measures to enable the mangroves to keep pace with sea-level rise (IUCN 1991b).

Environmental economics

The most effective way of influencing decision makers to consider plans and projects which will have a direct or indirect impact upon the environment is to provide them with reliable information on the cost of further degradation of the mangrove resource. Such information can then be built into economic cost-benefit analyses.

The process of environmental economic evaluation is still in its infancy, especially for wetland areas. However, the project is developing a methodology for such a study in the Indus Delta.

Achievements

Although these are early days in the life of the project, the replanting of mangroves appears to have become well-established. In 1991, about 100 ha of *Rhizophora* were planted and a 90% success rate recorded. A further 400 ha were planted in 1992. This consolidates the experience gained earlier by the Sindh Forest Department, and is a stepping stone to more extensive plantations under the World Bank project. Mangrove planting planned around the mouth of the Left Bank Outfall Drain, carrying irrigation water out of waterlogged agricultural lands, will serve to stabilize the drain and act as a nodal point for future mangrove growth.

Within Government there has been a gradual understanding of the importance of the mangrove resource. Recognition of the need to release at least 12 billion m^3 of freshwater into the Indus Delta is a significant step forward. Similarly, Government has commissioned consultants to study the hydrological aspects of the downstream flows below Kotri, the lowest barrage on the Indus. The freshwater issue is perhaps the major national issue for the future, especially in a country which has such low rainfall overall. This debate is just beginning.

Public awareness has been increased through newspaper articles and television programmes, and increasingly many of these have been independently written. The project has also been involved in public exhibitions and has responded to unsolicited requests to plant mangroves.

Similarly, awareness about particular pollution hazards, in particular what to do about tannery wastes, has taken a significant step forward, although the difficult institutional and financial questions are still to be resolved.

Awareness in coastal villages is a much slower process, and this requires long-term commitment and the continued presence in the villages of the project staff involved with this aspect.

Lessons learned

Despite the limited achievements so far, there are a number of lessons for wise use projects which have emanated from this project.

1. Wise or sustainable use of natural resources depends upon people; the villagers, those who buy resources from them, those who discharge their wastes into the surrounding

environment, and those making decisions about areas without ever having visited them. Wise use projects must attempt to work, directly or indirectly, with all these different levels of people. The most important people to convince of the necessity to conserve the environment and the natural resource are the local people whose livelihood depends upon them.

2. It is important to provide local users with non-destructive economic uses of the resource; e.g. honey production, fuelwood production, appropriate shrimp culture, and wildlife tourism, as well as encouraging the use of alternative sources of fuelwood and fodder.

3. Wise use projects should attempt to involve the different sectors affected by, or influencing, the natural resource. (It should be recognized that direct action may not always be possible and that a project's role may be more facilitative.) Balances between the different interest groups must also be struck; e.g. use of freshwater upstream must be balanced against use of the resources in the delta, or against using the creeks as a sink for industrial pollution.

4. It has to be recognized that environmental stresses are inevitable. In the context of the Indus Delta, the reality is that the Indus is not the river it once was. Population pressures will further increase the demand for drinking, industrial and agricultural water supplies. The project should therefore look towards developing a strategy with this in mind; e.g. by planting species or strains which appear to have greater salt tolerance, and by concentrating planting efforts in areas where there is likely to be more freshwater and nutrient availability.

5. Sea-level rise needs to be incorporated into long-term management planning. This may mean planting species with a greater capacity to cope with rising sea-level; encouraging the accumulation of sediments amongst existing mangrove stands so that they can raise the levels of their substrate at the same rate as sea-level rise; and identifying, preparing and replanting areas which will become progressively inundated by the tide.

6. Wise use projects should attempt to guide and channel tourism developments so that the environment is protected, but made accessible. Interpretation of the natural environment, especially one often regarded as a wasteland, is a very important aspect in gaining protection for it.

7. In terms of managing relatively pristine environments, this is no longer possible in Pakistan. The ecosystems represented are still significant and unique, both in terms of size and in the ecological services they provide, but they are nevertheless stressed by natural and man-made forces. Under such circumstances, 'wise use' means finding ways and means of mitigating such forces, and 'helping' the ecosystem to adapt without losing its essential character.

P.J. Meynell, Coastal Ecosystem Unit, IUCN Pakistan Office, 1 Bath Island Road, Karachi 75530, Pakistan.

M. Tahir Qureshi, Divisional Forest Officer, Forest Department, Government of Sindh, Pakistan.

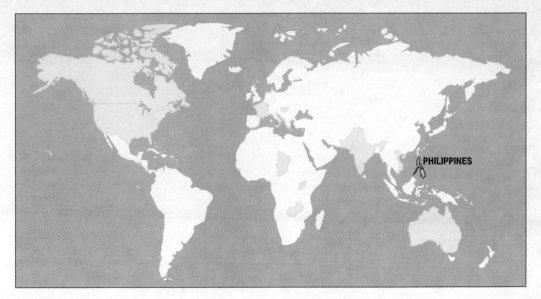

Wise use and restoration of mangrove and marine resources in the Central Visayas Region of the Philippines

Lyndo Villacorta and Jeroen C.J. van Wetten

Introduction

The Central Visayas Region lies at the heart of the Philippine archipelago and covers about 14,950 km². The region accounts for approximately 5% of the total land area of the country and comprises the island provinces of Cebu (the regional centre), Negros Oriental, Bohol and Siquijor. It has a tropical climate with two monsoon seasons and an annual rainfall of about 1,500-2,500 mm. Typhoons are common, especially between July and October, and can cause severe damage to coastal areas and habitation.

The islands of the Visayas Region have some 1,450 km of shoreline, encompassing about 9,500 ha of brackish water and tidal flats, 13,000 ha of mangroves, and 15,000 ha of coral reefs. The islands are traversed by rivers forming about 43 watersheds. Upland areas range from 500-2,000 m above sea level, dropping down to alluvial and coastal lowlands which are mostly cultivated for agro-forestry, palm plantations and rice irrigation. The topography of Central Visayas is generally rugged with limited flat land, mostly along coastal fringes. The area devoted to agricultural production (39%) is planted with crops such as sugar cane, corn, rice, coconut and tobacco. The forest areas (38%) have been used for various purposes, including agro-forestry and pasture. Open areas and grasslands account for about 19% and the remaining areas are used for settlement, mining (copper and gold) and aquaculture.

The coastal shelves around the islands account for just 12% of the marine waters but support almost all marine fishery activities. The productivity of the waters depends on the condition of adjacent coral reefs, mangroves and estuaries. The inshore waters of the coral reefs are the most productive, yielding 20-32 tonnes/year/km² (Wells 1986; White & Savina 1987). Mangroves and tidal flats provide a variety of resources, e.g. construction materials and fuelwood; food such as mussels, clams, shrimps and prawns; and tannery, coloring and medicinal products.

Mangroves play an important role in fisheries since they serve as nursery and spawning grounds, while coral reefs are unique for their biodiversity. A total of 488 coral species and 971 benthic algae are found in the Philippines (World Bank 1989). In good condition, coral reefs are the main reproduction areas for both coral reef and pelagic fish.

The problem

Central Visayas is one of 13 administrative regions and has 4.8 million people, making it one of the most populous in the country. Most of its people are concentrated in the coastal zone and the lowlands. The economy in the region is dominated by the industry and service sector. Agriculture, limited by the amount of suitable land, contributes only 23% of the gross domestic regional product. While the economy of the region has grown steadily, the increase has largely been in the industrial sector, leaving agriculture, forestry and fisheries behind. Upland dwellers live mostly in poor rural conditions, farming on small family plots and carrying out slash and burn agriculture in the remaining upland forest sites. Some 300,000 people live in municipal coastal fishery communities. Although commercial fishing forms 40% of all marine activity, municipal fisheries, which form 48%, provide the livelihood for 99% of coastal fishermen.

Environmental degradation and natural resource depletion

Coastal mangroves, seagrass beds, tidal flats, coral reefs and marine shelves are all affected by environmental degradation in upland areas. Despite efforts to control the utilization of forest resources, logging, together with slash and burn agriculture, has greatly reduced the forest cover of Central Visayas, such that by 1982 only 7% remained. During the rainy season, severe soil erosion occurs in upland areas, resulting in siltation in the lowlands. Coastal areas, too, are seriously affected by erosion.

The destruction of the native forests has led to a growing demand for mangrove to fill the gap in wood and timber production. Logging, charcoal making and clearance of the mangroves for fishponds and aquaculture have contributed to the rapid deterioration of coastal areas (Yoa 1986). Of newly developed fishpond areas, 95% involve mangrove conversion (Parish & Prentice 1987). In the Philippines as a whole, 90% of the mangrove area, which formerly covered 176,231 ha, has been converted to fishponds. Of 32,173 ha of mangroves which once existed in Visayas, only 15,500 ha were left by 1982 (CVRP 1991) – and of this area 9,890 ha have been earmarked for fishpond development. Only a few, well-off individuals with sufficient capital to invest have benefited from the aquaculture industry, to the detriment of the poorer local communities. Poor management and unsustainable practices have led to the abandonment of 20-40% of fishponds, leaving bare and degraded salt-flats or acid-sulphate soils. Leaching of artificial feeds, fertilizers and pesticides from intensive aquaculture has caused severe pollution of nearby mangroves and coastal waters. Waste from sugar cane milling has added further to declining productivity of adjacent coastal waters.

Loss of mangroves has had, and continues to have, a detrimental effect on natural coastal defences. Erosion of more than 1 m/year has been reported from many coastal sites which lack the protection of fringing mangrove strips against tidal waves and severe storms.

Lack of ownership of, or authority over, resources by municipal communities, in both mangroves areas and municipal marine waters, has led to mismanagement, misuse and over-exploitation of resources. There is strong competition for mangrove forest and marine fishery resources between local communities with traditional fishery methods and commercial fishermen and entrepreneurs. Commercial fishery interests have introduced modern technology and detrimental techniques such as dynamite fishing, which have led to a reduction in the yields of the artisanal fishermen. This has led some fishermen to adopt illegal fishing methods, unaware of the ecological impact of blast-fishing, cyanide poisoning and the use of fine mesh nets. By employing these methods, the municipal fishermen have themselves played a part in the over-exploitation of fish stocks and the destruction of coral reef habitats.

In the Visayas only one third of the coral reefs are reported to be in good condition, the remainder degraded by dynamite fishing and the gathering of coral for construction purposes. Siltation of coastal waters, brought about by increased erosion in upland areas, and the decreasing sedimentation capacity of the few remaining mangrove stands, contribute further to the destruction of coral. Coral recovery from dynamite fishing is very slow, ranging from just 1-3% per year (Alcala & Gomez 1979), while recovery from natural disasters such as typhoons is reported to be 45% within one year (Alcala & Gomez 1990). Fish catches have dropped considerably as a result of dynamite, cyanide and muro-ami fishing (Alcala 1988a,b; Alcala & Russ 1990); for example, the total catch in reef areas fell from 36 to 16 tonnes/km^2 within two years of the start of dynamite fishing. Catches in municipal marine waters fell by 13% over a five-year period (CVRP 1982). Fry fishery stocks in shallow coastal waters also disappear once adjacent mangroves are cleared.

Government efforts to maintain a balanced ecosystem have failed to address the environmental problems in the region, due largely to a lack of funds and manpower to enforce regulations on the proper use of, and access to, the resources. Although Government agencies were organizationally linked, their activities and efforts lacked cooperative cohesion. Government, non-government organizations and research and scientific communities have, in the past, proposed a number of programmes and projects to develop the region's natural resources. Very little success was achieved, largely because local community involvement in the identification, planning and implementation of the programmes was lacking.

The challenge facing the Central Visayas Region is to improve the social and economic well-being of its people, whilst at the same time conserving, protecting, restoring and making sustainable use of the region's resources.

The approach

Restoring the natural resource

A variety of techniques have been developed in Central Visayas in the last 10-15 years in order to increase the productivity of its coastal marine resources. A ban on mangrove cutting, introduced in 1992, was aimed at preventing the loss of remaining stands, while former mangrove areas have been replanted. Coral reef reserves have been established. Other restorative methods have been tested. Artificial reefs and devices such as rafts to attract fish have been created to simulate natural ecosystems, and have proved to be very effective in increasing productivity, especially in fish and shellfish production.

Mangrove reforestation

Mangrove species all bear viviparous seeds (propagules), which are very easy to collect, transport and plant, and 70-95% of planted propagules survive. Planting seeds at a distance of 1 m^2 apart (10,000 seeds/ha) requires a labour input of 5 man days/ha. Subsequent maintenance, such as removing barnacles from infested stems, is sometimes necessary. Tidal inlets, sandy fringes and muddy tidal flats are best for *Avicennia officinalis* and *Sonneratia* species. *Rhizophora apiculata* or *R. mucronata* can be planted in the sandy belts adjacent to tidal inlets. Further inland, waterlogged areas and riverbanks with clayey soils are best for *Nypa fructicans, Ceriops* and *Brugenia* (Serrano 1987). Thinning can start some 10 years after planting.

Within two to three years, fishermen have reported increasing fish and shrimp catches, and increasing yields of shellfish and mussels in and around the young plantations. Coastal erosion ceases soon after planting and by the end of the third year large root systems cover the soil and form a firm mat, breaking the impact of strong waves and water currents. Newly planted mangroves reach a height of 4.5 m after six years and help to lessen the effects of typhoons. Sediments build up at a rate of 5 cm/year. The cost of planting is about US$416 per ha, including labour costs; US$100 excluding labour costs.

Artificial reefs and fish decoys

Reef modules, constructed of bamboo poles, concrete and old tyres, placed at depths of approximately 15 m provide shelter for fish and settlement opportunities for algae, coral species and seaweeds. Pelagic fish are caught in substantially higher numbers in artificial reefs, while in dense clusters of 34 modules/ha, coral reef species become more abundant. Construction costs are approximately US$400 per module.

Fish decoys in the form of palm leaves attached to bundles of bamboo poles floating in an upright position also help to increase fish yields. Algae grow on the dead leaves and poles, providing food and shelter for small fish which, in turn, attract larger predatory species such as tuna *Scombridae* spp.. The decoys are placed either on top of artificial reefs or in open water. Fish catches have increased now that fishermen are able to catch pelagic species which were formerly beyond their reach. Decoys have to be renewed annually to remain effective, at a cost of US$250/decoy.

Upland reforestation in the Central Visayas Region of the Philippines is followed by attempts to implement agro-forestry. Photo: J.C.J. van Wetten/CML

Marine sanctuaries and reserves

The reefs and shallow coastal waters are highly productive fishing grounds. The reproductive success of pelagic fish and other marine organisms often depends on the condition of the coral reef. Research by the Silliman University has shown that areas where fishing is completely banned make ideal breeding grounds (Russ 1985; Alcala & Abregana in press). In the waters around Apo Island and Sumilon Island, where 10-20% of the waters were designated as a fish sanctuary and a ban was imposed on non-sustainable fishing methods within an 11.5-km zone in adjacent municipal waters, the number of fish increased by 25% within two years, and catches nearly doubled within two to five years.

Upland micro watershed-soil protection and forest restoration

Measures to conserve soil and prevent erosion, e.g. by hedgerow planting and the creation of rainwater diversion channels, are effective and can easily be carried out by farmers. Agro-forestry is suitable in areas with gentle slopes which are less prone to severe soil erosion. Farmers are more willing to protect a planted forest if fruit trees, at a ratio of 70:30, form part of the plantation. Firebreaks need to be established in areas prone to drought and fires. By employing such methods to protect forests, water run-off can be considerably reduced and therefore retained for longer periods in the micro-watersheds.

Wise use projects

Two examples of the moves towards sustainable use of the natural resources are the Marine Conservation and Development Project (MCDP 1984-1986) and the Central Visayas Regional Project (CVRP 1984-1992).

Marine Conservation and Development Project

The concept behind the MCDP was the rehabilitation and conservation of coral reefs in the Central Visayas through community-based resource management. This was based on the premise that effective conservation of resources and management must be rooted in the local communities and that resources cannot be protected unless those who exploit them are committed to conserving them (Savina & White 1986). The five major objectives of MCDP were marine management, community development, agro-forestry, linkages and replication, and institutional development.

The marine management component aimed to establish an integrated marine conservation programme through the participation of the fishing communities. The success of maintaining a marine reserve and sanctuary system was believed to be attainable only if the community learned to view the resources with a long-term perspective. To begin with, small, informal training groups were set up to stimulate awareness and activity within the community. The main thrust of this developmental work was carried out by social workers who acted as community organizers and informal educators. Starting at grassroots level within the community, a gradual process of individual integration and team building and strengthening took place. Fish rearing sanctuaries and marine reserves were set up in three 'barangays' (communities) and management plans for the reserves were drawn up in close consultation with local people. Within three years, coral reef fish species had increased considerably (White 1989) and catches had doubled in size.

The project was then extended to neighbouring fishing communities, firstly on Balicasag Island, and then on Panglao Island in Bohol and on Dauin, Negros Oriental.

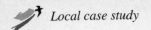

Central Visayas Regional Project

The CVRP was funded by the World Bank through an IBRD loan of US$25.6 million, plus a Government contribution of US$9.8 million: a total project budget of US$35.4 million. The project commenced in June 1984 and was due to end in December 1992.

The underlying philosophy of the CVRP consisted of four basic assumptions:

1. Community-based resource management is the best way to manage natural resources and protect the environment;
2. Tenure of and responsibility for natural resources is the major incentive for rural people to protect and manage resources in a sustainable way, also offering a measure of control over potentially harmful outside influences. (The issuing of Stewardship Contracts, a national policy that originated with this project, provides 25-year leases on government land on condition that sustainable resource management is undertaken.)
3. Centralized and uncoordinated activities of government ministries and agencies are ineffective in the management, protection and rehabilitation of natural resources;
4. Lowland and coastal environmental degradation occurs in part through the effects of upland soil and vegetation degradation, while encroachment by people into upland areas stems partly from declining resource productivity in lowland and coastal areas.

The objectives of the CVRP were threefold:

i) To raise the income and living standards of upland farmers, forest occupants and traditional fishermen in the region's rural areas;
ii) To improve the management of the forest, upland and inshore habitats by stopping the rapid degradation of the environment and improving the natural resource base;
iii) To assist the Government in its efforts towards administrative and budgetary decentralization, and implementation of development programmes and projects.

A key component of the CVRP was its holistic approach, based on watershed management from the uplands to coastal waters, with an emphasis on improving the natural resource base in six critical watersheds in the four provinces of the Central Visayas Region. The ecological zones within these watersheds were five agricultural sites, one forestry site and five inshore fishery sites.

Specific project management was undertaken by 11 Site Management Units (SMU), each coordinated by their respective Provincial Resource Management Office (PRMO). Overall implementation of the project was coordinated by the Central CVRP Office which came under the direction of the Regional Development Council (RDC). Responsibility for policy and decision-making lay with the CVRP Board which was composed of the Executive Director of CVRP, the four provincial governors, the Cebu city mayor, the regional directors of the departments of Agriculture, Environmental and Natural Resources, Public Works & Highways, and Interior & Local Government, private sector representatives from each province, and the National Economic Development Authority (NEDA).

The major role of the CVRP was watershed management in the areas of upland agriculture, inshore fisheries, social forestry and infrastructure, and provision of support and management services, including research, training, technical assistance, communications and project administration.

One of the project's major tasks was the creation of a committee structure within the communities, to encourage widespread grassroots participation. The project also provided security of tenure over primary resources on Government land through stewardship contracts, community timber utilization permits, timber concessions to smallholders, reforestation contracts, marine reserves and fish rearing sanctuaries, and licences for access to resources. Project activities also included better resource management through the application of new technologies in upland reforestation, mangrove reforestation, artificial reefs and fish decoys, livestock management, hill farming, soil conservation techniques and upland fishponds. Improvement of infrastructures such as roads, trails and village water supplies were also integral parts of the project.

Implementation

Project activities at the grassroots level were organized by the Site Management Units. Rural appraisals were conducted and surveys of resources and ecosystems were carried out. To begin with, the SMUs selected communities which were easily accessible and where resource rehabilitation was an urgent priority.

Project organizers and fieldworkers moved into the communities and began meeting and talking to people, first on an individual level, and then in group sessions. Once a nucleus of interested supporters had been found, training courses were run on subjects ranging from leadership, education and public awareness, to resource management and legal matters.

The community was then encouraged to write a management plan in which their needs were clearly addressed within the confines of sustainable resource management. The plan formed the basis of the activities undertaken by the SMU, after approval from Central Office and the CVRP Board. The SMU then supplied materials and technical or legislative assistance to the community. Constraints which hampered the implementation of resource management and rehabilitation were identified by both the community members and the SMU. It was the latter's responsibility to resolve such situations through cooperation with Community Environmental and Natural Resource Offices (CENROs), Provincial Environmental and Natural Resource Offices (PENROs) and Resource Access Committees, on which sat representatives of Government ministries, agencies and the legislature.

Although this bottom up approach proved to be successful, some problems could only be solved at a higher level, through the direct intervention of the project's Central Office and the CVRP Board, particularly where lack of coordination, political conflict and corruption were concerned. The CVRP's Executive Director had a non-voting role on the Board but played an important function in coordinating planning and development actions through the various Government agencies. In many cases the agencies became actively engaged in the community training and implementation programmes.

Once positive results had been achieved in the first communities to take part in the project, it was thought that neighbouring communities would be easier to involve. Through effective coordination, evaluation and sharing of experiences, pitfalls, mishaps and successes were immediately reported to other SMUs and their associated communities. Exchanges of community members between project sites also took place, giving the opportunity for fellow fishermen and farmers to extol the benefits of effective resource management, and helping to convince those with doubts about the viability of the scheme.

Achievements

Institutional restructuring

Membership of the CVRP Board covers a broad political and institutional spectrum, including provincial governors, regional directors of line agencies and representatives of the private sector. The CVRP's Site Management Units were each subject to the approval of the governor of the province. Close cooperation between the SMUs and the regional line agencies provided the basis for change to the agencies, making their function more appropriate for community based resource management and rehabilitation.

It is planned that Provincial Environmental and Natural Resource Offices and Community Environmental and Natural Resource Offices will take over the tasks of the SMUs after the project has ended. In the meantime, staff members of the PENROs and CENROs are involved in resource management training provided by the SMUs.

CVRP also established Resource Access Committees (RACs) to provide legal advice and other services, including training, to rural people. The RACs often mediate in conflicts over resource use and have proven to be an important factor in protecting the interests of rural people.

CVRP's Development Administration Task Force plays an important role in closing loopholes in regulations or in providing the incentives for major changes in policies. Logging bans, tenureship rights for rural people, introduction of the 1992 Local Government Code and the decentralization efforts are examples of changes which came about through the existence of the CVRP and its Task Force.

Coastal resource management

One of the most important achievements made by the CVRP was the heightened awareness of people involved in marine resource management. Not only did local fishermen become aware of the value of sound resource management to their livelihood, but so too did people within Government and Government agencies. The 1991 ban on mangrove cutting has brought about the curtailment of fishpond creation. Most municipal and provincial governments now realize that mangrove stands, which prevent shoreline erosion and benefit coastal fisheries, have a higher economic value than mangroves cleared for fishponds. Fishpond managers are now concentrating on improving the profitability of existing fishponds, rather than increasing the number of fishponds.

Replanting of mangroves initially covered 948 ha. By December 1991, 1,354 Stewardship Contracts had been issued, giving the planters exclusive rights to manage and use the resources of the mangrove in a sustainable way. While the provision of wood from mangrove plantations can only be realized in later years, more immediate benefits were apparent in the decreased rate of shoreline erosion, and an increase in crab and shrimp catches within a few months of replanting.

Fish catches in waters adjacent to 4-5 year old mangrove plantations increased by about 50%. The fishing community in Bohol reported 100%-150% increases in fish catches two years after the establishment of marine reserves and breeding sanctuaries.

About 180 coastal communities were involved in the creation of 982 artificial reefs along 154 km of inshore waters. Valuable coral reef remnants were protected in 3,368 ha of marine reserves where only sustainable fishing methods were allowed; 20% of these reserves were also designated as sanctuary areas in which no human disturbance other than swimming and diving was allowed.

Fishery yields were improved by the creation of 237 fish decoys, built by villagers through provision of materials by CVRP-SMU. The decoys helped to increase the catches of pelagic fish in inshore waters, as did smaller seaweed rafts, constructed and operated by fishermen.

Fishermen formed themselves into 'Bantay Dagat' (guardians of the sea) units to police their own municipal waters and prevent the use of illegal fishing methods. Fishermen's associations were given help by their respective SMU, or by the RAC, in taking cases to court. In 1991, an appeal to the country's Supreme Court by one group of fishermen successfully overturned a decision of a Municipal Court.

Upland resource management

The assistance provided by CVRP to 115 upland communities resulted in approximately 17,363 ha of forest, formerly Government-owned land with logging concessions, coming under the management of farmers and upland dwellers. Some 3,859 ha were reforested by contract labour or by voluntary labour provided by local farmers, who could then apply for Forest Lease Agreements.

The agro-forestry programme initiated fruit tree planting and soil conservation measures on farm plots covering some 6,437 ha. Micro-watershed protection through hedgerow planting along contours and tree planting was mainly carried out on nearby off-farm sites, covering an area of 1,116 ha. An additional 1,442 ha were reforested, mainly on bare hilltops and slopes, while a further 324 ha of grassland were set aside for natural regeneration. As in the fishing communities, 'Bantay Lasang' (guards of the forest) units were set up to prevent illegal logging. By the end of 1991, 465 Stewardship Contracts had been granted.

Infrastructures

Another benefit of the CVRP was the improvement made to the region's infrastructures – important to the success of the resource management and rehabilitation work. Bridges and small farm roads were constructed in order to facilitate the movement of goods to markets. Health services were also improved in the more remote areas. CVRP also provided funds for line agency activities catering for the needs of rural people; for example, the Department for Agriculture was given assistance with the development of veterinary programmes, and upland farmers were able to process timber into more valuable products such as furniture, instead of selling the wood at low prices to middlemen.

Lessons learned

There has been widespread recognition of the fact that combined initiatives by all of the Central Visayas Region's interest groups are needed if sustainable development is to be achieved. This includes the need for a high degree of involvement by the local community. Community based resource management has been successful in attaining wise use of wetland resources in Central Visayas. In areas where enforcement of laws and regulations by Government has been weak or absent, emphasis on local farmers and fishermen as the *de facto* managers proved to be decisive.

Wise use projects which temporarily deprive the rural poor of access to resources, such as fish rearing sanctuaries, should be complemented with income-generating components, especially in the critical transition period from the old ways to the modern methods of resource use and management.

Confidence building and awareness activities are needed within communities before effecting community based resource management. This should include awareness of ecological and environmental relationships and the impact of unsound resource utilization, as well as the social and political emancipation of communities and its members.

Wise use initiatives based on the premise that the local rural users are the *de facto* managers should attune the objectives, activities and methods to the existing social-cultural structure of the communities.

Deployment of capable, live-in community organizers and fieldworkers is a strong plus factor in initiating community support and effecting positive social change in terms of how a community values its finite natural resources.

Security of tenure and right of use over natural resources are essential factors in the willingness of participants to invest and accept sustainable resource management systems.

A legal framework to protect the interests of the *de-facto* resource managers is needed. Without any enforcement of this legislative protection, outsiders can easily step in and reap the benefits of a wisely used ecosystem, depriving the *de-facto* managers and the dependent community, and decreasing the socio-economic basis of wise use.

Sustainable exploitation of natural resources alone cannot in the long term support expanding populations or increasing economic demands. Diversification into other income-generating activities, such as the processing of fish or wood into more valuable products, are necessary if rural communities are to sustain their development.

Lyndo Villacorta, Institute for Environmental Management and Science, IESAM, Los Baños, Philippines.

Jeroen C.J. van Wetten, Centre for Environmental Science (CML), Leiden University, Leiden, The Netherlands.

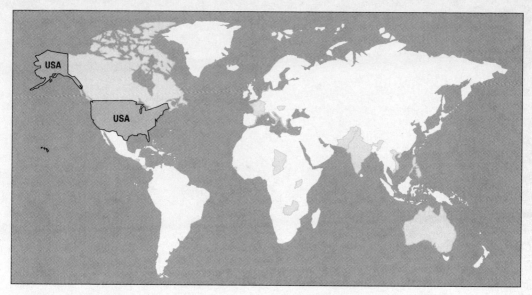

Wetland drainage and restoration potential in the Lake Thompson watershed, South Dakota, USA

Thomas E. Dahl

Introduction

The glaciated Prairie Pothole Region is an area of about 770,000 km^2 located in the central portion of the North American Continent. Within the United States, the Prairie Pothole Region encompasses an area of 274,000 km^2. It extends from central Iowa north to the Canadian border and includes portions of the states of Iowa, Minnesota, North Dakota, South Dakota and Montana (Figure 1). This region is characterized by small landscape depressions left behind as the glaciers receded from this part of the continent. These depressions, termed 'potholes', collect rainfall and snowmelt, forming small shallow wetlands and lakes.

These wetlands play a vital role in the maintenance of nearly all forms of prairie wildlife (Harmon 1970). Prairie potholes are commonly referred to as the 'duck factory of North America' because of their critical importance to breeding waterfowl (Crissey 1969; Bellrose 1979). Other values that pothole wetlands provide include water retention and forage production for livestock (Higgins *et al.* 1985), and economic and aesthetic values (Linder and Hubbard 1982).

This case study deals with the drainage of wetlands within the Lake Thompson watershed of South Dakota. It is a history of unwise land use resulting in lost wetland values and functions and the attempts to regain those benefits through wetland restoration.

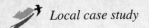
Figure 1. The prairie pothole region of North America.

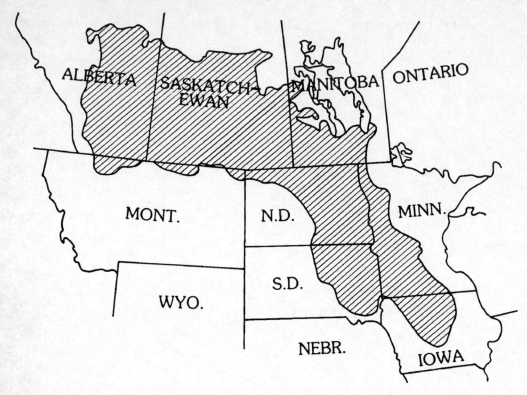

The problem

Wetland loss in the United States

During the past 200 years, wetlands in the United States have been regarded as a hindrance to productive land use. Of the 89.5 million ha of wetlands originally found in the 48 conterminous United States, 53% have been lost (Dahl 1990). Over the past two decades the United States has developed a better understanding of the benefits provided by wetlands. Along with this understanding comes recognition that the loss of wetlands must be curtailed. To accomplish this, losses must be reduced and, where wetland losses are unavoidable or in instances where functions need to be enhanced, restoration should be considered. Due to past wetland losses, the Prairie Pothole Region of the United States is a candidate for such restoration activity.

Despite their importance, extensive drainage has converted millions of hectares of prairie pothole wetlands, primarily to agriculture. In Iowa and portions of western Minnesota, drainage has been so extensive that the vast majority of pothole wetlands have been eliminated (Figure 2).

Within the Lake Thompson watershed in South Dakota, it has been estimated that over 8,000 ha of wetland were eliminated from this 192,000-ha watershed by the mid-1980s. The result has been increased flooding (amplitude and duration) within the Lake Thompson area. Damage to homes, personal property, roadways and other infrastructure has resulted. It is now believed that wetland drainage within this watershed has had an adverse impact on the flood control benefits that wetlands provide to human populations.

The approach

Wetland restoration as an alternative

In the United States the concept of wetland restoration is fairly new. While effective wetland protection involves the preservation of natural wetlands as a first choice (Schneller-McDonald *et al.* 1990), balancing wetland losses with restoration is a potentially viable means for achieving the 'no net loss of wetlands' policy goal. Restoration and creation of wetlands have been advocated for the following purposes:

* To restore or replace wetlands already degraded or destroyed;
* To compensate for additional, unavoidable losses;
* To reduce the impacts of activities in or near wetlands; and
* To serve various functions such as waste water treatment, aquaculture, and wildlife habitat (Kusler & Kentula 1989).

Currently there are no national comprehensive estimates of the area of wetlands that have been restored, created or rehabilitated. However, in localized communities, more attention is being diverted into restoration and rehabilitation efforts of both wetland function and area.

The plan for the Lake Thompson watershed

The Lake Thompson watershed is approximately 192,000 ha in size and is located in the south-eastern portion of the state of South Dakota in an area of prairie coteau historically dotted with small wetlands (Figure 3). The coteau region has generally not developed natural surface drainage systems. The larger watershed is made up of smaller, closed watersheds with the Lake Thompson basin at the terminus. Run-off water is stored in each of these closed depressions until overflow level is reached. Flooding of the Lake Thompson basin and surrounding areas can result.

Figure 2. Areas of extensive drainage in the prairie pothole region of the USA.

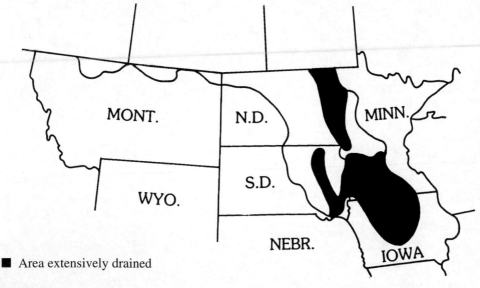

■ Area extensively drained

Figure 3. Lake Thompson watershed, South Dakota.

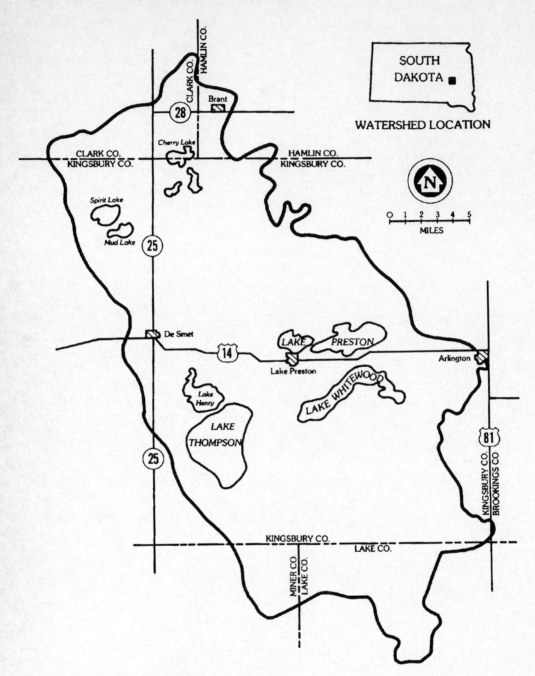

Within the Lake Thompson watershed about 90% of the land is cultivated with corn, wheat and other cereal grains comprising about 70% of the cropland (USFWS 1988). Data indicate that from 1952 to 1984, an estimated 1,286 wetland basins amounting to an area of 3,905 ha had been drained. The size of the basins drained ranged from 0.5 ha to over 240 ha. The majority of this drainage was due to conversion of land for agricultural production. Wetlands had been drained either by surface ditches or subsurface drainage tile. This is important information since the feasibility of wetland restoration is often tied to land use. This has increased the size of the contributing drainage area within the watershed.

The problems caused by wetland drainage within the Lake Thompson area became very apparent during the period 1984 to 1986. It was during this time that increased precipitation caused severe flooding around Lakes Preston, Whitewood and Thompson, resulting in damage to crops, property, and road systems. In an effort to alleviate the flooding problem, the Governor of South Dakota convened a task force to make recommendations to reduce flooding and enhance wildlife habitat. The task force proposed wetland restoration as a means to reduce the frequency and duration of severe flooding in the area. Acting on these recommendations, the Governor requested that a wetland preservation and restoration committee, initially composed of the US Fish and Wildlife Service, South Dakota Game, Fish and Parks, and the National Wildlife Federation, develop and implement a wetland restoration plan for the Lake Thompson watershed.

A consortium of non-government organizations and State and Federal resource agencies established the following objectives for the Lake Thompson project:

- Approximately 4,000 ha of wetland within the watershed should be restored. These wetlands should include all sizes and be distributed throughout the watershed;
- Drained wetlands identified on public lands should be restored first;
- Sites for water management should be identified;
- Land should be acquired wherever available in the watershed to restore wetlands;
- Conservation practices on private lands should also be developed throughout the watershed;
- Small watersheds should be identified and wetlands protected from drainage by offering a package involving perpetual easements, grassland easements, leases.

Half-drained prairie pothole wetlands, South Dakota. Photo: US Fish & Wildlife Service

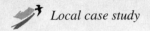

Achievements

Attaining wise use retroactively

There are a number of ways to measure achievements: e.g. the number of wetland basins restored; the number of hectares rehabilitated; the number of ducks produced. All of these actions are ongoing within the Lake Thompson watershed project. However, there are more subtle achievements that also have important consequences.

To employ wetland restoration techniques implies that there has been unwise use of wetlands. Wetland values have been lost or degraded to the point where restoration of these values is paramount. In this portion of the United States wetland drainage has been emphasized for many years. In hindsight, wetland drainage lacked sound environmental planning and as a consequence corrective measures are now needed to re-instil the wise use concept. Recognition of the consequences of the unwise use of wetlands by the scientific and governmental communities and the general public is in itself an achievement.

Other achievements of the Lake Thompson case study include the following:

1. Consensus of Government and non-government organizations. A mix of public and private expertise and funding has been proposed to accomplish the work. Local government organizations and citizens were involved in the planning meetings.
2. Restoration was technically and economically feasible. Wetlands on agricultural lands can be fairly easily restored by plugging surface ditches or putting risers on drain tile outlets (Madsen 1985). Land acquisition costs can be reduced by contracting volunteer landowners. (Some landowners may be willing to restore wetlands because of the problems associated with crop production on marginal lands.)
3. Restoration of functional values was not overly restrictive. While the flooding problems within the watershed ultimately stimulated actions, the restoration of specific wetland values did not preclude other values or benefits from the project. Virtually every hectare

Drained farmland – before wetland restoration work...

of wetland restored helped lessen the flooding problem. This allowed wetland managers to select basin restoration sites that would also serve as wildlife habitat, particularly for waterfowl production. This is an important concept since our knowledge of restoration specific to functional value is limited (Kusler & Kentula 1989).

Lessons learned

In terms of 'lessons learned' from the Lake Thompson experience, there are several things that are noteworthy:

- Wetland restoration is a learning process. Man's ability to engineer outcomes directed at replicating or restoring functional values is limited. Cairns (1985) has discussed the ecological end points for wetland 'restoration' efforts. He points out that while the objective may be restoration of the original habitat conditions and values, in reality this may amount to only partial rehabilitation of original functional values or creation of a different sort of system.
- Wise use probably can be achieved where wetland restoration, rehabilitation or creation seeks to alleviate past unwise use.
- Factual information is needed. Without a current wetland inventory and, in this instance, an inventory of drainage or historic wetlands, achieving the desired results would be difficult.
- Objectives and procedures must coincide. Restoration of hectares may not necessarily meet narrowly defined goals for restoration of values.
- Restoration as a means to achieve wise use is not cheap. Estimated costs to achieve the objectives in the Lake Thompson example could exceed US$1.3 million annually.

Thomas E. Dahl, US Fish and Wildlife Service, National Wetlands Inventory, 9720 Executive Centre Drive, Suite 101, Monroe Building, St Petersburg, Florida 33702, USA.

...and after restoration work. Photos: US Fish & Wildlife Service

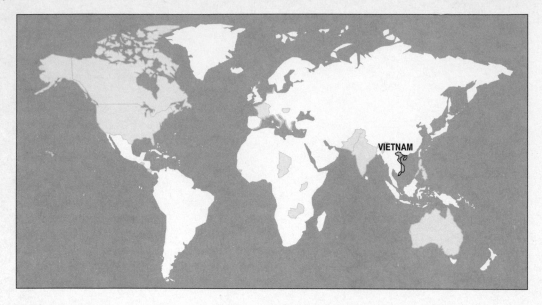

Rehabilitation of the *Melaleuca* floodplain forests in the Mekong Delta, Vietnam

Le Dien Duc

Introduction

The Mekong Delta is one of the largest and most complex wetland systems in South East Asia. It is also one of Vietnam's most productive land areas, as well as being one of the most densely populated parts of the country. With an area of 3.9 million ha, it supports over 14 million people: about 20% of the Vietnamese population on 12% of the total land area.

As Vietnam's population increases and the economy develops, pressure on the delta's ecosystems is increasing rapidly. There is therefore an urgent need to plan land use, taking account of the ecological capacity of the delta's ecosystems while protecting areas of greatest importance for biological diversity. In some instances, this will require rehabilitation of areas which have already been degraded as a result of human intervention. This case study describes current efforts to pursue rehabilitation of one high priority wetland community in the Mekong Delta – the *Melaleuca* floodplain forests.

The problem

Estimates of the *Melaleuca* forests dominating extensive areas of the seasonally flooded alluvial plains in the Mekong Delta are difficult to obtain. However, there are an estimated 280,000 ha of *Melaleuca* mangrove in the Vietnamese section of the Mekong Delta, plus a further 189,358 ha in Uh-Minh Province and more that 30,000 ha in the Thap Muoi closed floodplain.

The *Melaleuca* forests contain some 77 plant species, many of which are of direct economic importance in terms of timber and secondary products, such as firewood and fodder for animals. In addition, the forest system provides between five and six litres of honey per ha from wild bees, while a species of insectivorous plant is used to make a medicine for treating diarrhoea, and many forms of animal are harvested for food.

The nature conservation values of these forest systems are also of great significance. The Tram-Chim Sarus Crane Reserve has been established, with foreign financial assistance, on 9,000 ha of *Melaleuca*. Similarly, an area of relatively undisturbed forest in Uh-Minh district is a breeding area for the Lesser Adjutant Stork *Leptotilos javanicus*.

These *Melaleuca* wetlands are decreasing rapidly in the three southern provinces of Vietnam which lie in the Mekong Delta. Many of the forests have been drained or sprayed with defoliants and herbicides, and some were napalmed during the last war. The practice of draining the *Melaleuca* was continued after the war in an attempt to control flooding and to lower the water table to assist in the reclamation of land for rice-based agriculture. However, the agricultural potential of much of the area normally colonized by *Melaleuca* is limited. Reclamation of areas with acid sulphate potential soils and peat of more than one metre has led to very poor agricultural returns and the subsequent abandonment of large areas. In the province of An Giang, the extent of the *Melaleuca* forest is reported to have declined from 40,000 ha to 4,000 ha in the last decade (16% to 1.6% of the provincial area), while in the Tri Ton area of the northern part of the Long Xuyen region, more than 350,000 ha of *Melaleuca* have been degraded.

The *Melaleuca* forest has many very important ecological and economic functions. It is the only arboreal vegetation capable of growing on the acid soils which dominate about 25% of the province. In these areas, the forest provides an important habitat for a wide range of wetland birds, some of which are rare or endangered. On acid soils, the forest helps to improve soil quality by reducing acidity, as well as purifying water.

In economic terms, the *Melaleuca* forest is a major source of fuel for the local population, as well as poles, which are used for construction locally and are exported as far afield as Ho Chi Minh city. The severe depletion of the resource means that fuelwood is now imported into the region, mainly from mangrove forests near the sea, with the consequence that those forests are now also coming under threat. It means, too, that the price of fuelwood is increasing, causing economic hardship amongst the poorer members of the community. The small upland forest areas within the province are also coming under increasing pressure for fuelwood as the *Melaleuca* resources are depleted.

The remaining *Melaleuca* forest is only capable of sustaining a fuelwood supply of perhaps 30,000-40,000 m^3/year, though at present it may be supplying two to three times that amount and depleting existing stocks. The fuelwood demand for the province, with a population of 1.85 million, is likely to be 900,000-1,500,000 m^3/year, of which an unknown but probably large proportion is coming from trees around houses and agricultural residues. However, the proportion of fuelwood coming at present from mangroves is far greater than that from alternative supplies. As much as 3,000-4,000 ha of mangroves may be being destroyed annually to meet this demand, all of which could be met from *Melaleuca* if a substantial proportion of the wetlands on the acid soils were restored.

The approach

In view of the importance of *Melaleuca* in the Mekong Delta and the severity of its degradation, rehabilitation of the *Melaleuca* forest is now receiving substantial political support at both national and local government levels. Local communities increasingly recognize that the wise use of the forest provides a greater measure of economic and social benefit than reclamation for agriculture. A number of initiatives have therefore begun with the aim of rehabilitating the *Melaleuca*.

Rehabilitated forests

The provincial authorities have already begun to plant *Melaleuca* in several areas. The forests are established by sowing seed by hand, and this has so far achieved acceptable results, with reasonably uniform stocking in most areas, and densities in the range of 30,000-50,000 trees per ha. On the better sites this results in a dense canopy which shades out all grasses and ground flora. On the poorer sites, where tree height is lower, grasses grow strongly in open patches. However, in the absence of management (thinning), intense competition between young trees results in a very limited diameter growth in the majority of trees. In addition, because no thinning is undertaken, the opportunity for an early yield from small diameter trees is lost. Similarly, the accumulation of dead and dry litter under the trees is probably a factor in increasing the fire hazard.

The precise seed source for all of the trees is unknown and, judging by the poor form of a majority of the trees, it may well be that this is collected from poor, stunted, shrubby trees from which it is easy to collect seed, rather than from a genetic resource with desirable characteristics. The species being established also has less potential for growth than *Melaleuca leucodendron*; the latter is also reported to produce better quality honey. It is therefore essential that if this work is to continue, a good quality seed source must be established.

Similarly, in view of the scarce resource available, it is important that the sites undergoing rehabilitation are prioritized. At present, indications are that many of the sites are too acid. The capacity of *Melaleuca* to grow in soils of differing acidity therefore needs to be tested and sites selected on the basis of their acidity and acceptability to *Melaleuca*.

In view of the risks associated with fire, the technique of controlled burning should be carefully developed by the Forest Department. At the outset, small isolated blocks of *Melaleuca* should be subjected to controlled burning.

Reformation of land holdings and the design of a land use management system to promote sustainable forest utilization

Under the socialist Government, the *Melaleuca* forests are public lands. As such, they form common property resources and the task of conserving and rehabilitating the forest has proved to be beyond the capabilities of the Government. To help overcome this problem, local forestry officials are now giving local people a proprietary role in the management of the forest and are allocating 10-ha plots of former forest on long-term leases to local farmers. The objective is to form a forest reserve surrounded by a series of 10-ha plots where a system of agroforestry is practised by farmers. Each farmer will be required to plant 7.5 ha with *Melaleuca* and to practice permanent agriculture on the remaining 2.5 ha. Space for a dwelling is to be included in the 10 ha.

Soil surveys have not, however, been conducted by forestry staff and it is likely that many field crops will be unsustainable due to soil acidification. Therefore, although this model is innovative in that it encourages farmers to rehabilitate and protect the forest by granting them rights of use, more thought needs to be given to designing a more diversified farming system based upon an intensive mixed cropping system on 0.25-0.3 ha in order to provide food, fodder, fuelwood, medicinal plants and cash crops such as citrus. Reafforestation should also have a higher priority than field crops, especially if this is combined with diversification of secondary resources, such as honey production, and diversification of the economic opportunities available to farmers, such as the distillation of essential oils from the *Melaleuca* and the collection of medicinal plants.

Diversification of forest products

To increase diversification, a pilot initiative is under way to establish household-managed beehives, and community-managed stills for extracting essential oils from *Melaleuca*. Carried out through the provincial authorities, this work is designed to increase the economic value of the natural forest to the communities, thus providing alternatives to agriculture.

Restoration of the delta's hydrological regime

A large part of the Mekong Delta has had a complex system of canals dredged for agricultural and access purposes, and to form firebreaks to help protect reafforestation sites. This has led to the oxidation of peat, subsidence of the soil, compaction and acidification of the surface soils, loss of organic mineralized soil nutrients, and acidification of waters in adjacent streams and canals.

At present, dikes are constructed, at enormous expense, around established blocks of forest. The canals resulting from the extraction of the soil for dike construction are often kept filled with water for all or part of the dry season by pumping water from the rural canal system, the aim being to keep the soil within the forest moist throughout the year. The dikes are intended to retain water within the forest as the water level falls after the rainy season. However, losses through evaporation and groundwater seepage mean that the levels can only be maintained for part of the dry season. Therefore, in some areas, it is proposed to pump water back in from the surrounding land.

Since the acid sulphate soils, unsuitable for rice, occur over extensive areas of the delta, and in particular in An Giang province, it would seem to make more economic sense to investigate ways in which the water regime could be managed over an extensive tract, perhaps by

Life in the Mekong Delta, Vietnam – a family takes home 'Melaleuca' for use as fuel.
Photo: Hervé Lethier

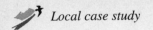

restricting the flow in the main canal system with the aid of sluices. The Department of Agriculture is already investigating a number of new canal schemes which need to be integrated with the available soils information and the Forest Department's resources, to develop a rational, overall land use plan for the province. If such investigations are linked with the growth and yield of the *Melaleuca*, a much more coherent and economically sound rehabilitation programme can be formulated.

Achievements

Although *Melaleuca* rehabilitation has been attempted in the Mekong Delta for almost two decades, much more needs to be done. Nevertheless, *Melaleuca* has been restored in selected areas, and there is substantial support at all levels, from central Government to the local communities, for further investment in this project. Most of the efforts currently under way are local initiatives.

Lessons learned

1. Rehabilitation needs to be carried out as a joint initiative involving central Government, provincial authorities and local people. In the absence of local support, it will be virtually impossible to maintain the forest plantations.

2. The national enthusiasm for managing *Melaleuca* needs to be supported by substantial technical assistance. Most of the problems so far encountered are a consequence of limited technical understanding of the soil and water characteristics of the delta and the dependence upon them of agriculture and forestry practices. The Government is currently emphasizing the need for integrated, ecologically balanced development and plans to reafforest more than 70,000 ha. A mixture of *Melaleuca* forest plantations to address environmental issues and commercial wood production is envisaged.

3. This case study focuses on the rehabilitation of one wetland type. However, while this specific resource yields many benefits for local communities, by restoring *Melaleuca* and demonstrating an economically productive, sustainable resource use which is dependent upon the maintenance of the natural system and restoration of the hydrological system, the work being undertaken will play a key role in restoring the natural wetland system over large parts of the delta. Had this wise use project not been undertaken, demonstrating clearly how the resources of the delta can be used sustainably, it is unlikely that there would have been sufficient Government support for the investment required to maintain the hydrological system. The alternative would have been further investment in more intensive irrigated agriculture in smaller areas, consequent acidification and degradation of the remainder of the delta, and continuing loss of biological diversity.

Le Dien Duc, University of Hanoi, 19 le Thank Tong, Hanoi, Vietnam.

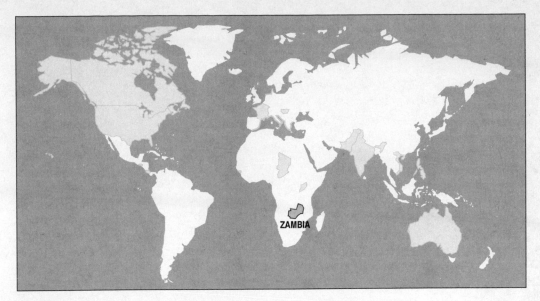

Wise use of floodplain wetlands in the Kafue Flats of Zambia

Richard C.V. Jeffery

Introduction

The Kafue Flats are a vast shallow basin of the Kafue River, formed on deep floodplain sediments underlain by ancient faulting between the Itezhi-Tezhi Gap and Kafue Gorge in Central-Southern Zambia. The periphery of the wetland is moderately heavily populated by peoples of the Ila-Tonga groups, the wetland itself by descendants of the BaTwa and recent immigrants. Pastoralism, agriculture, hunting, trading and fishing are the main activities of local people. Major national and international commercial interests include hydro-electric power generation, irrigation and water supply, agriculture and livestock production, hunting and tourism. The Kafue Flats are a wetland of major ecological, industrial and socio-economic significance for Zambia.

The problem

The WWF-Zambia Wetlands Project's activities in the Kafue Flats project area firmly link floodplain wetland management with human socio-economic development at the local and supra-local community levels. Such efforts face a crisis of objectivity, because the statutory responsibilities of the Government towards the project area's protected National Parks and Game Management Area (GMA) are at odds with the *ad hoc* human activities which have developed there. With rising pressures on land and resources, such activities are leading to an environmental crisis which in turn will constrain the socio-economic development of resident communities.

Which issues, therefore, should be addressed first in a project of this nature: environmental problems or those of socio-economic development? The assumption upon which the project has in fact been based is that the Kafue Flats project area will remain primarily a protected area for wildlife management purposes. However, this assumption is qualified by accepting that the principal human interventions which have developed on the Kafue Flats are a reflection of real human needs, and should therefore be integrated into a wetlands management agreement for the GMA, whilst maintaining the integrity of the Lochinvar and Blue Lagoon National Parks (which are relatively small proportions of the project area, and have been designated for the Ramsar List). The Wetlands Project is therefore addressing *both* issues by developing natural resource management as a *means* of community development.

The fundamental principles of community participation, upon which the Wetlands Project is based, are not experimental. They are proven principles established by the Lupande Research Project and the subsequent Lupande Development Project (Kaweche & Lewis 1985; Lewis *et al.* 1989).

The Wetlands Project's overall objectives are to conserve and manage the Kafue Flats and Bangweulu Swamps project areas, in order to maintain or enhance natural productivities for the sustainable use and development of resident communities and the nation as a whole.

The project area

The Kafue Flats core project area covers approximately 6,000 km^2, comprising two National Parks and a Game Management Area, the latter being occupied by some of the subjects of seven chiefdoms. The chiefdoms overlap the boundaries of the core project area and extend into a peripheral zone, the total human population of which is some 120,000 people. The target communities are predominantly Ilas and Tongas who are traditional cattle pastoralists. To a lesser extent, target communities also include immigrant populations (mainly fishermen), and employees of the various Government departments and other organizations concerned with the management, regulation and use of the project area's resources.

Current human activities and relationships with natural resources

Indigenous local communities are principally engaged in rearing (and increasingly in marketing) cattle. The traditional cattle population depending on dry season grazing of the Kafue Flats probably exceeds 250,000 (Bingham 1982). Local people are also involved in subsistence and small-scale commercial farming in the peripheral zone, maize, cotton and sunflower being the chief crops. Irrigated agriculture is mainly practised at the eastern extremity of the Kafue Flats by large-scale commercial farming concerns. By far the largest of these is the Nakambala Sugar Estate which produces sugar for national requirements and export. Whilst this scheme is undoubtedly of great national significance, local people still harbour resentment against a development which largely overlooked local needs, and claimed traditional grazing lands. Less obvious is the fact that irrigated agricultural schemes are major consumers of the Kafue Flats water resources.

No major industrial activity is practised by the local communities, whose wealth lies largely in cattle. However, there are many small-scale (village) industries, such as farming and brick-making, which have considerable potential for development.

Few Ilas or Tongas engage in fishing enterprises, which are largely in the hands of the BaTwa and a myriad of immigrant fishermen. Average annual fish production between 1966 and 1985 was 7,700 tonnes (Subramaniam 1992), making the Kafue Flats fisheries one of the most important in the country.

For both local and non-resident communities, hunting plays an important social and economic role in everyday life, but in most cases this activity is conducted illegally. There is growing evidence that the greater part of this pressure emanates from the urban (i.e. non-local) areas of Zambia. Nevertheless, the wildlife resource of the Kafue Flats remains productive in spite of serious over-exploitation over the last 30 years. By 1991, it was estimated that there were about 68,000 Lechwe *Kobus leche,* from a historical population of over 200,000 which had decreased to about 40,000 in the early 1980s (Howard & Jeffery 1983), and 5,000 Zebra *Equus berchelli* (Jeffery *et al.* 1991). Over 90 species of wild mammals and 400 species of birds (including the endangered Wattled Crane *Bugeranus carunculatus*) have been recorded. Recent estimates of over 3,000 Wattled Cranes reveal that the Kafue Flats is one of Africa's most important refuges for this species (Howard & Aspinwall 1984; Malambo pers. comm.). Some mammals such as Aardwolf *Proteles cristatus,* Cheetah *Acinonyx jubatus,* Wild Dog *Lycaon pictus,* Lion *Panthera leo,* Leopard *Panthera pardus* and Eland *Taurotragus oryx* are now believed to be extinct in the area. The wildlife resource supports important and expanding tourist and hunting industries.

The Kafue Flats water resources are of major significance for industrial and urban water supply (for Kafue Town and Lusaka City), and for hydro-electric power production.

The Kafue Gorge Dam power station has a generating capacity of 900 MW, and flow for this is regulated by the Itezhi-Tezhi Dam some 450 km (channel length) upstream of Kafue Gorge (Balasubrahmanyam & Abou-Zeid 1982). The intervening Kafue Flats project area is profoundly affected by these dams which artificially regulate water flow and flooding regimes, principally of course for the production of power. However, the design of these impoundments did allow for moderation of flow for other purposes, and it is a provision that a 'freshet' of a minimum of 300m^3/second be released in March of every year to help minimize change to the ecological balance of the Kafue Flats. The Zambia Electricity Supply Corporation which operates the dams has also invited scientists to provide information on which further regulations to meet ecological requirements can be based. Unfortunately, the minimum provisions required of the dam's operators are not always met; neither have ecologists maintained pressure on the authorities to apply or improve these provisions. Nevertheless, hydro-electric power production is of major significance to Zambia's national economy, particularly as power is exported to neighbouring countries. The waters of the Kafue system are of further international significance since they contribute to the Zambezi River system which flows through Zimbabwe and Mozambique.

Another valuable resource of the Kafue Flats is gypsum (chiefly used in manufacturing cement), which is found in shallow deposits, particularly on the south bank and within Lochinvar National Park. Whilst the Kafue Flats deposits have long been subject only to localized, low-level exploitation, there is a possibility of demand growing in the near future and threatening the integrity of Lochinvar National Park.

Rationalizing competing land use demands

Continued uncoordinated development on the Kafue Flats poses the threat of bitter conflicts between the various interest groups. However, by rationalizing competing demands, it is possible that all major current interests could be adequately catered for, if regulated at sustainable levels, within the framework of a wetland management agreement.

For the indigenous local communities, the most important activities which need safeguarding are pastoralism (including commons grazing on the Kafue Flats), agriculture (in peripheral areas), fishing (to a lesser extent), and wildlife utilization. Local community interests in hunting are based largely on game meat as a highly appreciated food luxury. By itself, it is not an important source of protein for local people, who thrive on local beef, fish and crops; wildlife trophies (e.g. skins) have a fairly low traditional utility value. However, it should be noted that local community concern for wildlife was once woven into the very fabric of traditional society. The cultural significance of wildlife has been diluted during the colonial and immediate post-colonial administrations in Zambia, which disenfranchised local people from their traditional resources through a highly centralized system of government. With the current trend of decentralization, the stature of wildlife amongst local communities is growing rapidly, particularly as an economic resource.

Apart from maintenance of a traditional life-style, the priority needs of the local communities are principally improved water supply, health, education, extension and marketing facilities. Some of the costs of satisfying these needs could be borne by the sustainable use of the Kafue Flats' natural resources.

From the national viewpoint, it is accepted that irrigated agriculture, industrial and urban water supply, hydro-electric power, fisheries, livestock, tourism and wildlife are important uses of the Kafue Flats' resources, and should continue to contribute materially and economically to the nation's development. However, local communities must be given greater opportunities for participating in the management of such activities, and a greater share of their benefits. Thus, any initiatives to expand or initiate activities in the project area must win the approval of local communities, as well as satisfy the legal and technical conditions necessary for integrating the proposed interventions with existing land uses and social structures. The responsibility for approving and implementing wetland management agreements must increasingly lie with the local communities who stand to gain the most in the long term from the sustainable management of natural resources. It is thus appropriate that the local communities also contribute some of the costs of such management.

The approach

In developing and implementing a wetland project with the objectives and constraints as outlined, stepwise progression is required which is both decisive but adaptive. The following

Life at the water's edge in the Kafue Flats, Zambia. Photo: Richard Jeffrey

inputs by the project have been designed, implemented and adapted, using and thus strengthening existing infrastructures as a matter of policy.

Natural resource management infrastructure

The principal statutory player in natural resource management of the project area is the National Parks and Wildlife Service (a department of the Ministry of Tourism). Thus, by 1989, the Wetlands Project had been integrated with the department by formal agreement, as one of its 'special projects'. This immediately created a working relationship with the department and its Administrative Management Design programme for GMAs (ADMADE) with which the Wetlands Project has close generic links. This crucial step has facilitated project implementation by using well-tested methods, and has laid the foundations for the project's long-term continuity. This measure has also enabled the project to gain the immediate support of the existing National Parks and Wildlife Service/ADMADE facilities, infrastructures and staff in the field, allowing project staff and resources to supplement and strengthen them in an 'institution building' role. The intention is for key senior project staff to join the department through the Civil Service, thus providing Government with trained and experienced professional personnel.

One drawback to this approach is that it could exclude the interests of other disciplines, so important in the overall task of wetland floodplain management. This has partly been overcome by the project having a sociologist seconded by the Ministry of Labour, Social Development and Culture, and by formal collaborative agreements with organizations such as the Ministry of Health, Department of Fisheries, the University of Zambia, and the National Environment Council. The proposed establishment of a Professional and Technical Advisory Committee, chaired by the Director of the National Parks and Wildlife Service, will further elaborate the multi-disciplinary nature of the Wetlands Project. It is possible that a 'Projects Directorate', already established at senior staff level in the department, may fulfil this role. Through such a committee, it is important that the department as a whole develops its multi-disciplinary function.

Natural resource management integration with local communities is being effected by representation of management staff (including the project leader, project sociologist, management biologists, wardens, rangers, management unit leaders, and extension workers) on local committees. Integration is enhanced by the employment of local people as 'village scouts' who participate in the management of wildlife through the ADMADE programme's input to the project area.

Funding for natural resource management is provided by central Government through the various line departments (such as the National Parks and Wildlife Service, and Fisheries Department), and is currently supplemented by the Wetlands Project. Limited (but potentially greater) funding is available specifically for local wildlife management initiatives from a proportion of funds generated in the project area from local wildlife utilization activities; these contributions represent the local communities' share of the wetland management costs. It is not anticipated that the entire natural resource management needs for the project area will ever become self-sufficient from such revenues. The project area as a whole probably generates a net surplus of national funds, so continued investment by central Government in natural resource management of the project area is probably justifiable on economic grounds alone.

The inputs of natural resource management in the project area should include maintenance and development of physical infrastructures (e.g. airstrips, roads, canals and buildings), law enforcement (including anti-poaching and fisheries patrols), natural resource monitoring (including wildlife censusing and fish-stock assessments), environmental management (including fire management, habitat manipulation and erosion control), and overall environmental monitoring and evaluation. The extent to which such inputs are applied varies according to the means available to managers. Until recently, the project had only two vehicles and two boats operational in the Kafue Flats project area, although the project has just completed the rehabilitation of a Government vehicle, a tractor and trailer. WWF-International has also acquired a light aircraft which spends part of its time assisting with project activities on the Kafue Flats. The incorporation of other natural resource management teams from other departments and organizations into a coordinated programme may ultimately lead to increased facilities and data being available for the project.

Community development infrastructure

The elaboration of a community development infrastructure has been a painstaking process, even though it too has been moulded about an existing framework of socio-political organization. Exhaustive consultations and public meetings with local communities, traditional leaders, and senior Government and political officials confirmed that the chiefdoms should provide the springboard for the project's community-based programmes. Community Development Units (CDU) were formed and members elected in six of the seven chiefdoms making up the project area. The seventh chiefdom has yet to join the project following its loss of grazing lands to the Nakambala Sugar scheme. The chiefs of the other six chiefdoms were automatically designated Patrons of their CDUs and were in most cases also elected Chairmen. Extension workers and other officers actively serving the chiefdoms' communities were in some cases elected or co-opted onto the CDUs as members or observers. The Wetlands Project's CDUs are the equivalent of wildlife management sub-authorities in other parts of the country where the ADMADE programme has been implemented. In order to provide an interface between traditional and contemporary authority in the project area, two Wetlands Management Authorities (WMA) were established (Lochinvar WMA for the south bank, and Blue Lagoon WMA for the north bank) under the principal District Councils of the two areas. The Chairmen of these authorities are the District Governors of the Principal Districts. Chiefs, CDU Chairmen, MPs and Ward Chairmen from the project area are automatically members of the authorities. Other officials and members are elected from CDU members. Because the authorities operate under the aegis of the District Councils, they have natural links with district, provincial, and thus central Government infrastructures. Indeed, the authorities may collaborate with district development officers, line department staff, and staff of other organizations to reinforce and coordinate community development activities. Some of these officials may serve as members or observers on the authorities. The majority of elected CDU and WMA members are local people. These infrastructures are thus truly decentralized and autonomous bodies representing the interests of local communities.

Extension work of the project promotes the integration of local community interests with environmental interests. However, a major aim of the project's extension programme is to catalyse and invigorate the inputs of existing extension workers stationed in the project area with a number of departments and organizations.

Participation of local communities in natural resource management activities has been initiated through ADMADE's Village Scout programme on the Kafue Flats. This programme is presently managed by ADMADE and its Wildlife Conservation Revolving Fund but, in time, indigenous inputs to natural resource management will be the WMAs' responsibility. Whilst technical research and management of natural resources must remain the responsibility of the various professional agencies, the CDUs and WMAs provide a platform for local communities to negotiate actively with national interests for larger shares in the benefits of sustainable management of natural resources. Meanwhile, the WMAs will make their own decisions regarding the use of information, funds and resources available to them for their own programmes, within the framework of existing legislation and management plans. Furthermore, through the Village Scout programme, and other training opportunities created by the project, more local people are finding professional employment within their home areas.

Economic infrastructure

At present (1992-93), the Wetlands Project has been supplementing central Government, provincial and district expenditures in the project area by about ZK40 million/annum from WWF funding. The figure is difficult to calculate in other currencies due to rapid devaluations of the Zambian kwacha over the last few years (from about ZK170 to ZK370 to the Swiss franc between September 1992 and June 1993).

The project has used the ADMADE programme policy framework to establish a means of funding the activities of the two WMAs from wildlife revenues. This facility allows the authorities to retain 50% of statutory (Government) revenues and all non-statutory revenues from certain categories of wildlife utilization, including revenues from hunting, cropping and donations. These revenues are accrued in the first instance by the Wildlife Conservation Revolving Fund, which then apportions them to the authorities for allocation according to the following formula:

- 40% to local wildlife management activities;
- 35% to local community development activities;
- 15% to NPWS costs of programme administration;
- 10% to ADMADE costs of programme administration.

It should be noted that the system does not prevent the authorities from developing their own income-generating schemes and allocating the revenues as they wish.

The two authorities have recently established 'development accounts' to accrue revenues for the member CDUs. Community development activities were receiving aid before the accounts were set up, from grants, donations and from the Wetlands Project itself. Whilst the new accounts will continue to receive such assistance, they will also generate funds from their own enterprises, such as community-run shops, grinding mills and safari camps. Unlike natural resource management of the project area, community development activities will be expected to become self-sufficient.

The authorities may soon open their own 'wildlife management accounts' to accrue funds for indigenous wildlife management initiatives (such as the Village Scout programme). These funds will accrue from the 40% proportion of project area funds generated from wildlife utilization and currently held by ADMADE's Wildlife Conservation Revolving Fund. In time, this provision may be extended to cater for local initiatives aimed at supplementing management of a broader range of natural resources.

Between 1988 and 1989, the Kafue Flats project area generated approximately ZK380,000 from non-statutory hunting revenues and a small Lechwe cropping scheme (150 animals). This amount has been apportioned to the two authorities, which have allocated 35% to community development and 40% to wildlife management in the project area. The rather low figure reflects, firstly, the low legal offtake of wild animals from the Kafue Flats and, secondly, the higher official values of the Zambian kwacha against the US dollar in 1988 and 1989.

From 1990, the Government agreed that 50% of statutory hunting revenues generated in the project/ADMADE areas would be returned to the WMAs, as long as they are divided as per the ADMADE formula. This boosted the 1990 revenue to at least ZK1,205,460 from hunting rights fees and 50% of hunting licence fees. Assuming that poaching will be reduced, the Kafue Flats project area could earn hundreds of millions of kwacha (at present rates of exchange) per annum from the same wildlife resources. Together with other sources of income (e.g. from community shops, camps, grinding mills, donations), the authorities have a high potential for generating income, the majority of which could perhaps come from wildlife.

Achievements and Lessons learned

The WWF-Zambia Wetlands Project's activities in the Kafue Flats Project Area represent an important case study of current initiatives in Zambia, which firmly link floodplain wetland management with human socio-economic development at the local and supra-local community levels. The project has gone a long way towards establishing an integrated system of wetland floodplain management. The salient features of the system are:

1. Recognition of the dual objectives of the project in terms of the management of protected areas, and participation of local communities under the principal jurisdiction of the National Parks and Wildlife Service;
2. Recognition of the local, national and international roles of the Kafue Flats in ecological, economic, social and political terms;
3. Development of the project as an institution-building mechanism for a coordinated natural resource management system, integrating the roles of the key organizations at the professional and technical levels;
4. To provide the means for local communities to participate in natural resource management, to implement their own community development programmes, and to develop their capacities for active professional and business inputs to their home areas;
5. To demonstrate the profitability of regulated, sustainable wildlife management and utilization for the benefit of local communities and the nation as a whole;
6. To demonstrate that coordination of social needs and existing land-use practices into a regulated wetland management framework can cater for most interests with a minimum of conflict;
7. To develop a wetland management agreement to maximize the local and national benefits from existing and proposed land-use practices, based on the principle of sustainable natural resource utilization.

It is recognized that the project has a long way to go before socio-economic benefits are widely felt (particularly at the household level) and effective natural resource management is reinstated. Consolidation of the project's current transitional phase is expected to take up to three years (from June 1991). It is also appreciated that the project has not yet invested sufficiently in monitoring the inputs and outputs of project activities. Now that its organizational structure in the field is virtually complete, the project should begin to address this issue, particularly as evaluation of the project is of concern to other agencies interested in developing similar floodplain wetland management schemes (Casley & Lury 1982).

Richard C.V. Jeffery, WWF-Country Representative Zambia, P.O. Box 50551 RW, Lusaka, Zambia.

Chapter 3
Distilling lessons from the case studies

In adopting a definition of wise use, and subsequently providing guidelines and guidance for its implementation, successive Conferences of Contracting Parties to the Ramsar Convention have provided substantial encouragement to countries seeking to improve management of their wetland resources. The present volume takes a significant step further by providing specific examples of the ways in which a wide diversity of countries have pursued wise use. Thus, while it would be imprudent to claim that any yet provide a clear demonstration of lasting success, these case studies provide a wealth of information and encouragement to those institutions that are seeking to grapple with the application of the wise use principle.

This is perhaps one of the most important messages to emerge from the present review. Wise use is a complex task which takes time to yield lasting results. The work described here therefore needs to be seen as a first compendium of examples of approaches to applying the wise use guidelines adopted in Montreux (Ramsar, 1990).

The second consequence of this complexity is that these case studies do not provide easy solutions for pursuing wise use. Rather they emphasize that, even in the simplest cases such as Laguna Jocotal in El Salvador, wise use is a complex task and requires action at several levels, adjusted to national conditions. Ideally, wise use should be pursued through a comprehensive national programme addressing information, awareness, policy, planning, management and institution building. However, while in several countries, such as Uganda and Canada, there is sufficient awareness of the values of wetlands and concern for their conservation to lay the basis for such an approach, this may be totally inappropriate in many others where such awareness is absent, or institutional capacity limited. Here a more pragmatic approach is required, one which, while viewing a comprehensive national programme as a long-term goal, pursues intermediate steps such as site-specific management, or sub-national planning approaches to wise use. In reviewing the case studies, readers therefore need to consider the lessons they provide and assess their relevance to their own context. The purpose of the general recommendations set out here is to assist in this task.

Guidelines and guiding principles

Upon its formation in 1987, one of the first tasks of the Wise Use Working Group was to prepare guidelines on implementing the wise use requirement. These guidelines, adopted by the Fourth Conference of Contracting Parties in 1990, provide a broad framework within which each country can examine its priorities and the approach most adapted to its individual needs. Rather than focus attention upon this framework, which already sets the scene effectively, the wise use project has concentrated upon illustrating how specific actions can be best pursued. It has done so by examining the case studies presented here, considering the specific actions taken by governments and non-government organizations to improve management of wetlands, and distilling from them broad guiding principles that can be used by Contracting Parties in pursuing wise use through national, sub-national and site-specific action.

While guidelines provide a framework and guiding principles provide a philosophy, it is essential to note that neither provides rigid instruction. Rather, wise use, whether at national or site specific level, will not be achieved by applying some ready-made package, but by measures which are freshly designed to meet the specific conditions of the country and site in question. Indeed one of the conclusions of the wetland management workshops held before the Montreux Conference in 1990 is that there is no fixed recipe for wetland management. Rather, in most countries the critical requirement for effective wetland management is development of the appropriate conservation ethic rather than acceptance of a detailed 'hands on' management methodology.

There are, however, some strong guiding principles underlying this ethic and which the wise use case studies underline:

i) Social and economic forces are the main reasons for wetland loss and therefore need to be of central concern in wise use programmes;

ii) Special attention needs to be given to the local populations who will be the first to benefit from improved management. Devolution of control over resources from central government to local structures may be a critical element in the success of approaches to wise use, and ways of achieving this need to be examined in all field projects.

iii) Although one agency may be responsible for coordinating national action to conserve wetlands, other public or private institutions have expertise which is of importance to effective long-term wetland management. Wise use programmes should seek to involve, and where appropriate, work through these partners.

iv) Specific site projects may often demonstrate the need for more general institutional requirements for the wise use of wetlands.

v) Wetlands form an integral part of a wider coastal zone or catchment; wise use must also take into account the problems of the surrounding coastal zone or catchment. It is from this wider geographical setting that many of the pressures upon each wetland originate, whether they be water diversion or direct human pressure.

vi) While comprehensive understanding of the ecological constraints of a wetland system should be sought, when such knowledge is not available, activities affecting wetlands need to be governed by the 'precautionary principle'. In other words, if the impact of specific actions is not clearly understood, then these actions should be prohibited even if there is insufficient evidence to prove a direct link between the activities and resulting wetland degradation.

The case studies provide tangible demonstration of how governments and NGOs have pursued these principles. Thus, while they do not provide recipes, they do demonstrate the importance of certain ingredients, notably the concern that needs to be given to social and administrative issues.

In addition to these guiding principles there are two other issues which provide a wider context for the increasing investment in wise use. First, wise use of wetlands will only be successful in the long term if it is carried forward as part of a wider investment by government and NGOs in pursuit of an integrated approach to conservation and development goals across the natural landscape, and through both national and local economies. While a growing number of countries profess allegiance to this wider goal, few, if any, pursue it effectively. Many have established National Conservation Strategies (NCSs) and the World Bank is currently exhorting all borrowing nations to develop National Environmental Action Plans (NEAPs). However, these need to be seen as part of a long-term process which needs much greater investment and more courageous action by governments and public alike. In pursuing wise use, the Ramsar Convention has the potential to provide leadership by providing further encouragement for development of such comprehensive approaches to environmental management.

The second issue is a logical, but elusive, consequence of a country's commitment to both wise use of wetlands and the wider goals of a NCS or NEAP. In embracing the message that environment and development are inextricably linked and that sustainable use of wetlands can bring benefits to a broad section of society, governments should be committed to applying the principles of wise use both at home and abroad. In other words, wise use should govern relations with neighbours over shared wetlands and river systems and, for industrialized nations, should govern the terms of their development assistance. These goals remain elusive however and more careful attention to them is needed.

How can guidance be used?

The challenge to countries is, of course, to move beyond the case studies and guidelines and establish processes through which they can pursue nationally adapted approaches to applying the wise use concept, both in managing individual sites and over natural landscapes as required by the Convention. However, guidance by definition is designed to assist institutions and individuals that are already actively searching for solutions to specific problems. It is of little value in countries where there is little serious concern for wetland conservation, while in many where such concern exists, the national institutions need to be strengthened considerably if they are to pursue this mandate effectively. Wise use initiatives therefore need to be complemented by substantial efforts to build awareness of the importance of wetland conservation, while investing substantial financial resources to strengthen institutions and assist them in applying the guidance provided. National, sub-national and site-specific initiatives are required, all of which should be complemented by investment in training. Training should be provided for a wide range of disciplines, including irrigation engineering and rural development planning. At present, relatively few examples exist of institutions which are effective in pursuing integrated wetland management. However, the example of Uganda, where an inter-ministerial committee has been established, has considerable merit, and this example should be monitored and lessons learned.

The challenge faced by most countries will be to distil from the guidance a clear set of actions that can be followed to strengthen wise use measures, while working to ensure that there is truly effective government and public support for this, as well as institutions capable of implementing the necessary action. Some will feel that much has already been achieved in their countries and that relatively little immediate action is required. However, the continuing pattern of wetland loss worldwide suggests that there is little room for complacency, even in those countries which have already established a commendable record in wetland conservation. Every country will benefit from a careful review of wetland conservation actions, to assess whether these indeed mirror the guidance provided by successive resolutions of the Contracting Parties. In doing so, and in assessing those actions required to meet any gaps, the lessons of the case studies reviewed here provide an important reference point.

To date a number of countries have engaged in comprehensive reviews of wetland conservation issues and needs. Canada has devoted special attention to this process and elaborated a federal wetland policy. In the developing world, Uganda has led the way, while Kenya, Tanzania, Zambia, Zimbabwe, Bangladesh, the Philippines, Vietnam, Colombia, Peru and Venezuela have all held national workshops designed to lay the basis for long-term programmes of support to wise use. These initiatives have drawn encouragement from the attention being given to wise use by the Ramsar Convention. However, they are but the start of what will need to be long-term programmes of investment at many levels. The case studies provide an important resource upon which these further efforts, and the new initiatives of other countries, can draw.

Detailed technical guidance: constraints and opportunities

To complement the broad guidance provided by the guidelines, case studies, and the guiding principles, detailed technical guidance is required on the potential and constraints of wetland ecosystems, on the types of wetland use that yield long-term benefits, and, conversely, on those that have been shown to yield substantial costs.

Many forms of guidance of this type are already available, while others are in preparation. Thus there are manuals on wetland classification and assessment, a handbook of mangrove management, lake management guidelines, diverse publications on aquaculture in wetland systems, guidelines on the management of large dams, and many other similar volumes. Handbooks on the management of tidal wetlands, tropical peatlands, and tropical floodplains, and a field guide on wetland interventions are in preparation. These can provide important complementary materials which will support the wise use guidelines and case studies, while providing a strong technical base upon which Contracting Parties can draw in applying wise use on the ground. Further work of this nature needs to be encouraged and designed to contribute to the elaboration of the wise use process.

Conclusion

The case studies examined during the course of the Ramsar Wise Use Project provide diverse examples of approaches to sustainable use of wetland ecosystems at site-specific level. However, neither alone nor together do these provide a recipe, or recipes, for wise use. Rather they provide tangible examples of promising approaches to achieving wise use. As such, they can serve as a source of encouragement and guidance to the Contracting Parties as they pursue their obligations under the Convention. The challenge over the coming years will be for Contracting Parties to build upon this and to apply wise use more widely, both at home and in their relations with other countries.

Patrick J. Dugan
Director of Regional Affairs
(formerly Coordinator IUCN Wetlands Programme)
IUCN - The World Conservation Union
Gland
Switzerland

Bibliography

Alcala. A.C. 1988a. Effects of marine reserves on coral fish abundances and yields of Philippine coral reefs. *Ambio* 17:194-199.

Alcala. A.C. 1988b. The effect of marine reserves on fisheries yields. UNEP Regional Seas Reports and Studies, No.97, pp. 29-34.

Alcala, A.C. & Abregana, B.C. in press. Scientific Basis and Psychosocial Determinants of Protective Management of Living Coastal Resources. Silliman University, Dumaguete City, Philippines.

Alcala, A.C. & Gomez, E.D. 1979. Recolonization and growth of hermatypic corals in dynamite-blasted coral reefs in the Central Visayas, Philippines. Proc. Int. Symp. Mar. Biogeogr. and Evol. S. Hem. 2:645-661.

Alcala, A.C. & Gomez, E.D. 1990. Recovery of a coral reef from typhoon damage at Pescador Island, Cebu, Central Visayas, Philippines. UNEP Regional Sea Reports and Studies No. 106, pp. 105-115.

Alcala, A.C. & Russ, G.R. 1990. A direct test of the effects of protective management on abundance and yield of tropical marine resources. *J. Cons. Int. Explor. Mer.* 46:40-47.

Anonymous 1992. *A strategy to stop and reverse wetland loss and degradation in the Mediterranean basin.* IWRB and Regione Friuli-Venezia Giulia, Trieste, Italy. 40 pp.

ASSAILD 1990. Note de Presentation. ASSAILD, Moundou, Chad.

ASSAILD 1991. Project Documents, unpublished. ASSAILD, Moundou, Chad.

Balasubrahmanyam, S. & Abou-Zeid, S.M. 1982. The Kafue River Hydro-electric Development. In: G.W. Howard & G.J. Williams (eds.). Proceedings of the National Seminar on Environment and Change: The Consequences of Hydroelectric Power Development on the utilization of the Kafue Flats. KBRC, University of Zambia, Lusaka. Pp. 63-68.

Baldock, D., Long, T. & Maltby E. 1988. *Study of integrated management of coastal wetlands in countries outside the European Community.* Institute for European Environmental Policy, London. Final typescript report to EEC/DG XI.

Bellrose, F.C. 1979. Species distribution, habitats, and characteristics of breeding dabbling ducks in North America. In: T.A. Bookout (ed.), *Waterfowl and wetlands - an integrated review.* Proceedings of a symposium, 39th Midwest Fish and Wild. Con., 5 December 1977. Madison, Wisconsin.

Bingham, M.G. 1982. The Livestock Potential of the Kafue Flats. In: G.W. Howard & G.J. Williams (eds.). Proceedings of the National Seminar on Environment and Change: The Consequences of Hydroelectric Power Development on the utilization of the Kafue Flats. KBRC, University of Zambia, Lusaka. Pp. 95-104.

Blache, J. 1964. Les Poissons du bassin du Tchad et du bassin adjacent du Mayo Kebi, Etude Systematique et Biologique. ORSTOM, Chad. 483 pp.

Blache, J. & Miton, F. 1962. Premiere contribution a la connaissance de la pêche dans le bassin hydrographique, Logone-Chari-Lac Tchad. Aspects general des actives de la pêche et de la commercialisation des produits, description des engins de pêche et leur moi. ORSTOM, Paris. 143 pp.

Bond, W.K., Cox, K.W., Heberlein, T., Manning, E.W., Witty D.R. & Young, D.A. 1992. Wetland Evaluation Guide: Final Report of the Wetlands Are Not Wastelands Project. Sustaining Wetlands Issues Paper, No. 1992-1. North American Wetlands Conservation Council (Canada). Ottawa, Ontario. 121 pp.

Boulot, S. 1991. Essai sur la Camargue. Environnement, état des lieux et prospective. Actes Sud, Arles, France.

Cairns, J., Jr. 1985. Facing some awkward questions concerning rehabilitation management practices on mined lands. In: R.P. Brooks, D.E. Samuel, and J.B. Hill (eds.), *Wetlands and water management on mined lands, proceedings of a workshop.* Pennsylvania State University, School of Forestry Resources, University Park, PA. Pp. 9-17.

Casley, D.J. & Lury, D.A. 1982. *Monitoring and Evaluation of Agriculture and Rural Development Projects.* John Hopkins University Press, Baltimore and London.

Cataudella, S., Ardizzone, G.D., Rossi, R. & Belluscio, A. 1988. *Etude relative aux exigences de l'aquaculture pour la gestion intégrée de zones humides côtières du type méditerranéen.* Final typescript report to EEC/DG XI.

Clark, P. & Lowe, E. 1990. *Chowilla Saltwater Interception Scheme: Options for future Management of Crown Land in the NSW component of the Chowilla Anabranch System.* Western Lands Commission, New South Wales.

Collingham, E.B. 1990a. Technical Discussion Paper: *Basic Hydrogeology of the Chowilla Area.* EWS Dept Paper.

Collingham, E.B. 1990b. Technical Discussion Paper: *The Influence of Hydrogeologic Processes on Soil Salinity in the Chowilla Anabranch.* EWS Dept Paper.

Collingham, E.B. 1990c. Technical Discussion Paper: *The Influence of Hydrogeologic Processes on Fish Habitat in the Chowilla Anabranch Floodplain.* EWS Dept Paper.

Common Wadden Sea Secretariat 1991. The Wadden Sea. Status and developments in an international perspective. Wilhemshaven, Germany.

Crissey, W.F. 1969. Prairie potholes from a continental viewpoint. In: Saskatoon wetlands seminar. Can. Wild. Serv. Rept. No. 6.

CVRP 1982. Progress Report, Central Visayas Regional Project, Cebu City, Cebu, Philippines.

CVRP 1984-92. Progress Report, Central Visayas Regional Project, Cebu City, Cebu, Philippines.

CVRP 1991. Progress Report, Central Visayas Regional Project, Cebu City, Cebu, Philippines.

Dahl, T.E. 1990. Wetland losses in the United States 1780's to 1980's. U.S. Dept. of the Interior, Fish and Wildlife Service. Washington, D.C. 13 pp.

de Groot, R.S. 1992 *Functions of Nature: evaluation of nature in environmental planning, management and decision making.* Wolters Noordhoff. 315 pp.

Drijver, C. & van Wetten, J.C.J. 1992. *Sahel 2020, Changing Development Policies or Losing the Best of Sahelian Resources.* ICBP, Cambridge. 39 pp.

Dugan, P.J. 1990. Wetland Conservation: a review of current issues and required action. IUCN, Gland, Switzerland. 96 pp.

Environment Canada 1986. *Wetlands in Canada: A Valuable Resource.* Lands Directorate, Fact Sheet No. 86-4. Ottawa, Ontario. 8 pp.

Gillespie, D.I., Boyd, H. & Logan, P. 1991. *Wetlands for the World: Canada's Ramsar Sites.* Canadian Wildlife Service, Environment Canada, Ottawa, Ontario. 40 pp.

Government of Canada 1990. Canada's Green Plan. Ottawa, Ontario. 174 pp.

Government of Canada 1991. The Federal Policy on Wetland Conservation. Environment Canada, Ottawa, Ontario. 14 pp.

Harmon, K.W. 1970. Prairie potholes. *National Parks and Conservation* Vol. 45(3): 25-28.

Higgins, K.F., Fulton, G.W. & Barker, W.T. 1985. *Wetlands and forage.* South Dakota Cooperative Wildlife Research Unit. U.S. Fish and Wildlife Service. Brookings, S.D. FS-826.

Hollingsworth, I.D. 1989. *A Reconnaissance Soil Survey of the Chowilla Anabranch System of the River Murray in SA and NSW.* SA Dept. Agriculture for the M-DBC, Canberra.

Howard, G.W. & Aspinwall, D.R. 1984. Aerial censuses of shoebills, saddlebilled storks and wattled cranes at the Bangweulu Swamps and Kafue Flats, Zambia. *Ostrich* 53: 207-212.

Howard, G.W. & Jeffery, R.C.V. 1983. Kafue lechwe population status, 1981-1983. Report to the Director, NPWS, Chilanga, (Mimeo).

IUCN 1987a. Rapid Assessment of Industrial pollution in the Korangi-Phitti Creek. IUCN-Pakistan, Karachi.

IUCN 1987b. Survey of marine pollution in the Korangi-Phitti Creek. IUCN-Pakistan, Karachi.

IUCN 1987c. Socio-economic and public health survey - Korangi-Phitti Creek, near Karachi. IUCN-Pakistan, Karachi.

IUCN 1991a. Possible effects of the Indus Water Accord on the Indus Delta ecosystem. IUCN-Pakistan, Karachi.

IUCN 1991b. Sea-level rise - possible impacts on the Indus Delta. IUCN-Pakistan, Karachi.

IUCN 1992a. Phytosociological survey of mangroves of Korangi Creek Area, Karachi. IUCN-Pakistan, Karachi. (in prep.)

IUCN 1992b. Survey of benthic fauna and associated bird populations in the mangroves of Korangi creek area, Karachi. IUCN-Pakistan, Karachi. (in prep.)

IUCN 1992c. Survey of resource use in the coastal villages around Korangi creek, Karachi. IUCN-Pakistan, Karachi. (in prep.)

IUCN 1992d. Wastes discharged from the Korangi tanneries - a review of the current situation. IUCN-Pakistan, Karachi.

Jeffery, R.C.V., Kampamba, G. & Kamweneshe, B. 1991. Large wild Mammal Surveys of the Kafue Flats 1991. Report to the Director, NPWS, Chilanga, (Mimeo).

Kaweche, G.B.& Lewis, D.M. 1985. Lupande Research Project. National Parks and Wildlife Service of Zambia, Chilanga.

Klein, R. 1988. Explanatory note: Preparatory action concerning integrated management of coastal wetlands of Mediterranean type (environmentally sensitive areas in the sense of budget line 6611). Commission of the European Communities DG XI B-3. 7pp. Typescript.

Koumaru, M. 1993. Wise Use of the Kushiro Shitsugen (Marshland). Pp 177-181 in: H. Isozaki, M. Ando & Y. Natori (eds.). Proc. of the Asian Wetland Symp. October 1992, Otsu and Kushiro, Japan.

Kusler, J.A. & Kentula, M.E. 1989. *Wetland creation and restoration: The status of the science.* Vol. I: Regional Reviews. U.S. Environmental Protection Agency EPA 600/3-89/038, Corvallis, OR. 473pp.

Kyle, R. 1992 The utilisation of renewable resources in the Kosi Bay Nature Reserve by rural indigenous people. KwaZulu Bureau of Natural Resources, KwaNgwanase, S. Africa. 50 pp.

Lean, G., Hinrichsen, D. & Markham, A. 1990. *Atlas of the Environment.* Arrow Books, London. 192 pp.

Lewis, D.M., Mwenya, A.N. & Kaweche, G.B. 1989. *African Solutions to Wildlife Problems in Africa. Insights from a Community Based Project in Zambia.* National Parks and Wildlife Service, Chilanga.

Linder, R.L. & Hubbard, D.E. 1982. Wetland values in the Prairie Pothole Region of North America. In: Proceedings of the Great Plains Agricultural Council, North Platte, NE, June 7-9.

Lynch-Stewart, P. 1992. No Net Loss: Implementing "No Net Loss" Goals to Conserve Wetlands. In: Canada. Sustaining Wetlands Issues Paper, No. 1992-2. North American Wetlands Conservation Council (Canada). Ottawa, Ontario. 35 pp.

Madsen, C. 1985. Wetland restoration on private lands – a pilot effort. 40th Annual Meeting of the Soil Conservation Society of America. St. Louis, MO.

Malakou, M., Jerrentrup, H., Kyriazis, A., Hatzantonis, D. & Papayannakis, L. 1988. *Integrated management of coastal wetlands of the Mediterranean type. Northern Greece.* Panorama Cultural Society, Athens. Final typescript report to EEC/DG XI.

Maltby, E., Immirzi, C.P. & McLaren, D.P. 1992. *Do not disturb: peatbogs and the greenhouse effect.* Friends of the Earth, London. 55 pp.

Maltby, E., Hughes, R. & Newbold, C. 1988. *The dynamics and functions of coastal wetlands of the Mediterranean type.* Final typescript report to EEC/DG XI.

Martos, M.J., Pardo, R. & Perea, J. (eds.) 1989. *Estudio de la gestion integrada de las zonas humedas costeras en Andalucía.* Junta de Andalucía, Agencia de Medio Ambiente, Sevilla, Spain.

National Wetlands Working Group 1988. Wetlands of Canada. Ecological Land Classification Series, No. 24. Environment Canada, Ottawa, Ontario. 452 pp.

North American Wetlands Conservation Council (Canada) 1991. Report on Canadian First Step Projects for the 1988 to 1990 Period. Report No. 91-1. NAWCC (Canada) Secretariat. Ottawa, Ontario. 24 pp.

North American Wetlands Conservation Council (Canada) 1992. Report on Canadian Second Step Projects for the September 1988 to March 1991 Period. Report No. 92-1. NAWCC (Canada) Secretariat. Ottawa, Ontario. 60 pp.

O'Malley, C. & Sheldon, F. 1991. *Chowilla Floodplain Biological Survey NCSSA.* Independent study by the NCSSA.

Parish, D. & Prentice, C. 1987. *Wetland and Waterfowl Conservation in Asia.* Asian Wetland Bureau/IWRB, Kuala Lumpur. 222 pp.

Pergantis, P.C. 1988. *Study on the integrated management of coastal wetlands in Western Greece.* Final typescript report to DG XI.

Pierce, B.E. 1990. *Chowilla Fisheries Investigations.* SA Dept. of Fisheries for the M-DBC, Canberra.

Robinson, N.A. 1992. Agenda 21 and the UNCED proceedings. Third series, International Protection of the Environment.

Ramsar Convention Bureau 1990. Guidelines for the implementation of the Wise Use concept. REC. C.4.10 (Rev.). Annex III. Pp. 177-182 in Proceedings of the Fourth Meeting of the Conference of the Contracting Parties, Montreux, Switzerland, 27 June to 4 July 1990. Vol. 1. Gland, Switzerland. 306 pp.

Rubec, C.D.A., Lynch-Stewart, P., Wickware, G.M. & Kessel-Taylor 1988. Chapter 10, pp. 379-412. In: *Wetlands of Canada.* Ecological Land Classification Series, No. 24. Environment Canada, Ottawa, Ontario. 452 pp.

Rubec, C.D.A. & McKechnie, M.R. 1989. From theory to practice: promoting policy and actions towards sustainable development on Canada's wetlands. Pp. 37-44 in: Proceedings, International Symposium on Wetlands and River Corridor Management. Association of State Wetland Managers, Berne, New York.

Rubio, J.C. & Martos, M.J. 1991. *Estudio de la gestion integrada de las Marismas del Odiel.* Junta de Andalucía, Agencia de Medio Ambiente, Sevilla, Spain.

Russ, G. 1985. Effects of protective management on coral reef fishes in the central Philippines. Proc. 5th Int. Coral Reef Congr. 4: 219-224.

Savina, G.C. & White, A.T. 1986. A Tale of Two Islands: Some Lessons for Marine Resource Management. *Environmental Conservation ,* Vol. 13, No.2:107-113.

Schneller-McDonald, K., Ischinger, L.S. & Auble, G.T. 1990. Wetland Creation and Restoration: Description and Summary of the Literature. U.S. Fish and Wildlife Service, Washington, D.C. *Biol. Rept.* 90(3). 198 pp.

Serrano, C.R. 1987. State of the Art. Mangrove Research. Philippine Council for Agriculture and Natural Resources, Research and Development. PCARRD, Los Baños, Laugujna, Philippines, Forestry Research Series No. 4, 83 pp.

SNV-Tchad 1989. Rapport Annual 1989, N'Djamena, Tchad.

Szijj, J. 1988. Ecological requirements for the integrated management of coastal wetlands of Mediterranean type. Final typescript report to EEC/DG XI.

Social and Ecological Assessment Pty. Ltd. in association with Pak-Poy and Kneebone Pty. Ltd. 1989. Chowilla Recreation Study. DEP Report for the M-DBC, Canberra.

Subramaniam, S.P. 1992. A brief review of the status of the Fisheries of the Bangweulu Basin and Kafue Flats, pp 45-55. In: R.C.V. Jeffery, H.N. Chabwela, G. Howard & P.J. Dugan (eds.). Managing the Wetlands of Kafue Flats and Bangweulu Basin. Proceedings of the WWF-Zambia Wetlands Project Workshop, Musungwa Safari Lodge, Kafue National Park, Zambia, 5-7 November 1986. IUCN, Gland.

Sustaining Wetlands Forum 1990. Sustaining Wetlands: International Challenge for the '90s. Secretariat, North American Wetlands Conservation Council (Canada). Ottawa, Ontario. 20 pp.

U.S. Fish and Wildlife Service 1988. A Prospectus for Lake Thompson Watershed Project South Dakota. A component of the North American Waterfowl Management Plan. U.S. prairie Pothole Joint Venture. U.S. Fish and Wildlife Service, Washington, D.C. 16 pp.

Waterhouse, J. (Feb 1989). *The Hydrogeology of the Chowilla Floodplain.* Status Report, M-DBC, Canberra.

Wells, S. 1986. A future for coral reefs. *New Scientist* 112:46-50.

White, A. 1989. The marine conservation and development program of Silliman University as an example for Lingayen Gulf. Pp. 119-123 in: G. Silvestre, E. Miclat & T.E. Chua (eds.), Towards sustainable development of the coastal resources of Lingayen Gulf, Philippines. ICLARM Conf. Proc., Philippine Council for Aquatic and Marine Research and Development, Los Baños, Laguna, and International Center for Living Aquatic Resources Management, Makati, Metro Manila, Philippines.

White, A.T. & Savina, G.C. 1987. Reef fish yield and nonreef catch of Apo Island, Negros, Philippines. *Asian Marine Biology* 4:67-76.

World Bank 1989. Philippines, Environmental and Natural Resource Management Study. A World Bank Country Study, Washington DC, USA.

Yoa, C.E. 1986. Mangrove reforestation in Central Visayas. *Canopy International* Vol. 12, No.2:6-9.

APPENDIX 1

REC. C.4.10 (Rev.)

CONVENTION ON WETLANDS OF INTERNATIONAL IMPORTANCE ESPECIALLY AS WATERFOWL HABITAT

Fourth Meeting of the Conference of the Contracting Parties
Montreux, Switzerland : 27 June to 4 July 1990

GUIDELINES FOR THE IMPLEMENTATION OF THE WISE USE CONCEPT

RECALLING that the Third Meeting of the Conference of the Contracting Parties approved Recommendation 3.1 which called for the establishment of a Working Group "to examine the ways in which the criteria and guidelines for identifying wetlands of international importance might be elaborated, and the wise use provisions of the Convention applied, in order to improve the worldwide application of the Convention";

NOTING that a "Working Group on Criteria and Wise Use" was established by the Standing Committee at its Third Meeting on 5 June 1987, with the participation of seven Contracting Parties (Australia, Chile, Iran, Mauritania, Norway, Poland and USA - one from each of the Standing Committee's regions);

AWARE that the Working Group met on the occasion of the Fourth Meeting of the Standing Committee in Costa Rica in January 1988 and elected Norway as Chairman of the Working Group, and that observers from many other Contracting Parties took part in this meeting of the Working Group, as well as in subsequent deliberations;

TAKING NOTE of the Report of the Working Group, circulated to all Contracting Parties with Bureau Notification 1989/3 (31 March 1989), and revised according to comments received from Contracting Parties;

EXPRESSING ITS APPRECIATION to the Working Group and its Chairman for their work in clarifying the criteria and developing the guidelines on wise use;

RECONFIRMING that the concept of wise use extends to all phases of wetland conservation including policy development, planning, legal and educational activities, and site specific actions;

NOTING with pleasure the support being provided to the Convention Bureau by the Netherlands Ministry of Foreign Affairs for promoting application of the wise use concept in developing countries;

ACKNOWLEDGING the need for a Convention Working Group to provide guidance to the Bureau in promoting the wise use concept;

THE CONFERENCE OF THE CONTRACTING PARTIES

RECOMMENDS that the "Guidelines for implementation of the wise use concept of the Convention", contained in Annex III of the Working Group's report, discussed at the present Conference and appended as an Annex to the present document, be adopted and applied by Contracting Parties;

FURTHER RECOMMENDS that a Working Group on Wise Use be reconstituted under the supervision of the Standing Committee, with sufficient representation from each of the Convention's regions and assisted by invited experts from concerned organizations, to continue the wise use work of the Convention by:

(a) overseeing the work of the Bureau in implementing the Netherlands Wise Use project;

(b) fostering further development and refinement of the "Guidelines for implementation of the wise use concept" contained in the Annex, to apply to a diversity of wetland types, regions, resources and uses, concerning such areas as:

1. organizational and institutional processes;
2. inventory and classification;
3. development of management plans, policies, and alternative conservation strategies;
4. environmental education and outreach programmes;
5. effective training programmes;
6. ongoing monitoring and research programmes; and
7. available partnerships for further assistance;

(c) disseminating examples of site-specific wise use from regions throughout the world;

(d) disseminating practical examples of the interrelation between human activities and wetlands; and

(e) providing information about the process of developing national wetland inventories and policies; and

FINALLY RECOMMENDS that the Working Group report back to the next ordinary meeting of the Conference of the Contracting Parties.

Annex to REC. C.4.10 (Rev.)

GUIDELINES FOR IMPLEMENTATION OF THE WISE USE CONCEPT OF THE CONVENTION

Introduction

Article 3.1 of the Convention states that the Contracting Parties "shall formulate and implement their planning so as to promote the conservation of the wetlands included in the List, and as far as possible the wise use of wetlands in their territory".

The third meeting of the Conference of the Contracting Parties in Regina, Canada from 27 May to 5 June 1987, adopted the following definition of wise use of wetlands:

"The wise use of wetlands is their sustainable utilization for the benefit of humankind in a way compatible with the maintenance of the natural properties of the ecosystem".

Sustainable utilization is defined as "human use of a wetland so that it may yield the greatest continuous benefit to present generations while maintaining its potential to meet the needs and aspirations of future generations".

Natural properties of the ecosystem are defined as "those physical, biological or chemical components, such as soil, water, plants, animals and nutrients, and the interactions between them".

The wise use provisions apply to all wetlands and their support systems within the territory of a Contracting Party, both those wetlands designated for the List, and all other wetlands. The concept of wise use seeks both the formulation and implementation of general wetland policies, and wise use of specific wetlands. These activities are integral parts of sustainable development.

It is desirable in the long term that all Contracting Parties should have comprehensive national wetland policies, formulated in whatever manner is appropriate to their national institutions. However as recognized by the report of the Workshop on Wise Use of the Regina Meeting, elaboration of national wetland policies will be a long term process, and immediate action should be taken to stimulate wise use. The guidelines presented below therefore include both elements for comprehensive national wetland policies and priority actions.

Establishment of national wetland policies

National wetland policies should as far as possible address all problems and activities related to wetlands within a national context. These may be grouped in different sections:

1. Actions to improve institutional and organizational arrangements, including:

(a) establishment of institutional arrangements which will allow those concerned to identify how wetland conservation can be achieved, and how wetland priorities can be fully integrated into the planning process; and

(b) establishment of mechanisms and procedures for incorporating an integrated multidisciplinary approach into planning and execution of projects concerning wetlands and their support systems, in order to secure wetland conservation and sustainable development.

2. Actions to address legislation and government policies, including:

(a) review of existing legislation and policies (including subsidies and incentives) which affect wetland conservation;

(b) application, where appropriate, of existing legislation and policies of importance for the conservation of wetlands;

(c) adoption, as required, of new legislation and policies; and

(d) use of development funds for projects which permit conservation and sustainable utilization of wetland resources.

3. Actions to increase knowledge and awareness of wetlands and their values, including:

(a) interchange of experience and information on wetland policy, conservation and wise use between countries preparing and/or implementing national wetland policies, or pursuing wetland conservation;

(b) increasing the awareness and understanding of decision-makers and the public of the full benefits and values, within the terms of wise use, of wetlands. Among these benefits and values, which can occur on or off the wetland itself, are:

- sediment and erosion control,
- flood control,

- maintenance of water quality and abatement of pollution,
    - maintenance of surface and underground water supply,
    - support for fisheries, grazing and agriculture,
    - outdoor recreation and education for human society,
    - provision of habitat for wildlife, especially waterfowl, and
    - contribution to climatic stability;

(c)   review of traditional techniques of wise use, and elaboration of pilot projects which demonstrate wise use of representative wetland types; and

(d)   training of appropriate staff in the disciplines which will assist in implementation of wetland conservation action and policies.

4.   Actions to review the status of, and identify priorities for, all wetlands in a national context, including:

(a)   execution of a national inventory of wetlands including classification of the sites;

(b)   identification and evaluation of the benefits and values of each site (see 3b above);

(c)   definition of the conservation and management priorities for each site, in accordance with the needs and conditions of each Contracting Party

5.   Actions to address problems at particular wetland sites, including:

(a)   integration from the outset of environmental considerations in planning of projects which might affect the wetland (including full assessment of their environmental impact before approval, continuing evaluation during their execution, and full implementation of necessary environmental measures). The planning, assessment and evaluation should cover projects upstream of the wetland, those in the wetland itself, and other projects which may affect the wetland, and should pay particular attention to maintaining the benefits and values listed in 3b above;

(b)   regulated utilization of the natural elements of wetland systems such that they are not over-exploited;

(c)   establishment, implementation and, as necessary, periodic revision of management plans which involve local people and take account of their requirements;

(d)   designation for the Ramsar List of wetlands identified as being of international importance;

(e)   establishment of nature reserves at wetlands, whether or not they are included in the List; and

(f)   serious consideration of restoration of wetlands whose benefits and values have been diminished or degraded.

Priority actions at national level

Whether or not national wetland policies are being prepared, several actions should receive immediate attention at national level in order to facilitate the preparation of national wetland policies, and to avoid delay in practical implementation of wetland conservation and wise use.

Contracting Parties will naturally select actions, according to their own national priorities and requirements, from those listed above under 'Establishment of national wetland policies'. They may wish to carry on institutional, legislative or educational measures (such as those listed under sections 1, 2, 3 above) and at the same time initiate inventories or scientific work (such as those listed under section 4); in this way the institutional, legislative and educational instruments will be available in time to deal with scientific results.

Equally, Contracting Parties wishing to promote wise use of wetlands without waiting until national wetland policies have been developed, may, based on their situation and needs, wish to:

(i)   identify the issues which require the most urgent attention ;

(ii)   take action on one or more of these issues;

(iii)   identify the wetland sites which require the most urgent action; and

(iv)   take action at one or more of these wetlands, along the lines set out under 'Priority actions at particular wetland sites' below.

Priority actions at particular wetland sites

As at national level, immediate action may be required in order to avoid destruction or degradation of important wetland values at particular wetland sites. These actions will undoubtedly include some elements listed in section 5 above, and Contracting Parties will select those appropriate to their own national priorities and requirements.

Whenever planning is initiated for projects which might affect important wetlands, the following actions should be taken in order to promote wise use of the wetland:

(i)   integration from the outset of environmental considerations in planning of projects which might affect wetlands (including full assessment of their environmental impact before approval);

(ii)   continuing evaluation during their execution; and

(iii)   full implementation of necessary environmental measures.

The planning, assessment and evaluation should cover projects upstream of the wetland, those in the wetland itself, and other projects which may affect the wetland, and should pay particular attention to maintaining the benefits and values listed, in 3b above.

APPENDIX 2

RES C. 5.6

CONVENTION ON WETLANDS OF INTERNATIONAL IMPORTANCE ESPECIALLY AS WATERFOWL HABITAT

Fifth Meeting of the Conference of the Contracting Parties
Kushiro, Japan : 9-16 June 1993

WISE USE OF WETLANDS

RECALLING Article 3.1 of the Convention which stipulates that "the Contracting Parties shall formulate and implement their planning so as to promote ... as far as possible the wise use of wetlands in their territory";

REFERRING to Recommendation 4.10, adopted by the Fourth Meeting of the Conference of the Contracting Parties, which calls on Contracting Parties to:

-    adopt and apply the "Guidelines for the implementation of the wise use concept";

-    reconstitute the Wise Use Working Group established by the Third Meeting of the Conference; and

-    receive the report of the Working Group at the Fifth Meeting of the Conference;

THANKING the Government of the Netherlands for its generous initiative in providing the Convention Bureau with finance for the coordination of a three-year project on the wise use of wetlands, which has been carried out since the Fourth Meeting of the Conference of the Contracting Parties;

TAKING NOTE of the report of the Wise Use Working Group and the conclusions of the Wise Use project;

THE CONFERENCE OF THE CONTRACTING PARTIES

CALLS ON the Contracting Parties to implement in a more systematic and effective manner, and at international, national and local levels, the guidelines on wise use adopted by the Fourth Meeting of the Conference of the Contracting Parties;

NOTES the "Additional guidance for the implementation of the wise use concept" contained in the Annex to the present resolution and urges Contracting Parties to implement its applicable provisions;

INVITES the Contracting Parties to strengthen international co-operation between developed countries and developing countries, or those whose economy is in transition, for the implementation of the wise use guidelines and additional guidance, and appropriate project activities; and

DECIDES that the follow-up to the work of the Wise Use Working Group, and in particular evaluation of the application of the wise use guidelines and additional guidance on wise use, be carried out by the Scientific and Technical Review Panel established at the present meeting.

RES C. 5.6 (Annex)

ADDITIONAL GUIDANCE FOR THE IMPLEMENTATION OF THE WISE USE CONCEPT

INTRODUCTION

Article 3.1 of the 1971 Ramsar Convention provides that the Contracting Parties "shall formulate and implement their planning so as to promote the conservation of the wetlands included in the List and, as far as possible the wise use of wetlands in their territory".

In the early years of the Convention, the wise use provision proved to be difficult to apply. Most attention was focused upon the designation of sites onto the Ramsar List in line with global priorities to secure the conservation of internationally important areas. Over time, as the essential need to integrate conservation and development has become recognized throughout the world, the Contracting Parties to the Ramsar Convention have made wise use a central theme for the functioning of the Convention.

The wise use concept was defined at the Third Meeting of the Conference of the Contracting Parties held in Regina, Canada, in 1987 (Recommendation REC C.3.3), as "the sustainable utilization of wetlands for benefit of humankind in a way compatible with the maintenance of the natural properties of the ecosystem".

The Third Meeting of the Conference of the Contracting Parties also decided to establish a Working Group on Criteria and Wise Use (Recommendation REC C.3.1), charged *inter alia* with the development of draft guidelines for the implementation of the wise use concept. These guidelines were adopted by the Fourth Meeting of the Conference of the Contracting Parties at Montreux, Switzerland, in 1990 (Recommendation REC C.4.10).

In addition to adopting the guidelines, the Contracting Parties requested the Wise Use Working Group to undertake additional tasks including "fostering further development and refinement of the guidelines to apply to a diversity of wetland types, regions, resources and uses ..."

In 1990, the Ramsar Convention Bureau initiated the coordination of a three-year project on the wise use of wetlands funded by the Government of The Netherlands. The Wise Use Working Group was also requested by the Montreux meeting to oversee the implementation of this project, which comprises a series of case studies demonstrating applications of the wise use concept in different ecological and socio-economic situations throughout the world.

Several basic conclusions can be drawn from the case studies considered under this project:

1) Social and economic factors are the main reasons for wetland loss and therefore need to be of central concern in wise use programmes.

2) Special attention needs to be given to the local populations who will be the first to benefit from improved management of wetland sites. The values that indigenous people can bring to all aspects of wise use need special recognition.

3) Although one agency may be responsible for coordinating national action to conserve wetlands, other public and private institutions have expertise which is of importance for effective long-term wetland management. Wise use programmes should seek to involve and, where appropriate, work through these partners.

4) Specific site projects may often demonstrate the need for more general institutional requirements for the wise use of wetlands.

5) Where wetlands form an integral part of a wider coastal zone or catchment, wise use must also take into account the problems of the surrounding coastal zone or catchment.

6) While comprehensive understanding of the ecological constraints of a wetland system should be sought, activities affecting wetlands need to be governed by the "precautionary principle" when such knowledge is not available. In other words, if the impact of specific actions is not clearly understood, then these actions should be prohibited even if there is insufficient evidence to prove a direct link between the activities and resulting wetland degradation.

In view of the lessons learned from the case studies and further analysis by the Wise Use Working Group, additional guidance is proposed to the Contracting Parties to the Ramsar Convention for the application of the wise use provision of the Convention. This guidance must be applied in the light of other national and international obligations for nature conservation, including the conservation of biodiversity, climate change and pollution control measures, as adopted by the UN Conference on Environment and Development (UNCED, Rio, 1992) and in other international fora.

The 1992 Convention on Biological Diversity is of special relevance for the conservation and wise use of wetlands, and the preparation of national biodiversity strategies, action plans and programmes as required under the Convention on Biological Diversity may provide good opportunities to include wetland conservation and wise use on a wider scale.

The following points of guidance address the main elements for the application of the wise use concept. They are meant to amplify the Wise Use Guidelines by providing further assistance to those officials responsible for the application of the Ramsar Convention. As the wise use concept is central to all aspects of the convention, this guidance is also relevant for action to be taken under several of the obligations of the convention, including international cooperation, reserve creation and the conservation of listed sites.

The Scientific and Technical Review Panel established at Kushiro by Resolution 5.5 has among its tasks "evaluation of the application of the Additional guidance on wise use".

I. ESTABLISHMENT OF NATIONAL WETLAND POLICIES

I.1 Institutional and organizational arrangements

1)   The main message given by the wise use guidelines is that the wise use of wetlands requires a coordinated approach on a national scale; this necessitates planning, which can be in the framework of wetland policies, conservation policies or policies with a broader scope (environment, application of water laws, or resource planning); institutional and administrative arrangements should be made.

Obstacles to the development of national wetland policies may however include:

-   a lack of institutional mechanisms designed to encourage the involvement of both public and private sectors of the society, at regional or local level as well as at national level;

- insufficient coordination among public agencies;

- policies that discourage conservation and wise use objectives;

- inadequate policy research programmes; and

- lack of cooperative arrangements with neighbouring countries for joint management of shared wetlands or wetland species.

2) There are many different ways in which countries may attempt to overcome these obstacles.

A few examples can be given:

- At international level, countries may wish to establish cross-boundary water commissions or other coordinating boards to avoid action in one country adversely affecting wetlands in another country and to guarantee that water quality and quantity are maintained in such a way as to preserve the functional values of wetlands. In addition, countries that are range states for migratory species dependent on wetlands may wish to establish coordinated conservation programmes for those species and set common guidelines on development aid in the field of conservation and wise use of wetlands.

- At national level, countries might create inter-ministerial boards or commissions, national wetland committees or other bodies to oversee coordination and cooperation for wetland management. These bodies should include a wide representation (based on a catchment approach) from the authorities with responsibility for wetlands and might include government agencies dealing with environment, nature conservation, agriculture, forestry, aquaculture, hunting, fishing, shipping, tourism, mining, industry, health, development assistance, and other relevant subjects; they should also include interested governmental and non-governmental conservation organizations.

- At local level, countries might establish procedures to guarantee that local populations are involved in the decision-making process related to wetland use and to provide local populations with sufficient knowledge of planned activities to assure their meaningful participation in this decision-making process.

There should be established working groups or advisory boards representing users, NGOs and local authorities.

I.2 Policy/Legislation and other appropriate measures

Governments can use several instruments to promote policy such as legislative tools; five different mechanisms are necessary in order to implement wise use in practice:

1) Periodical review of existing legislation to ensure that it is generally compatible with the wise use obligation, and make adjustments if necessary; this applies to particular legislation regarding mandatory wetland destruction or to that which encourages such destruction through tax benefits and subsidies.

2) General wise use legislation for wetlands should consider the following:

- inclusion of wetlands in the zones of land-use plans which enjoy the highest degree of protection;

- institution of a permit system for activities affecting wetlands. This should include a threshold under which a permit would not be required, as well as a general exemption for activities which, because of their nature, are deemed to be compatible with any performance obligation;

- execution of an environmental impact assessment in order to determine if a proposed project is compatible with the general requirements of wise use and the maintenance of the ecological character of the wetlands concerned. Special rules relating to the contents of an environmental impact assessment will be needed in order to ensure that no important factor specifically related to wetlands is overlooked. The cumulative effects of separate projects should also be taken into consideration.

Environmental impact assessments should also be prepared not only for activities and projects in the wetlands concerned but also for activities outside these areas when they may have significant effect on wetlands. Environmental impact assessments should also cover the long-term effects of proposed activities, projects, plans and programmes as well as interactions between all components of the water system at the catchment level.

- monitoring of the effects of authorized actions and carrying out unbiased environmental audits of these actions when they have been completed;

- institution of a system of management agreements between relevant government agencies, landowners and landusers to provide for positive management measures by the latter when this is required for the maintenance of the ecosystem;

- provision of financial incentives including taxes and subsidies to encourage activities which are compatible with the maintenance of wetlands, and which promote and contribute to their conservation. Financial tax incentives should not permit activities which have detrimental effects upon wetlands;

- obligation to refrain from introducing invasive alien species, and to take preventive measures to minimize the risk of accidental introductions; existing guidelines for these purposes need to be taken into consideration;

- obligation to make all appropriate efforts to eradicate introduced and translocated species which may cause significant ecological disturbances in water systems and, in addition, provide for the possibility of claiming civil damages from those responsible for unlawful introductions; and

- right of appeal by private organizations against governmental agency decisions which might violate obligations laid down by law.

3) Legislation for the conservation and wise use of specific wetland sites (e.g. Ramsar sites, ecologically sensitive areas, areas with a high degree of biodiversity, sites containing endemic species, wetland nature reserves).

Such legislation will generally apply to large wetland areas where human activities compatible with the conservation of the ecosystem should be maintained, encouraged and developed for the benefit of local populations. This legislation will be in addition to those provisions laid down in the previous paragraph in respect of wetlands in general. It should consider the following points:

- definition of a special legal status for large wetland areas allowing for the control of any potentially damaging activity, including agriculture, forestry, tourism, fishing, hunting, aquaculture;

- division of those wetlands into different zones with particular regulations applying to each type of zone; these regulations would be defined to ensure that the carrying capacity of the area concerned is not exceeded in respect of each activity authorized;

- encouragement of traditional and other ecological and sustainable activities in these areas through incentives and advice;

- establishment of a management system in each area which should have legal support and of a management body to oversee the implementation and to ensure that regulations are observed;

- association of populations living in or close to the area with its management, through appropriate representation; scientific institutions and conservation NGOs should also be associated with management, at least in an advisory capacity;

- application of special environmental impact assessment rules to these areas in view of their particular environmental sensitivity; and

- submission of activities which may have adverse effects on the area, to environmental impact assessment or to other forms of evaluation. Such activities should only be authorized when the evaluation has shown that no significant damage to the area will occur.

4) Review of division of jurisdiction among government agencies.

This issue, which concerns both territorial and functional matters, often constitutes a considerable obstacle to integrated management of wetlands since it needs to be based on a catchment-wide approach.

A review of legal and administrative constraints which prevent management at the correct scale (e.g. catchment-wide management) should be undertaken with a view to developing appropriate solutions to jurisdictional problems. Particular attention should be paid to the need to manage coastal wetlands as single units, irrespective of the usual division of jurisdiction between land and sea.

5) Development of cooperative arrangements for water systems shared between two or more countries to achieve wise use.

This will entail the conclusion of agreements for the conservation, management and wise use of such systems as required by Article 5 of the Convention. As relevant, elements of the present guidance should be used in the development of these agreements. Furthermore, such actions need to be pursued in coordination with or through other existing treaties such as the 1992 Helsinki Convention on the Protection and Use of Transboundary Watercourses and International Lakes, the 1979 Bonn Convention on the Conservation of Migratory Species of Wild Animals and the 1991 Espoo Convention on Environmental Impact Assessment in a Transboundary Context.

II. KNOWLEDGE OF WETLANDS AND THEIR VALUES

In order to manage wetlands, it is necessary to have adequate knowledge of their functioning. To promote and apply the wise use of wetlands, inventory, research, monitoring and training activities should be undertaken.

The values of wetlands need to be much more widely promoted in educational programmes and to the general public. Special attention should be devoted to targeting audiences by taking geographical, economic, and political considerations into account. Different mechanisms should be used to approach each target audience.

Some countries have had considerable experience in the application of the wise use concept. Important sources of information are the case studies on wise use published by the Ramsar Convention Bureau. The Bureau, with the assistance of its partners, could be used as a focal point for information pertaining to wise use implementation.

II.1 Inventory

Inventories can produce information in the form of maps, check-lists, regional analyses, narratives of ecological or cultural resources. However, they need not be elaborate to be useful. The goals of an inventory may vary so that defining goals will help to determine the methods and extent of each inventory.

1) Some goals for an inventory may include:

    - identification of resources (ecological, cultural and traditional);

    - determination of these resources in geographic or socio-economic context;

    - identification of known uses of wetlands;

    - identification of priorities for research (improved knowledge base), management and protection;

    - identification of present and potential problems;

    - provision of a tool for future planning and monitoring.

    A wetland inventory should not be seen as a final document, but rather as a continuing process. It can be a long term commitment for both collecting and updating information. Inventories may include input from various disciplines, such as ecology, limnology, hydrology, social sciences, agronomy, wildlife management, fisheries, as well as input from policy makers.

2) Possible applications of an inventory may include:

    - base-line information for land-use and management planning;

    - base-line for future monitoring;

    - information for impact assessments;

- availability of data through publication of regional, national or local inventories such as those carried out for Africa, Asia, the Neotropics and Oceania;

- provision of quantifiable data for future management application;

- tools for recognizing diminishing or threatened types of wetlands;

- drawing associations between wetland types/sizes with socio-cultural uses and needs to help develop standardized approaches for these classifications; and

- setting of priority actions whether for research, policy or management.

II.2 Monitoring

Monitoring is the process of measuring change in ecological character in any wetland over a period of time.

1)   The following points should be observed in any monitoring effort:

- The need to produce objective information;

- The need to follow up any activity taking place in a wetland;

- The knowledge gained from a specific project or activity, but also from activities taking place in similar wetlands.

Monitoring can be carried out at different levels of intensity, depending on available funding and/or technology. It should be noted that monitoring does not automatically require sophisticated technology or high investment.

2)   The following approaches might be used:

- Changes in wetland area or catchment utilization can be monitored by remote sensing or field observations;

- Ecological character and productivity can be monitored using available information or quantitative sampling techniques;

- Changes in social values and uses may be monitored by participatory observation.

II.3 Research

Research can be anything that expands upon basic knowledge. Particular areas that may deserve attention are both identification and quantification of wetland values, sustainability of wetland use, and landscape functioning and modification. Contracting Parties should take positive steps to acquire and, when possible, share any knowledge developed on wetland values, functions and uses.

1)   Priority research actions may include:

- The development of a vocabulary of terms, understandable world-wide;

- The development of means to emphasize landscape or catchment approaches in management;

- The development of techniques for monitoring ecological change and forecasting the evolutions of wetland characteristics under the pressure of present uses;

- The improvement of the knowledge base of wetland functions and values, especially the socio-economic values of wetlands, in order to learn about the traditional management techniques of the local populations and their needs;

- The improvement of the knowledge of the scientific classification of wetlands micro-organisms, plants and animals, and the lodging of study specimens with museums or other appropriate institutions;

- The development of methodologies to evaluate sustainable practices;

- The provision of the data on which alternative/wise use technologies can be developed;

- The development of techniques for restoration of wetlands.

2) The above-mentioned research questions represent an indication of needs. In practice, it can be expected that the number of specific research questions to be addressed will increase as progress is made in natural resource programmes. Research priorities must be based on management needs.

II.4 Training

1) Attention should be devoted to four aspects of training:

- The definition of training needs

- The differing needs between regions, countries and sites

Expertise may not always be available and some key aspects of wise use may not be covered in the existing programme. These key aspects must be considered as priorities for further training activities. Therefore, the first step in establishing a training programme should be to carry out a training needs analysis.

- The target audience

There is a huge difference between educational and awareness programmes and professional training. Generally, it can be said that while the general public and senior policy makers should be made aware of ecological, cultural, social and economical values of wetland ecosystems, training should be provided for those who are directly involved in administering and practising wetland management. Training sessions should focus on the most up-to-date methods for implementing wise use. Such sessions need also to be organized for judicial authorities and other law enforcement officials.

- The subject

Training should furnish wetland managers and administrators with the professional knowledge needed for establishing, defending, and implementing the concept of wise use of wetlands.

2) Three broad types of training appear to be of particular relevance for wetland professionals:

- Courses on integrated management

Training should seek to bring together specialists from different fields to generate a common understanding and a common approach to wetland management and planning;

- Courses on wetland management techniques

Training should seek to provide the participants with the most up-to- date and effective techniques of inventory, planning, monitoring, environmental impact assessment (EIA) and restoration;

- Courses for field staff

Wardens and rangers need to have a very basic understanding of the concept of wise use and to be able to deal with day-to-day situations such as enforcement of legislation and public awareness;

The development of training manuals and other resource materials should be an important long-term goal for any training programme.

3) Training methods and resources

Training activities and transfer of appropriate knowledge should be an integrated component of all wise use projects. Those activities should be as catalytic as possible, and seek to train potential trainers at regional level who can then pass on their expertise to lower levels, and involve the cooperation of governmental and non-governmental organizations, using local resources and institutions whenever possible.

II.5 Education and public awareness

Education and public awareness (EPA) are fundamentally different from the training required by professional staff in order to manage wetlands wisely. Education is the deeper and longer-term process of change in individuals, and their development of longer-term skills and values; awareness is an individual's state of knowledge, which often precedes and stimulates more interest, and leads to further learning and action.

The values of wetlands have not yet been communicated effectively to the public at large through EPA programmes. Most people do not know what wetlands are and, even if they do, they tend to see them as wastelands, which do not generate the public support that has been generated for tropical forests. Improving EPA for wetlands is fundamental to achieving wise use. The following activities are required:

- definition of the target audiences

Awareness programmes should be designed for management authorities, landowners, local government officials, communities depending on wetland resources for their livelihood, and the general public.

- market research

This should identify the most appropriate techniques for increasing awareness of the values of wetlands in different regions of the world.

- EPA campaigns

EPA will only work through a bottom-up approach. However, a great deal could be achieved through globally or nationally coordinated campaigns, which would enable sharing of materials and expertise, as well as generating the necessary momentum to raise the global profile of wetlands.

III. ACTION AT PARTICULAR WETLAND SITES

III.1 Ecological aspects

Wetland management should be an integrated process, taking into account the criteria of time and space. It needs to incorporate long term, sustainable goals. It also needs to take into account the catchment approach. As an integrated process, it needs to incorporate different uses and activities that are compatible with sustainability.

This management also needs to incorporate an inter-disciplinary approach that reflects the wide variety of human endeavours, drawing inter alia upon principles of biology, economics, policy and social sciences. In many cases, it also needs to respond to global concerns, especially as they relate to shared species, shared water systems, and to the issue of global change.

III.2 Human activities

In order to achieve wise use of wetlands, it is necessary to attain a balance that ensures the maintenance of all wetland types through activities that can range from strict protection all the way to active intervention, including restoration.

Wise use activities therefore can be varied in nature, ranging from very little or no resource exploitation, to active resource exploitation as long as it is sustainable. It must be recognized, however, that there are very few wetlands that are not currently being utilized by local populations in some way.

Wetland management should be adapted to specific local circumstances, sensitive to local cultures and respectful of traditional uses. Management therefore is not a universal concept that can be broadly applied; rather, it needs to be adapted to suit local conditions.

III.3 Integrated management planning

Wetland management may be implemented by the development of management plans or strategies for a specific area or region. Workshop C of the Kushiro Conference reviewed draft "Guidelines on management planning for Ramsar sites and other wetlands", later adopted in plenary session (see Annex to Resolution 5.7).

These guidelines emphasize that management planning applies not just to wetland reserves but to all wetlands, and that it is a process subject to constant review and revision. Management plans should therefore be regarded as flexible, dynamic documents.

1) In general, a management plan is organized as a four-part unit:

   - Description (this provides the factual basis on which management decisions can be taken, and may be revised in the light of improved knowledge of a site);

   - Recognition of the past modifications of the sites and of the possible threats;

   - Evaluation and objectives (from the description, the goals of management can be defined, in terms of both long term objectives and of immediate operational objectives for the short term);

   - Action plan (definition of work to be done in order to achieve the objectives; activities to be considered include: habitat management; species management; usage; access; education, interpretation and communication; and research).

Monitoring is an integral part of the planning process. Annual and longer term reviews of the plan need to be undertaken, and may lead to amendment of the description, objectives and action plan.

2) A management authority charged with the implementation of the management process should be appointed; this may be particularly relevant in large wetlands where planning must take account of all interests, uses and pressures. Strong cooperation and participation from governmental and non-governmental agencies, as well as from local people, needs to be achieved.

3) When appropriate, management plans should incorporate both traditional and modern technologies. The plan must reflect the overall carrying capacity of the system. Implementation should optimize the sustainable use of existing resources.

Wetland management needs to be incorporated into overall national policies, as already indicated in the Montreux guidelines. These policies should reflect the best technical information available. Specific technical information can be obtained through the Ramsar Bureau and its partner organizations.

III.4 Technical issues

For many regions of the world, wise use is not a new concept. Humans have been building civilizations around wetlands for thousands of years, and have developed technologies of utilization.

Many of these technologies are sustainable, and should therefore be identified, studied and promoted as a matter of urgency. In the cases where these technologies are not sustainable, they should be refined and adapted to optimize their sustainability.